The Politics of Imprisonment

*How the Democratic Process Shapes
the Way America Punishes Offenders*

VANESSA BARKER

OXFORD
UNIVERSITY PRESS
2009

OXFORD
UNIVERSITY PRESS

Oxford University Press, Inc., publishes works that further
Oxford University's objective of excellence
in research, scholarship, and education.

Oxford   New York
Auckland   Cape Town   Dar es Salaam   Hong Kong   Karachi
Kuala Lumpur   Madrid   Melbourne   Mexico City   Nairobi
New Delhi   Shanghai   Taipei   Toronto

With offices in
Argentina   Austria   Brazil   Chile   Czech Republic   France   Greece
Guatemala   Hungary   Italy   Japan   Poland   Portugal   Singapore
South Korea   Switzerland   Thailand   Turkey   Ukraine   Vietnam

Copyright © 2009 by Oxford University Press, Inc.

Published by Oxford University Press, Inc.
198 Madison Avenue, New York, New York 10016

www.oup.com

Library of Congress Cataloging-in-Publication Data

Barker, Vanessa.
The politics of imprisonment: how the democratic process
shapes the way America punishes offenders / Vanessa Barker.
p. cm.
Includes bibliographical references and index.
ISBN 978-0-19-537002-7
1. Criminal justice, administration of—United States—States.   2. Criminals—United States—
States.   3. Imprisonment—United States—states.   4. Equality—United States.
5. Discrimination in criminal justice administration—United States—states.   I. Title.
HV9950.B357 2009
365'.973—dc22   2008055085

9 8 7 6 5 4 3 2 1

Printed in the United States of America
on acid-free paper

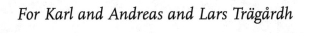

For Karl and Andreas and Lars Trägårdh

Preface

Driving through the light rain, we sat stone-cold silent, numbed
by our visit to a maximum security prison. Located deep in the pine
forest, hours away from town, this "close management" prison
confines inmates for nearly twenty-three hours a day in near total
isolation. An hour has passed before anyone spoke. The first words
were barely audible. "Why?" Someone asked plaintively.

This book is motivated by a desire to understand this profound
human experience. When someone breaks the law, how do we as a
society respond? Are we afraid, angry, resentful, vengeful? Are we
compassionate or merciful? What do penal sanctions look like? How
do they represent justice? The value of human life? How do they
express our fear and indignation? Our humanity? Our indifference?

This book has been inspired by the work of David Garland. He
has written extensively about punishment as a complex social
institution and its centrality to social science research. I have been
deeply influenced by this view. I express my sincere thanks for his
generosity, insight, and encouragement. His critical comments on
various research memos, the dissertation upon which this book is
based, and subsequent book chapters have been invaluable.

This study would not have been possible without the generous
financial support provided by the National Science Foundation, the
Public Policy Institute of California, New York University, Florida

State University, and the Law and Public Affairs Program (LAPA) at Princeton University. I thank Kim Scheppele and the LAPA fellows for creating a lively intellectual environment in which I could transform my dissertation into a book manuscript. I thank Mark Baldassare, David Lyon, the research fellows and associates, and the staff of the Public Policy Institute of California for supporting my research on California and completion of the dissertation.

I also thank James Cook, my editor at Oxford University Press, for taking interest in this project and making it a reality; David Greenberg for challenging me to do the numbers and supporting this project from beginning to end; and Edwin Amenta, Jonathan Simon, and Joachim Savelsberg, whose criticisms over the years have improved this project immensely. I thank all of the anonymous reviewers, Jeff Goodwin, Nitsan Chorev, Neil Brenner, Aaron Kupchik, Joseph DeAngelis, Karen Snedker, members of the NYU Workshop on Power, Politics, and Protest, and Ted Chiricos and Tom Blomberg at Florida State University for their feedback on earlier versions of this work. And I thank Jo Dixon for introducing me to sociology.

I am indebted to the librarians, archivists, researchers, and research associates at the following institutions for their excellent assistance: Rockefeller Archive Center; Washington State Library and Archive; New York Department of Correctional Services; Washington State Department of Corrections; Data Analysis Unit of the California Department of Corrections, California History Library; Paul Gann Archive; Dace Taub at the University of Southern California; Paul King at the Institute of Governmental Studies, University of California at Berkeley; New York State Library; Schomberg Center for African America History; New York Public Library; and the Public Policy Institute of California.

Some of the case study material on the democratic process and crime victims in California and Washington appeared as "The Politics of Pain: A Political Institutionalist Analysis of Crime Victims' Moral Protests," *Law & Society Review* 41.3 (2007). I thank Blackwell Publishing for permission to include this material. An early statement of the argument was published as "The Politics of Punishing: Building a State Governance Theory of American Imprisonment Variation," *Punishment & Society* 8.1 (2006)—thanks to Malcolm Feeley. I also thank Darwin Stapleton and the Rockefeller Archive Center for permission to quote from Governor Nelson A. Rockefeller's gubernatorial papers.

Special thanks to my family for enduring years of this grim topic. I especially thank my husband Lars Trägårdh for his excitement about life in general and about this project in particular. His critical attention to each chapter helped me clarify key points and develop my arguments. His unwavering support buoyed me through the most difficult moments— for that I am forever grateful. This book is dedicated to him and to our sons, Karl and Andreas, who were born the same day I received the book contract.

Contents

The Politics of Imprisonment

I

Imprisonment and the Democratic Process

The Transformation of U.S. Imprisonment

Punishment in America has radically changed over the past thirty years. The United States has increased its reliance on confinement to unprecedented levels, imprisoning more people than ever before and for longer periods of time in rather austere prison conditions. Today, there are over two million people in prison or jail, a historic record, and a 500 percent increase in the incarceration rate since the early 1970s.[1] One of every 100 adults is currently imprisoned, a rate that is five to seven times that of other advanced industrial democracies such as France, Germany, and Sweden and a figure that surpasses Russia and South Africa, countries with comparatively high incarceration rates.[2] Across much of the United States, rehabilitation, the underlying principle of punishment, has been replaced by retribution as many policy makers, politicians, and correctional officials have given up efforts to reform inmates and instead simply punish them, sometimes quite harshly.

The poor, undereducated, unemployed, and racial and ethnic minorities have been especially hard hit by these policies, often with long-lasting consequences. African Americans and Latinos make up about half the prison population despite their smaller proportion in the general population. Problems with prisoner "reentry" into mainstream society—difficulties with employment, marriage, child care, education—have tended to further alienate ex-offenders and destabilize community life for their families and neighbors.[3] Such heavy reliance on imprisonment over the years has not only driven up the cost of government in a time of growing budgetary crisis but has created intractable social problems for the entire country.

State-Level Variation

What is less well known is how the individual American states contributed to this massive prison build-up and how some states confounded this trend. The United States does not have a uniform nor coherent punishment policy because all criminal justice policy is a subnational responsibility. Individual states tend to punish differently from one another and punish in ways that have not been fully documented, understood, or explained.

First, consider varying state-level imprisonment rates. Currently, Louisiana imprisons over 800 inmates per 100,000 population, Texas nearly 700, and Mississippi just over 700.[4] These stunning figures, substantially higher than the national average of 447, tower over the rates of Maine and Minnesota (159 and 181, respectively), states with the lowest imprisonment rates in the country. The gross disparities in imprisonment rates cannot all be explained away by varying crime rates. Many states with high crime rates tend to have high imprisonment rates, but this not a fixed relationship. Some states with low crime rates also have high imprisonment rates. Mississippi, for example, ranks thirty-first in violent crime but third in the nation in imprisonment rates. Others, like New York, with relatively high crime rates (until very recent years) have created bifurcated imprisonment rates, high for certain crimes and low for others. New York imprisons drug and violent offenders at relatively high rates but simultaneously diverts and paroles nonviolent offenders, practices that support a surprisingly moderate imprisonment rate of 322.

Second, the intensity and character of penal sanctioning varies dramatically from place to place. Some states have embraced the full force of penal sanctioning, instituting policies and practices designed to humiliate and degrade offenders, to use James Whitman's apt terminology. Some, like Arizona, have reintroduced modern-day chain gains, complete with antiquated striped prison garb and public road crews. In Louisiana, the Angola

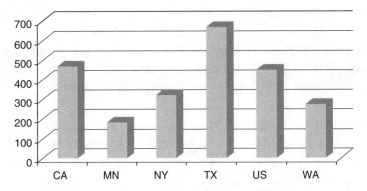

FIGURE 1.1. Subnational imprisonment rates, selected U.S. states, 2007.

prison sits on a former plantation and deploys extensive prison labor, reviving "days gone by" with white correction officers on horseback overseeing predominantly black inmates in the fields.[5] In Texas, the death house at Huntsville is so overworked that many longtime staffers have quit, and the warden, once a solid supporter of capital punishment, has reconsidered his views.[6]

Less sensational but no less intense, some states have adopted a set of policies and practices that mandate prison terms instead of probation for first-time offenders, lengthen prison terms, create severe penalties for specific crimes, and eliminate early release from prison. California's "three strikes and you're out" law, for example, significantly increased prison sentences for repeat offenders and created a twenty-five years to life mandatory sentence for third-time felony offenders, including nonviolent offenders. California's indiscriminate imprisonment of first-time offenders, parole violators, and repeat violent offenders—its "wide net"—has driven up imprisonment rates, placing this once liberal state fifteenth in the nation with its rate of 471 inmates per 100,000 population.

At the same time, however, some states have bucked this punitive trend. Some have developed policies that reduce the intensity of penal sanctioning. Some have even pursued a quiet policy of de-escalation, seeking to reduce state reliance on confinement through diversion and other means. Washington State, for example, relies extensively on community sanctions, penal sanctions that tend to depress imprisonment rates as offenders are diverted from prison to noncarceral settings. Washington currently imprisons about 273 inmates per 100,000, ranking forty-first in the nation. Like Washington, Oregon tends to favor community sanctions over imprisonment with nearly three times the number of offenders in community supervision compared to prison.[7] Ohio has initiated similar policies through sentencing guidelines reform, which promotes community sanctions for nonviolent offenders.[8]

Many other states have recently tried to lessen the severity of punishment by decreasing prison terms. Eighteen states, including Connecticut, Indiana, Delaware, Michigan, Missouri, and Louisiana, have either abolished or reduced their mandatory minimum prison terms for low-level nonviolent offenders.[9] North Dakota, Mississippi, Maine, Colorado, Maryland, Iowa, Illinois, Oregon, Montana, and Hawaii have instituted similar penal reforms.[10]

In the 1980s and 1990s, prison construction could barely keep pace with new admissions to prison. Today, many states have halted prison construction and have either consolidated or closed entire facilities. Some states have been forced to do so in response to major budget cuts, but others have actively sought to reduce their prison populations for political and social reasons. California, Florida, Georgia, Illinois, Massachusetts, Michigan, Nebraska, Ohio, Pennsylvania, New York, Texas, and Virginia have either consolidated or closed prisons.

Variation in penal sanctioning is not only significant across the American states but is substantial within individual states. Many states often lack internal consistency in punishment, deploying a wide range of penal sanctions, using both structured and unstructured sentencing, and mismatching penal philosophies (e.g., rehabilitation and retribution). Some states may promote stiff criminal penalties on the front end but generous early release policies on the back end. Some manage to use both indeterminate and determinate sentencing, fixing penalties for certain crimes but not others. Some may tout the rehabilitative ideal but simply warehouse inmates. Others may promote more "progressive" policies but are merely refashioning state coercion under friendlier names: community sanctions, substance abuse treatment, and prisoner reentry programs.

American penal sanctioning is fragmented, multidimensional, and often contradictory. It is an odd mix of policies and practices that are ad hoc, reactive to current events, and sometimes the result of long-term planning. The reality of American penal sanctioning is much more complicated, uneven, and obscure than the discussion of national trends allows.

Comparing Penal Regime Variation in Three Cases

This book seeks to document and explain variation in American penal sanctioning. It is an important empirical pattern that has been downplayed in
the existing literature in its attempt to identify and explain general trends.[11]
This study compares the ways in which three American states, California,
Washington, and New York, developed their distinctive penal regimes in the
late 1960s and early 1970s, a critical period in the history of U.S. crime control
policy. A penal regime includes the discourse on crime, conceptualizations of
justice, the rational for punishment, the character and type of sanctions, and
imprisonment rates. At this juncture, Washington introduced the *principle
of parsimony*, relying on the least repressive sanctions possible; whereas
California pursued *retribution*, more punitive and mandatory penal sanctions;
and New York adopted *managerialism*, sorting certain offenders into prison and
diverting others away.

What is puzzling here is why the states did not pursue the same kind of
policies in response to the same kinds of policy problems. Each faced a historic
rise in crime, increases that quickly overloaded criminal justice systems
around the country and called into question the rehabilitative ideal. For nearly
eighty years, most states had tried to follow a rehabilitative approach to crime, a
penal philosophy that assumed crime was caused by social deprivation rather
than moral depravity and required the treatment and correction of offenders'
failed socialization. This crisis in criminal justice took place within the context
of major social change that further undermined the public's confidence and
trust in government to handle pressing social problems. The rise of a youth
counterculture, antiwar demonstrators, contentious racial politics, and a backlash against the welfare state not only overturned traditional social hierarchies
and social norms but also challenged state authority.

Given these conditions, we might have expected state governments
to respond to rising crime and growing social unrest with repression, a
uniformly harsh response. Weakened political authorities tend to rely on
repression to temporarily restore social order during times of uncertainty
and social disintegration.[12] But many American states did not do so in any
consistent way.

It is critical to examine this early period because these initial changes
help explain the chronic long-term differences in penal sanctioning we continue to see across the American states, despite the national upward trend in

imprisonment. Understanding the past can be a useful way to explain the present. If we want to understand why recent efforts to reform California's three strikes laws failed, why Governor Arnold Schwarzenegger's much publicized Public Safety and Offender Rehabilitative Service Act may be a hollow reform, how Washington State muted the effects of its three strikes laws and prioritized diversion, or how New York has managed to shut down prison facilities and reform its drug laws, we need to understand the ongoing and cumulative effects of the past on current events. Past decisions and past policies have created resilient path dependencies that direct and shape contemporary penal sanctioning in each state. Consider that Washington has kept its imprisonment rates relatively low, California has had relatively high imprisonment rates, and New York has maintained moderate imprisonment rates, consistently hovering around the national average despite the state's infamous drug laws (see Figures 1.1, 1.2).[13] Figure 1.2 illustrates the long-term trends in imprisonment rates in the cases and the national average. It shows the secular upward trend across the cases since the 1970s and highlights the chronic long-term differences we see today.

In addition, these particular states may tell us something important about punishment in the other states because they are representative of broader trends in American penal sanctioning and deeper trends in American democracy, discussed shortly.

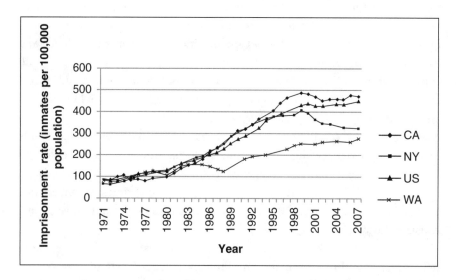

FIGURE 1.2. Long-term trends and imprisonment rates in the cases, 1971–2007.

Explaining Penal Regime Variation: The Democratic Process

This book is about the way Americans engage in the democratic process and how the democratic process shapes the way the nation punishes criminal offenders. Criminal law and penal sanctions can be explained by the logic of collective action, rather than the logic of supply and demand. Penal sanctions are the result of deliberate policy choices rather than automatic responses to crime. More crime does not mean more imprisonment, just as more home-lessness does not mean more housing. Societies make choices about how and why they punish, choices that are bound up in changing historical condi-tions and cultural and political processes. People struggle over the meaning and causes of crime, and they struggle over the ways states should respond to criminal violations. These struggles are embedded in broader conflicts over the meaning and practices of democracy.

Informed by political sociology, particularly the work of Theda Skocpol and Robert Putnam, this book develops an analytical framework of the demo-cratic process based on two theoretically and empirically significant features: political structures and collective agency.[14] *Political structures* refer specifically to the institutional and administrative organization of the state; *collective agency* refers to the mobilization of ordinary people in the policy-making process. These features shape how people take action in politics and how people understand the nature and meaning of their actions. Taken together, these two dimensions form modes of governance. They create an underlying texture of political life in a particular place. They form the organizing princi-ples, classification schemes, the taken-for-granted assumptions, the routines and habits of political interaction, or, in Pierre Bourdieu's terms, a *habitus* of political action. They significantly shape the way people make sense of political conflict and the ways they try to resolve it. This means that we are likely to see variation rather than uniformity in the ways people understand the very nature of political problems and how they try to solve, avoid, escalate, or defuse them.[15]

The subtle but crucial differences in the political institutions and demo-cratic traditions of the American states help account for penal regime variation. When we see significant changes in the political order, we are likely to see transformation in penal regimes; likewise, when we see variation or differ-ences between political orders, we are likely to see correlative differences in penal regimes.

The second major claim of this book is that penal regime change, continuity, and difference are significantly shaped by place. Penal regime variation is shaped by local and state-level institutional configurations as well as national and global trends. Crime and punishment tend to be experienced and made meaningful on a more local level even as these institutions are subject to and agents of broad social and cultural changes. People tend to experience and understand the common conditions of contemporary life in ways that are reflective of their immediate context, their past traditions, and in ways that help them make sense of the changing world around them.[16] Moreover, people tend to take action with the tools, schemas, and resources available to them in their particular contexts. As a consequence, we tend to see variation rather than uniformity in state-level responses to crime and other perceived problems of social order.

Comparative and historical methodology is used to develop these arguments, the first study of American punishment to do so.[17] This study not only takes into account the broad social conditions that underlie the development of particular penal regimes, it takes seriously the longlasting and cumulative effects of the cultural and political differences that give expression to the unique punishment practices in each state. For each case study, I analyze and compare a wide variety of data sources, including archival material, citizens' letters to political leaders, internal government reports and memos, written and oral public testimony, newspaper accounts, extensive secondary literature, and survey and statistical data. By taking advantage of underutilized data sources and the analytical leverage provided by a small number of cases, this study closely examines the dynamic interface between the state and civil society in the policymaking process.

Case Studies

In the California case, political actors operate within a neopopulist mode of governance with a high degree of democratization but intensive social polarization. Here, key actors such as the governor, state officials, and social activists are more likely to view crime as a result of moral depravity, individual failing, and social indecency. With their depressed sense of mutual obligation and heightened contentiousness and uncompromising, winner-take-all politics, citizens tend to support and often demand that state elites pursue a more retributive penal regime. California's retributive penal regime not only mandates penal sanctioning across crime categories, it changed the moral calculus of justice in the state, dramatizing the pain and suffering of crime victims as the justification for increased sanctions. It intensifies the repressive powers of the state to resolve social conflict, creating more exclusionary conditions of citizenship.

By contrast, in the Washington case, political actors operate within a more deliberative democracy, a mode of governance that emphasizes citizen participation, discussion, compromise, and self-governance. Here key actors such as state officials and public participants are more likely to view crime as a result of failed socialization and a common but unfortunate condition of affluent societies. With their well-developed norms of reciprocity and sense of mutual obligation, they tend to be reluctant to impose the repressive powers of the state on others, seeking at various times to de-escalate imprisonment. At the same time, the legacy of cooperatives and self-governance provide the cultural and institutional support necessary for officials to pursue noncustodial community sanctions based primarily on the discipline of labor and the perceived virtues but coercive powers of civil society. Taken together, these policies and practices restrain state coercion, creating more inclusionary but normalizing conditions of citizenship.

In the case of New York, political actors operate within a mode of elitist pragmatism. With its depressed democratization and heavy reliance on expertise, state officials are more likely to portray crime as a threat to public health, a contagion to be quarantined, defusing the emotional and moral dimensions of both crime and punishment. They develop a managerial penal regime, a triage approach to penal sanctioning that sorts and classifies perceived risks and allocates resources accordingly. This apparently reasonable and pragmatic approach to crime with its strategic use of state power nevertheless tends to suppress individual autonomy and liberty in favor of the perceived public good, creating restrictive conditions of citizenship.

Key Findings: Deep Democracy, Less Coercion; Thin
Democracy, More Coercion

By focusing on the complex political processes at the subnational level, this book challenges a taken-for-granted assumption about the democratic process and punishment. As this study shows, the apparent link between public participation, punitiveness, and rough justice is not only historically contingent but dependent on specific state structures and patterns of civic engagement, patterns that tend to vary within the United States and across liberal democracies. Public vengeance depends on certain political institutions and collective agency to give it a legal and political expression.

Perhaps more important, the research suggests a counterintuitive claim: increased democratization can support and sustain less coercive penal regimes. This study offers an analysis of an understudied and countervailing practice of de-escalation, a practice that should certainly be of interest to those challenging the massive prison build-up over the past thirty years. At the same time, the analysis suggests that at the aggregate level, depressed civic engagement, withdrawal from public life, and lack of public participation in the political process may underpin mass incarceration in the United States. Consider that fewer people vote in national and state elections, fewer people get involved in civic affairs and local politics, congressional and state-level elections are less competitive, and elite-driven professional organizations have replaced many of the locally run grassroots organizations that once buoyed American democracy for most for the nineteenth and twentieth centuries.[18] These trends have coincided and share affinities with the increased reliance on imprisonment and other coercive forms of state power, especially as it has been used against those who are the least politically and socially integrated, the poor, undereducated, and racial and ethnic minorities. We may be witnessing the retrenchment of American democracy and its repressive aftermath.

An understanding of penal sanctioning and the processes that bring them about are essential for understanding the nature and character of democracy and citizenship. Ever since the Enlightenment, the prison has been a major site of democratic state building as it created new institutions of crime control and new sites of state power from policing to sentencing.[19] The prison also helped establish new frameworks for understanding and classifying citizenship in democratic societies as it distinguished which people are subject to state sanction, which are not, and why. By setting the limits of what state authorities could do to someone who broke the law, penal sanctioning helped define individual rights and protections from state power. Moreover, by giving legal and political expression to polity members' feelings of scorn, resentment, pity, mercy, sympathy, and indifference, penal sanctioning also helps clarify which people are subject to social exclusion and which are candidates for reintegration.[20] As a mechanism of political integration, it identifies which people are valued and welcomed as full citizens and which are not. By doing so, punishment sorts and stratifies equality.

By taking up these themes, this book aims to contribute to a sociological understanding of the relationship between punishment and democracy, especially as punishment has helped define, classify, and sometimes change the nature of political authority and the conditions of citizenship and equality in democratic societies. If we think of the democratic process as how people self-govern and how they mobilize collectively to do so, it indicates how certain social groups dominate others, integrating and excluding individuals through particular policies and programs. The prison provides a vivid illustration of this collective process of categorization and social ordering, especially its exclusionary dimension.

Qualifying Penal Regimes

This study seeks to identify the most significant penal regime in each state. Because penal sanctioning tends to be multidimensional, overlapping, and sometimes inconsistent, I focus on the dominant penal regime rather than the entirety of criminal justice policies in each state. I identify and examine the discourse on crime, conceptualizations of justice, the rationale for punishment, the set, range, and intensity of penal sanctions, and imprisonment rates in each case.

It is important to clarify that a state's penal regime, including its imprisonment rate, is the result of continuous rather than discrete actions. A state's prison population, for example, cannot be created overnight by a dramatic piece of legislation nor by public outrage; nor can it be controlled by the actions of one person or interest group. Criminal justice policy spans multiple jurisdictions and multiple levels of government. It is organized around system-wide discretion in which the actions of a local beat cop can sometimes determine who ends up in prison. This means that a penal regime and its associated imprisonment rate are the result of cumulative actions, some of which are immediate, such as arrest rates, charging decisions, sentencing policies, and release decisions, while others are much slower and long-term, like changes in cultural values or political institutions that occur over time. In this kind of causal process, crime control policies can result in outcomes at times other than their proximity to the events under investigation.[21]

Just as natural scientists study the long-term and sometimes delayed effects of colder and deeper ocean currents on much warmer southern seas great distances away, we can think of causality in crime control in much the same way. By doing so, we can see that the war on drugs and certain three strikes legislation, for example, will probably continue to impact imprisonment populations for some time to come but are not sufficient explanations of contemporary penal regimes. By taking into account cumulative processes over time, we also gain an appreciation for the significant effects of past practices. In the early 1970s, as state officials adapted to a new set of governing conditions (namely, increasing crime), they experimented with new policy initiatives. But they could not simply break away from nor override the path dependencies established by previous penal policies.[22] The resulting penal regimes have the distinction of being both old and new simultaneously. To understand the present, we need to examine the past,[23] especially the complex processes of change and continuity.

Moreover, the book focuses on the use of imprisonment rather than policing, probation, jail, or parole. This restriction keeps the study manageable. I make no claims about mapping the entirety of crime control policies and practices in these states. During this thirty-year period, each state passed a broad range of criminal justice policy initiatives concerning but not limited to sentencing reform, parole reform, drug offenders, repeat offenders, sex offenders, community policing, juvenile justice, prison labor, crime victims compensation, victim impact statements, and new approaches to crime prevention—each of which was the result of a specific set of institutional and political configurations that are well beyond the scope of this study.

More important, I focus on imprisonment because the prison, although an early nineteenth-century invention, still occupies a privileged position in the repertoire of criminal justice because all states rely on imprisonment in response to crime—they just do so differently. More important, imprisonment is one of the most intrusive and tactile displays of state power. Through penal sanctioning the state reasserts its right to rule a territory and its people and do so with force if necessary. This kind of power is simply awesome in its sheer control over the life of another human being. Imprisonment makes visible the state's power to punish as the offender is literally encased inside the state. Imprisonment, like state execution (a relatively rare occurrence despite its hold on the public imagination)[24] and conscription into the military, is a raw and physical form of power that can subdue the minds and bodies within its grasp, especially as it infringes on a person's sense of autonomy and selfhood.[25]

Imprisonment captures something meaningful about the relationship between rulers and ruled in democratic societies. A liberal democracy like the United States is defined by the extent to which individual rights and autonomy are valued and protected from abuses of governmental power and from the intolerance of the majority. Imprisonment represents the extent to which democracies are willing to infringe on those rights and obligations, especially as they are determined by collective action. This book explores the conditions under which state officials and social groups in civil society are willing to impose on the sanctity of individual autonomy and why some U.S. states are more willing than others to engage in this practice.

Case Selection

So which states are more willing than others to infringe on the rights and liberties of convicted criminal offenders? Louisiana, Texas, and Mississippi imprison more people per capita than any other state, each with an imprisonment rate (excluding jail) of well over 600 inmates per 100,000 population.[26] Maine, Minnesota, and Rhode Island currently imprison the fewest people per capita, each with an imprisonment rate of under 200 inmates per 100,000 population.[27] Yet this book is about Washington, New York, and California, none of which fall in the top five or bottom five rates of imprisonment, none of which are the extreme cases. Instead, these states represent the general and differentiated patterns of punishment we see across the fifty states. They represent what this study refers to as de-escalation, managerialism, and retribution, respectively. At the beginning of the study, each state fell into the top, middle, and bottom third of state-level imprisonment rates. Currently, Washington imprisons 273 inmates per 100,000, ranking forty-first in the nation; New York 322, ranking thirty-seventh in the nation (it ranked thirtieth at the beginning of this study); and California 471, ranking fifteenth in the nation.[28] By looking at these particular states rather than others, this move allows me to examine trends that may be more common across a wide range of states while maintaining a tight analytical focus on a small number of cases. This strategy maximizes the potential explanatory power of the case studies.

Crime Rates

Some readers may be quick to point out that states with higher crime rates have higher imprisonment rates. For example, South Carolina has one of the highest violent crime rates in the United States, as well as one of the highest imprisonment rates.[29] Similarly, Maine has very low crime rates and very low imprisonment rates. This is an intuitive observation because every sentence of imprisonment is imposed in the wake of a criminal conviction. It is also an observation that is taken seriously by this study. However, what is less clear is why some states with similarly high crime rates may be less likely to rely on imprisonment or why states with low crime rates may rely heavily on imprisonment. Tennessee, for example, ranks second in violent crime but twenty-second in imprisonment rates; likewise, Alaska ranks sixth in violent crime but twenty-fifth in imprisonment rates.[30] Washington, California, and New York have all maintained relatively high crime rates for nearly thirty years but pursued different kinds of penal regimes. Violent crime in Washington is lower than in California and New York, but the overall crime rate in Washington has hovered well above the national average for over thirty years, at times higher than that in California or New York.[31]

It also less clear why the doubling of crime rates between 1965 and 1975 in nearly every state did not lead to the doubling of imprisonment rates in nearly every state. Many commentators view the increase in crime as simply a technological advance in which law enforcement improved its ability to record crime and a cultural change in which the public became more willing to report it—both imply an artificial rise in crime in a relatively short period of time.[32] Despite these doubts, however, many state officials, legislators, grassroots activists, and criminal justice officials experienced rising crime in the late 1960s as a real event with material consequences for the criminal justice system, an experience supported by increasing homicide rates.[33] The experience of high crime put tremendous pressure on understaffed, decentralized, and undermodernized criminal justice systems. So much so that many state and criminal justice officials began to rethink their approach to crime control, which by the 1970s seemed ineffective and perhaps even counterproductive. This book is about how and why certain state officials, legislators, grassroots activists, and criminal justice officials came to perceive and characterize the experience of rising crime as a policy problem in the first place, and how they did so in different ways in different political contexts.

There is no unmediated or pure experience of crime because it is a product of social interaction and requires interpretation. The interpretation of crime is in turn shaped by culturally available schemas or frameworks of understanding in particular places and times, schemas that are themselves shaped by varying forms of social organization.[34] For example, seventeenth-century Puritans perceived crime as sin, an unholy act against God that necessitated retribution and even purification. Likewise, the late nineteenth-century Women's Christian Temperance Union and the Anti-Saloon League associated drinking with sin, disease, disorder, and inevitable social disintegration, an interpretive act that led to social hygiene campaigns and increased state regulation of private life and community health. More recently in the 1960s, critical criminologists viewed crime as the result of class conflict and social deprivation, an inevitable act in an unequal society based on the exploitation of the poor and socially marginalized.

The shock of high crime in 1960s took on a different meaning and character in Washington, California, and New York as key actors interpreted this steep increase in different ways. In Washington, state officials, criminal justice actors, politicians, and engaged citizens tended to characterize crime as the consequences of social deprivation and as a common condition in affluent societies. In response, government officials asked citizens to alter their behavior to decrease the opportunities for crime and they promoted various work programs to make up for offenders' failed socialization. In New York, state officials interpreted crime in epidemiological terms, making an analogy between rising crime and the spread of infectious, contagious diseases, and they tended to favor policy responses based on the quarantine of perceived risks, particularly drugs and violent crime. In California, crime became associated with moral depravity and weakened social controls. Crime was characterized as an insult to the people who helped build and benefited from the Golden State's generous social policies and myths of limitless opportunity, both of which were undermined by the experience of high crime. As a consequence, crime policy in California became rather punitive, designed to punish offenders for this transgression and express resentment. How and why these states developed their particular punishment regimes is rooted to a certain degree in the historically contingent conceptualizations of the crime problem and is evidenced by the discourse on crime control.

Race

Some readers may point to racial differences in the cases as a plausible explanation for variation in penal regimes because researchers have established an important relationship between the size of a state's black population and imprisonment rates. According to this argument, a relatively large black population poses an economic and political threat to the white majority, subsequently leading whites to support and demand more punitive penal sanctioning.[35] To be sure, African Americans and other minorities are over-represented in U.S. prisons, and contentious racial politics clearly play a role. What we still need to theorize and explain is why and how different states developed different kinds of penal regimes. Recall that they all did not respond punitively to the changing social order or the success of the civil rights movement. New York's black population, for example, has been nearly twice that of California's since the 1960s,[36] yet state officials developed a managerial penal regime with lower imprisonment rates. Likewise, Washington's relatively small black population does not explain the character and meaning of the state's penal regime or why officials pursued de-escalation in the face of high crime and a rapidly increasing black population in the 1960s. An absence does not explain a presence. Racial politics rather than racial demographics shape imprisonment patterns and are likely to vary by political context.

Specifically, the political incorporation of African Americans may have played an important role in moderating punitiveness. In states where black Americans and their advocates increased black integration into the political process and codified antidiscrimination laws throughout the 1950s and 1960s, we might expect to see less reliance on coercive social controls. By contrast, in states that continued to exclude African Americans from full citizenship, restricting their political participation and weakening their economic viability, we might expect to see higher reliance on repression, including imprisonment. Black incorporation not only indicates a more inclusive notion of citizenship but also gives political actors opportunities to develop social trust and norms of reciprocity across social groups, an imperative in complex political communities that depend on compromise. Political incorporation may provide a buffer against the use of imprisonment as a blunt instrument of racial social control.

Already by the mid-1950s, both New York and Washington State passed fair employment antidiscrimination laws and created enforcement agencies; by the mid-1960s, both had passed fair housing and open accommodations antidiscrimination laws along with enforcement agencies.[37] New

York created the New York State Civil Rights Bureau along with strengthening antidiscrimination laws in employment, housing, and public accommodation and promoted equal opportunity.[38] Although California passed antidiscrimination laws in the 1950s, racial politics since the mid-1960s have been and continue to be much more polarized and exclusionary than in New York or Washington.[39] In the mid-1960s, California voters rejected pro-civil rights legislation, rejecting the Rumford Fair Housing Act, a far-reaching statute that would have protected blacks from widespread housing discrimination,[40] a move that most likely prompted the Watts Riots of 1965 and subsequent backlash.

Democratic Process

What makes California, Washington, and New York so interesting, especially for this study, is precisely the nature and character of their democratic processes. For example, the political structures and collective agency in California and Washington, like much of the west, are rooted in populism—more direct forms of citizen participation in governmental decision making. By the turn of the twentieth century, the populist movement and the progressive movement that followed led to the fundamental restructuring of government and expanded democratization.[41] With the introduction of voter initiatives, ordinary people could draft their own legislation, essentially bypassing elected officials and state legislatures, deemed at the time to be corrupt and unresponsive to the public's demands. More people had access to and were integrated in the political process. Today, California and Washington have some of the most open political institutions in the United States; both have had, for part of the twentieth century, some of the most generous social policies in the nation.

These two states are puzzling cases because they eventually diverged from this shared past and adopted distinctive forms of governance. By the mid-1960s, we can see the emergence of a more reactionary and antistatist form of populism in California, based on the deep distrust of both government and expert knowledge. Somewhat paradoxically, this form weakened citizen participation in political life and increased the protection of private self-interest over the pursuit of public goods. By contrast, in Washington, by the mid- to late 1960s, we can see the emergence of institutions and collective agency oriented toward open and public debates, and discussion—a set of institutions that values compromise, mutual cooperation, and self-governance. This more deliberative style of governance shares certain affinities with a more inclusive stance toward the provision of public goods and members' well-being.

New York provides a counterbalance to these states. It shares none of California and Washington's familiarity with populism and direct democracy. The populist movement and the various farmers' alliances failed miserably in New York. Instead political authority is highly centralized and insulated from public participation. Ordinary people have very little direct access to governmental decision making, the initiative process does not exist, and few people turn out to vote.[42] The executive branch, headed by the governor, is one of the most powerful in the United States in terms of its capacity to control the budget, veto legislation, make appointments to state agencies, and repeatedly run for reelection.[43]

Given these indicators of a somewhat limited public participation, it is surprising that New York has maintained some of the most generous social policies in the country. This practice, important for punishment policy, is itself rooted in the fertile period of political transformation that swept most of the country during the early part of the twentieth century. The progressive movement, dominated by middle-class professionals and other elites, made a serious challenge to New York's patronage and machine-based politics. The progressives ushered in a new form of pragmatic governance—a form that relied extensively on expert knowledge, professionals, technocrats, bureaucrats, and other state insiders to pursue public works in the most rational and efficient way possible. By the 1960s, we can see an almost idealized form of pragmatism in New York operating under the strong leadership of Governor Nelson Rockefeller.

New York is a complex case because political authority is highly centralized and collective agency tends to be pragmatic, reliant on expertise, and oriented toward problem solving, but it also shows tendencies toward elitism and the pursuit of private self-interest. From the time of Dutch settlements onward, state officials have consolidated power, concentrating it in the executive branch, and to a certain extent have restricted democratization. So what we see in New York is the continuity of elitism—the elite dominance of political power—but discontinuity in collective action. Collective agency shifts from patronage politics and the pursuit of private gain and self-interest to the ideals of progressive pragmatism and the pursuit of public works, without making a clean break from either one.

In the pages that follow, I develop an account of punishment that relates it to the character of the democratic process. Chapter 2 establishes the theoretical basis for this study. Chapters 3, 4, and 5 deploy the theoretical framework to sort out and make sense of the empirical variation in imprisonment in

California, Washington, and New York. The case studies show how differences in political structure and collective agency lead to differentiated penal sanctioning in the states. The case studies also locate these patterns in the broader social and historical context of the late 1960s and 1970s. The last chapter brings together the findings of the case studies to explain why and how the democratic process matters to any explanation of punishment. I highlight convergences and divergences in penal policy by trying to make some sense of the complicated nature of change and continuity in both American democracy and American punishment. The last chapter raises several important implications for understanding punishment in America as well as other advanced liberal democracies.

What about the South? Readers may wonder why the case studies do not focus on any of the southern states since the South tends to have the highest imprisonment rates. The South was excluded because this region has been and continues to be relatively underdemocratized compared to every other region in the United States. With its historical ties to feudal-like social and political hierarchies, slavery, weakened central government, and underdemocratized polity, the South has followed a different path of penal development than most other American states. That path includes the brutal use of convict leasing and state-sanctioned lynching, both of which involved a disproportionate number of African American men and high rates of mortality. These practices existed into the twentieth century, when most other states debated and many adopted the principles and practices of the rehabilitative ideal. With some exceptions, much of southern punishment has tended to favor relatively harsh penal sanctions for most of the twentieth and twenty-first centuries, imprisoning as well as executing the most people per capita in the nation. In a book that covers three other American states in some detail, I felt I could not do justice to the depth and complexities of southern punishment, especially since it has followed a different historical path. Southern punishment requires its own intensive study, a project I leave, for the moment, to others.

Rationale and Implications of this Study

One of the central aims of this project is to understand and try to provide some insight into the democratic process—its varying political structures and diverse forms of collective action—and its relationship to punishment. With a few important exceptions, it is a process that has been somewhat neglected and understudied by current scholarship in both political sociology and criminology.[44] In the academic division of labor, students of politics, power, and social movements for the most part have left questions of criminal justice, criminal law, and penal sanctioning to others, implicitly accepting official narratives about crime and punishment as beyond the realm of political contestation and social conflict. Nor has this field of study incorporated in any serious way the structuring role of punishment in the production of political authority, citizenship, and state legitimacy. Likewise, criminologists, concerned more about the causes of crime, for the most part have not taken up questions about the nature and character of democracy, governance, and state power in any way that goes beyond the instrumentalist neo-Marxian perspective that views the forms of punishment as mere reflections of existing economic relations and a function of social control—here the "state" is epiphenomenal, redundant, and beholden to economic imperatives.

This book seeks to address these oversights by building on recent work in the sociology of punishment, work that takes seriously the changing nature of governance in contemporary societies. My argument is consistent to a certain degree with current scholarship that has identified the changing nature of governance as bringing about increased harshness in American punishment.[45] As Jonathan Simon, David Garland, and Loïc Wacquant (among others) have pointed out, the nature of governance has taken on a more neoliberal character—that is to say, as it has prioritized privatization and market solutions to complex social problems and downplayed more inclusive welfarist policies intended to alleviate some of the ill effects of capitalist economies.[46] Subsequent to these shifts in governance, we have seen the intensification of state repression in response to crime and other perceived problems of order.

Although this book builds on common ground with many leading accounts, it takes important departures from current scholarship. It focuses on the chronic and long-term differences across the states, rather than the secular upward trend in imprisonment rates, paying more attention to differentiated experiences of crime and differentiated responses. As a consequence, this analysis points to variation rather than uniformity in the way that ordinary people and state officials try to resolve conflicts over social ordering, political community, and citizenship through penal sanctioning. By examining a differentiated democratic process, this analysis suggests that increased democratization can support de-escalation in imprisonment while retrenchment in democracy can lead to increased state coercion.

Moreover, an understanding of the democratic process and its relationship to penal sanctioning is crucial to understanding the changing nature of governance in the twenty-first century. It can help us understand how we are changing the way we live our daily lives. As many commentators have noted, the basic forms of government and social organization are slowly being reconfigured in real time. In response to the forces of globalization and its associated pressures of economic and political integration, the modern nation-state faces serious challenges to its sovereignty and legitimacy. With the expansion of supranational entities, such as the European Union, the World Trade Organization, and International Criminal Court, the modern nation-state no longer maintains exclusive control over law, regulation, and rule making.[47] As political theorist Jean Cohen explains, political sovereignty is becoming "disaggregated" and shared across jurisdictions as the nation-state no longer fully controls "its own territory, borders, resident population, as well as the internal hazards that threaten its citizens."[48]

In response to some of these pressures, many Western democracies have changed their basic approach to governing. Confronted by a globalizing economy, many have reorganized their once generous social welfare policies and programs, which are aimed not only at the poor but the middle classes, to keep up with international competition. Alongside these changes, we have also witnessed changes in the social relations that make up civil society as social trust and mutual identification have been slowly replaced by suspicion and resentment, animosity aimed especially at those social groups that are marginally integrated into political and economic life. At the same time, many American states and some European nations have become more willing to use imprisonment and other coercive forms of state power in response to crime and other complex social problems.

As these social transformations continue, the question remains which states will be more likely to pursue this particular policy response. An understanding of the diversity of states and democratic institutions and practices not only in America but in the post–cold war Europe may help us sort out which nation-states are more likely to rely on more coercive approaches to governance. An appreciation of the differences across democratic societies can helps us tease out which mechanisms, cultural resources, institutions, and practices—centralization, bureaucratization, deliberation, participation— depress or exacerbate state repression. By paying attention to the divergences in democracy as well as long-standing path dependencies, we may be able to explain why some states more than others are willing to use imprisonment and other policing mechanisms to redefine the conditions of citizenship and quite possibly undermine notions of political and social equality. We may be able to explain why some states more than others rely on the structural role of punishment to redefine political sovereignty and shore up legitimacy in the face of transnational realignment and globalization. This book aims to contribute to this conversation.

2

Explaining Penal Regime Variation

Political Structures and Collective Agency

This chapter presents the theoretical basis for the study. It seeks to develop an account of punishment, particularly of penal regime change, continuity, and difference, that is rooted in the structure of the democratic process in all its variation and complexity.

This chapter makes two central claims:

(C1) The character and intensity of penal regimes are deeply rooted in the structure and collective agency of the democratic process. When we see significant changes in the political order, we are likely to see transformation in penal regimes; likewise, when we see variation or differences between political orders, we are likely to see correlative differences in penal regimes.

(C2) Penal regime change, continuity, and difference are significantly shaped by localized institutional configurations as well as by national and global trends. Crime and punishment tend to be experienced and made meaningful on a subnational level even as these institutions are subject to and agents of broad social and cultural change. People tend to experience and understand the common conditions of late modernity in ways that are reflective of their immediate context, their past traditions, and in ways that help them make sense of the changing world around them.[1] Moreover, people tend to take action with the tools, schemas, and resources that are available to them in their particular contexts.

I base these arguments on a set of nested propositions:

(P1) Punishment and political orders are loosely coupled social institutions.[2] Under certain conditions, they tend to be bound together by a shared historical trajectory and institutional logic.

(P2) To understand the significance of penal regime change, continuity, and difference, the sociology of punishment needs a theory of the democratic state. The state is a set of institutions that not only structures social relations, in part through the legitimate use of force, but one that is structured and made meaningful by social mobilization. We can understand the state as a set of mutual obligations between public authority and citizens, but one that is subject to ongoing political struggle as well as changing historical conditions.

(P3) This understanding of the state is based, in part, on Max Weber's classic formulation but also on Anthony Giddens's structuration theory of action.[3] Structuration theory posits that people make up the social structures that organize, pattern, and give meaning to their lives at the same time that these structures organize, pattern, and give shape to human interaction. It is a theory of social life that incorporates the efficacy of human agency with the capacities and constraints of social structures.

Historical Background: State Change

The reproduction of American democracy is fraught with uncertainty and complexity given that the meaning of democracy is not settled, fixed, or universal. Instead, it is a highly contested social institution that has been and continues to be subject to intense political struggle across time and space.

In the mid-1960s and early 1970s, Americans began to seriously remake the democratic order. War, political protest, and loss of confidence in government all posed significant and historic challenges to the legitimacy of the political order. Specifically, dissent over the Vietnam War, corruption in the highest office, daily insecurity brought about by rising crime and what appeared to be lax law enforcement and weak social controls, demands to increase political participation, and demands to redistribute power and resources to marginalized social groups all exposed the hypocrisy and deficiencies of American democracy. They exposed the hypocrisy of a political order that promised not only individual freedom but equality, well-being, and security. This set of social conflicts raised distressing questions about the nature of state power, the conditions of full citizenship, and the limits of equality, and it strained the tenuous emotional ties across social groups in civil society, ties that are necessary to bind a diverse political community together.

Remarkably, out of this turmoil, new kinds of citizenship claims and entitlements appeared to remake American democracy into a much more generous and inclusive political order. The success of the civil rights movement, the women's movement, and to some extent poor people's movements changed the mutual obligations between public authority and its citizens, expanding the terms and conditions of full citizenship. Although democratization—that is to say, the expansion of citizenship, participation, and representation—seemed to be on an upward trajectory, the empirical reality, of course, was much more complex. These were partial and sometimes temporary gains for women and minorities and were offset by a series of unresolved cultural and moral conflicts that would animate politics for the next thirty years. Brewing resentment over the flattening of social hierarchies, increased social polarization, and the subsequent decline in political participation and social trust set in motion a major transformation of American political life—factors that eventually changed the democratic process itself. What has emerged from this set of conflicts has been the rise of a rights-based politics, a variant of the democratic process and a style of politics that has tended to sharpen social divisions rather than level social inequalities.

Already by the mid-1970s, the intensification of the criminal law and penal sanctioning began to remake American democracy into a much less generous and more coercive political order. The intensification of state violence through punishment quickly undermined a generation's utopian visions of a free, equal, and tolerant society. Yet the intensification of penal sanctioning did not spread across the fifty states in any kind of predetermined or uniform way. Instead, it was subject to the vagaries of collective action.

People across the states experienced this period of acute social and political conflict in their own and varied ways, some reeling from escalating crime and violence, others encouraging it, some desperately trying to defuse racial animosity, some seduced by ideology, others simply seeking new forms of pleasure, and many trying on new forms of social organization. Ordinary people, grassroots activists along with politicians and state officials, responded to a shared set of challenges, but they did so in distinct ways. Many retreated into the private sphere, some marched in the streets, and some turned their attention to government policies and programs, seeking ways to use public policy to realize competing visions of a "good society," to concretize the imagined "city on a hill" so central to the American ethos.

Informed by broad social changes, this set of reformers, civically engaged social groups, and various state actors tended to make demands and develop policy responses in ways that were firmly grounded in the localized political context in which they were operating. In response to increasing crime and other perceived threats to social order, state officials and politicians began to reform their nearly century-old penal regimes. Some simply increased penal sanctioning and stiffened penalties. But many others changed their penal regimes in ways that were not only different from one another but were expressive of their local character whose idiosyncrasies and particular view of crime made sense to the local actors involved. Some viewed crime as a disease to be quarantined rather than cured, others viewed crime as a natural consequence of social deprivation in a society based on material consumption, and many resurrected an older view of crime as a sign of moral depravity and individual wickedness. The state-level penal regimes developed, in part, around these different conceptualizations of crime in which some regimes emphasized containment and incapacitation, others discipline through labor, and many introduced harsh and punitive sanctions. These developments are discussed in the case studies. Even when faced with similar kinds of social conditions, penal regime change across the American states reflected a more localized rather than global or national understanding of crime. Penal regime change was patched together with the material, resources, and schemas of context specific institutions and actors.

In the late 1960s and early 1970s, Americans remade their democracy. They did so in part by expanding citizenship and also in part by intensifying the punishing powers of the state. This general process was accomplished in highly distinctive ways across the American states and in ways that were made meaningful by local practice and understanding.

To better understand these transformative moments in American political and social life, we need a theory of the state. As I argue in the pages that follow, the state was the axle through which Americans turned their political and social order. The state not only provided the raw material for this transformation, its coercive powers, and its legitimating authority, for example, but its multiple and differentiated institutional configurations shaped the contours of political struggle even as it was fundamentally altered by these political struggles.

This conceptualization of the state and its intrinsic relevance for punishment follows. It should be noted in the beginning that my own understanding of the state and its effects on punishment are intellectually indebted to Max Weber and a more general social theory of action, Anthony Giddens's *structuration theory*. Structuration posits that people make up the social structures that organize, pattern, and give meaning to their lives at the same time that these structures organize, pattern, and give shape to human interaction. As Giddens explains, social life is "fundamentally recursive" as it is made up of repeated and continuous cycles of interaction between people and the patterns of interaction they have already created. (William Sewell refers to this same process as the "duality of structure.") Human beings tend to create the patterns of interaction in the present with the raw material of the past, a process that leads to the stability and durability of social institutions. Institutions provide routine to daily life and help establish the long-term and persistent cross-cultural differences in political, family, and economic systems. However, institutions are themselves the result of repeated social interaction, repeated social interaction of human beings, a source of unpredictability and imagination. This process introduces an element of uncertainty and change into the very structure of social life. The patterns of social life must be reproduced, but they are not necessarily replicated in any straightforward way. This particular social theory of action seamlessly incorporates the efficacy of human agency with the capacities and constraints of social structures, building in sources of change in the very reproduction of social life. It provides this study with a useful framework for thinking about the dynamism of state institutions, especially how human agents can change the course of political development through their patterned interaction within state institutions.

The Development of State Theory in the Sociology
of Punishment: Overview

We can think of the state as a set of multiple and overlapping institutions invested with administrative, legal, extractive, and coercive powers.[4] The state is a highly complex organization, one that provides some of the most basic organizing principles of social life. Crowned with authority, the legitimate use of force, and material and symbolic resources, the state plays a central structuring role in the patterns and meanings of political and social life. Through state institutions certain kinds of politics, political identities, and public policies become possible. In other words, particular institutional con-figurations give expression to and make possible certain kinds of political demands, needs, and interests while suppressing others. The state structures social relations: it organizes the terms, the rules, the resources through which people come to understand the conditions of membership in a shared political community; it patterns the interaction and understanding between different social groups in civil society; and it shapes how citizens understand the character and nature of public authority and their relationship to it.

Yet this institutionalist view is incomplete. The state is not only a set of institutions that structures social relations but one that is structured and made meaningful by social mobilization. This study wants to avoid viewing the "state" as a coherent entity, moving through space and time in a unified manner, issuing commands to its passive subjects. Although the state is a set of institutions, these institutions are mobilized, put into action, and made meaningful through the interaction of human beings. Given the importance of human agents to reproduction of social institutions, it is clear why we need to incorporate people into a theory of the state. We can go beyond the convention-al state actors and politicians to think about ordinary people, citizens, and social groups in civil society. Democratic states are governed in part by the rule of the people. However naive that may sound to readers steeped in critical theory and contemporary politics, citizen participation nevertheless generates deep legitimacy to democratic political orders. The people who make up democratic political orders are both subject to authority, law, and regulation, but they are also citizens and participants in lawmaking. The withdrawal of citizen participation, the public's disengagement and indifference to public life, poses the most significant threat to the legitimacy of democratic order. We need to seriously consider how people, ordinary people, along with state officials, politicians, interest groups, and other relevant parties, actually engage and participate in the political process to make law.

It may be helpful to think of the state not as a solid, monolithic structure like a brick building or even as government but rather as a relationship between public authority and citizens. Specifically, it is a set of mutual obliga-tions between public authority and citizens, one that is subject to change. As a social contract, this set helps clarify the conditions of citizenship in a shared political community, it establishes the rights and entitlements group members can claim on state agents as well as the state agents' duties to recognize those rights. This set of mutual obligations imposes limits on the claims of citizen-ship but it also imposes limits on the use of force to sanction group members. In democratic orders, penal sanctioning has played a critical role in establish-ing the legitimacy of public authority in part through force but also by con-stituting the boundaries of citizenship and political subjectivity.[5] Despite its inherently repressive nature, penal sanctioning helps produce the citizens and subjects of a political order. It does so by classifying, expressing, and stratifying the conditions of citizenship, the very basis of political participation, and by dramatizing the reaches and limits of the intrusive, arbitrary, and coercive powers of the state. Penal sanctioning, a highly effective classification schema, sorts people into recognizable social categories and social groups.[6]

Second, we can think of the state as a set of mutual obligations that is nevertheless subject to ongoing political struggle as well as changing historical conditions. Although state institutions shape the contours of political struggle, establish the rules of the game, and open certain channels of action while closing others, social mobilization can change the terms and conditions of citizenship and authority, consequently transforming the state itself.

Political struggles over crime and punishment in the late 1960s and early 1970s, discussed shortly, led to the intensification of penal sanctioning in many places across the United States. This major policy change subsequently transformed the very nature of the state, reconfiguring group membership in the political community, and fundamentally altering citizens' relationship to political authority. The high rates of felon disenfranchisement is perhaps one of the most striking examples of this new political order. By denying many former and current inmates (many of them African American men) the rights and duties of full citizenship, felon disenfranchisement excludes an entire class of people from the benefits of and commitment to a shared political community.[7] By doing so, it quite possibly undermines the pretense of political equality in the United States. As Stuart Scheingold and many others have noted, increased state reliance on punitive and disciplinary measures makes it increasingly difficult to rebuild a political order based on inclusion and broad and full citizenship, let alone social justice.[8]

Below I place this conceptualization of the state in the field of the sociology of punishment to illustrate a few basic points of contention and clarify the distinctiveness of the account.

Prior Conceptualizations of the State in the Sociology of Punishment

By thinking more explicitly about state institutions, this formulation seeks to overcome some of the limitations endemic to current scholarship on punishment. Current accounts of punishment have done much to advance our understanding of how various social factors—racial demographics, economic marginality, crime patterns—influence imprisonment rates and broader punishment patterns.[9] Yet these kinds of accounts are insufficient explanations. Because they tend to undertheorize the state and overlook various political factors, they also may be misspecified. This means that current accounts may have misidentified the nature of the relationship between democratic order and punishment. This is obviously a topic that necessitates an extensive analysis that is not possible here. It is a project I turn to elsewhere.

With a few important exceptions, the state has not been explicitly theorized in more recent work of the sociology of punishment.[10] This is surprising given that the state, its institutions, resources, cultural schemas, legitimacy, brute force, and disciplinary power, has been central to classic analyses of the transformation of punishment in the modern era. The state has been central, in some shape or form, to the work of Michel Foucault, Norbert Elias, and David Garland. The idea of the state and its importance for punishment has not disappeared, rather, it has not been fully articulated, and when it has, it has been problematic. I impose a thematic framework to help us make sense of the unarticulated assumptions about the state in the sociology of punishment.

For the most part, studies of contemporary penal trends have implicitly rather than explicitly conceptualized the state as an arena, a black box, an empty vessel to be filled by either the public's demands or politicians' schemes. In other accounts, the state is epiphenomenal, a mere reflection of preexisting social relations, used as an instrument of class control or as a more insidious mode of repression, management, and social regulation.

In pluralistic versions, the state is a black box, an inanimate object to be filled by the demands and needs of competing interest groups. The state is simply a place where competing political interests negotiate their differences. Here the state is reduced to the actions and activities of politics. This perspective not only assumes all parties are equal at the bargaining table but places too much causal weight on the actions of autonomous, rationally calculating individuals to influence the policy-making process and bring about change. Even the most powerful executive with centralized power must contend with bureaucracy to get anything done. This perspective also overemphasizes the degree to which political actors are indeed rational, calculating, and strategic and downplays the extent to which political action is driven by moral outrage, emotion, or the desire to break or strengthen social ties—factors that clearly underpin debates about crime and punishment in contemporary America.

Perhaps more problematically, this view of the state assumes that interest group competition and electoral competition results in public policies. This assumption moves too quickly from "politics to policy," to invoke Hugh Heclo's efficient formulation. Political campaigns and public outrage (preceding and following those campaigns) about crime and punishment do not necessarily translate into public policy—quite the contrary. Most legislatures do not pass new legislation in any given session. As Darryl Brown puts it, "failure is the norm of legislative proposals."[11] Failure is the norm for crime control proposals, which may generate moral outrage, intense engagement, and a flurry of activity from both the public and legislators. To appreciate this point, we need to take seriously the mundane world of the policy-making process, including its arcane procedural rules and bureaucratic channels of action.[12] Simple rules of procedure, committee assignments, protocol, and veto power can prevent the least contentious bill from passing into law. Institutional configurations of the state and political process enable certain avenues of action while modifying or suppressing others.

In the second neo-Marxian or conflict perspective, the state does not exist on its own. At its best, it is only relatively autonomous from the interests and needs of the capitalist economy. At its weakest, the state is assumed to be an instrument of the ruling class or mechanism to regulate the labor market. This kind of account places too much causal weight on the structural force of the economy, as if nothing could resist or break the sheer power of economic interest and as if the economy moved as a unified and consistent force. In addition, as some commentators have recently noted, the state, its institutional configurations, norms, and actors have played a significant role in the transformation of the global economy, overstepping the needs and demands of certain sectors of the economy and privileging others.[13] Under certain historical conditions, the state has played the central structuring role in the formation of social classes. As a consequence of these conceptual limita-tions, variations of a neo-Marxian approach to the state often lead to overdeter-mined and somewhat hollow accounts of punishment—that is to say, they tend to say things like any and all forms and functions of punishment can be explained by the needs of capital and labor market. Economic relations, particularly as they shape social hierarchies, clearly play a role in the formation and impact of punishment policies. However, this kind of explanation is insufficient and unnecessarily totalizing and has had mixed empirical and historical support.

In still other accounts, scholars informed by Foucault have taken up a much more complex view of the state. Here the state is a node along an immense power grid that regulates various forms of social interaction. Specifi-cally, state power is dispersed through a wide range of social institutions, social practices, and human interactions. Rather than an instrument or property of a particular social group or economic class, state power emerges out of social interaction, a major conceptual advance. Yet despite its usefulness for thinking about the insidious ways state power shapes, informs, and constitutes social relations, privileging some forms and disciplining others, we are still left with a fairly shallow view of the state. The state disappears into a pure exercise of power. When applied to punishment, this approach reduces the state to a mode of repression or population management. Again, this kind of approach is far too structural to incorporate the people who actually make up the actions and activities of the state. This kind of approach suppresses the human agency that is necessary to put the state in motion and make its political authority and cultural schemas meaningful.

Punishment as a public policy does not neatly reflect the public will nor the will to power. Nor does it embody the needs of capital or easily respond to the electoral calculations of politicians or the power schemes of elites. Instead, public policies are messy, they often fail, and they can bring about just as many unintended as intended consequences. Public policies are the result of a dense political process that is in turn shaped by the legacies of past policies, administrative capacities and rules, and of course the broader institutional environment. The dynamic interaction between actors and institutions trans-lates public demands and elite desires into tangible public policies. At the same time, we need to consider how the interactions between agents and institutions structure and are structured by changing historical conditions—a factor that makes this process even more obtuse and subject to immense empirical variation and contingency.

To overcome some of these limitations, I develop an account of the state that seeks to integrate the structural constraints of political institutions with the power of human agency. By doing so, this work seeks to develop and specify the dynamic interaction between state institutions and social mobilization in ways that help explain how and why liberal democracies rely on the criminal law and penal sanctions to resolve complex social problems, including criminal victimization and other threats to social order. This approach may help sort out and clarify why we see such divergences in penal policies across space in spite of the social and political pressures towards convergence.

By taking up this line of argument, this book builds on and seeks to contribute to the emerging literature on the role of political institutions as a necessary explanatory factor of penal outcomes. This is a theoretical framework that emphasizes the primacy of state structures and political actors on penal processes as Joachim Savelsberg, John Sutton, Anthony Doob and Cheryl Marie Webster, Trevor Jones and Tim Newburn, and James Willis have demonstrated in their respective and comparative research on imprisonment rates in the United States, the United Kingdom, Germany, Australia, New Zealand, and Canada; the rise of private prisons in the United States and United Kingdom; and eighteenth- and nineteenth-century British penal transportation systems to America and Australia.

Differentiating Political Structures and Collective Agency

This book claims that the character and intensity of penal regimes are deeply rooted in the democratic process and the structure of the state. First, the state provided the crucial resources and cultural schemas—that is, its legitimacy, its repressive powers—out of which ordinary people, political elites, and state officials pieced together new forms and functions of punishment. Second, the state, as a complex set of multiple and overlapping institutions and obligations, mobilized and made meaningful by repeated social interaction, provided the terrain on which social actors struggled over and made sense of these transformations even as their political struggles eventually reconfigured the state and social relations in the process.

This section breaks down my understanding of the state and democratic process into discrete analytical components. This move helps clarify the key dimensions of the democratic process, enabling comparisons across cases. We should think of these analytical dimensions as heuristic devices meant to simplify the messiness and intricacies of empirical reality and bring out the significance of its underlying logic.[14]

Analytically, we can capture the core features of the democratic process, the interface between state and civil society, with two theoretically and empirically significant factors: political structures and collective agency. *Political structures* refer specifically to the institutional and administrative organization of the state; *collective agency* refers to the mobilization of ordinary people in the policy-making process. These features shape how people take action in the political field and how they understand the nature and meaning of their actions. Taken together, these two dimensions form *modes of governance*—that is, they create an underlying texture of political life in a particular place. They form the organizing principles, classification schemes, the taken-for-granted assumptions, the routines and habits of political interaction, or in Bourdieu's terms, a *habitus* of political action. As such, they significantly shape the way people make sense of political conflict and the way they try to resolve it. This means that we are likely to see variation rather than uniformity in the ways people understand the very nature of political problems and how they try to solve, avoid, escalate, or defuse them.[15] The consequences of this lead to variation in the policy-making process and policy outcomes.

Political Structures

Political structures refer to the institutional and administrative organization of the state. These institutional configurations establish the rules of the game, the legitimate channels of action, the appropriate flows of information and exchange. As such, they significantly shape how political decisions about budgets, public policies, political identities, and even governing philosophies and rationalities of rule are set into motion or realized in the political field. These institutional configurations shape, to a certain extent, the flow and exchange of knowledge and power across political systems. The institutional configuration of the state can work like a gravitational pull, attracting certain actions and repelling others. In many ways, it is much stronger than any individual actor, a president or political party, because it organizes the very interaction among political actors. It gives us a sense of why in certain political systems, political parties tend to dominate the business of government, while in others ordinary people (through their voting preferences or some other mechanism) seem to exert substantial control over the trajectory of public policies.

Political scientists and political sociologists have generally thought about the force of political structures in terms of the institutionalization of decision-making power or political authority. They have mapped political authority as the degree to which political systems distribute or share power across and between branches and levels of government and between the state and civil society.[16] This move provides a systematic method to capture the way power is exercised, distributed, and legitimated in a particular place and an effective way to capture the differences across localities. In a highly centralized political system, the executive branch (such as the president or governor) is likely to control decision-making power over legislation, budgets, and appointments. In a decentralized system, decision-making power is shared and dispersed across the levels and branches of government and may include forms of "direct democracy" in which nonelected ordinary people make legally binding decisions through the use of the ballot box, voting on initiatives, referendums, or recall measures.[17] The United States, for example, decentralizes power across and between levels of government, an institutional design of checks and balances meant to hobble, weaken, and restrain the "tyranny" of centralized government so feared by the Federalists in late eighteenth-century America.[18] In this decentralized system, power and the ultimate source of sovereignty, the right to rule, is invested in ordinary people, the citizens. In contrast, in more centralized systems, the right to rule is invested in state actors, including the executive, civil servants, and politicians.

The political structures of the state have consequences for the success and failure of mass movements and the efficacy of more mundane forms of political participation. For example, a high degree of centralization closes off the public's access and influence over government, a move that tends to dampen various forms of political participation because state insiders and state elites dominate the business of governing, discouraging public engagement or input. In contrast, a low degree of centralization provides multiple points of access, a configuration that can promote various forms of citizen participation, including grassroots mobilization and social protest.[19]

Institutionalized channels of action cannot be ignored or easily overcome by any individual actor or mass movement, no matter how determined they may be.[20] Paul Rock has demonstrated this point well in his analysis of the structural differences in the policy-making process in Canada and the United Kingdom, factors that shaped the voluntary organization of victim support in

Britain vis-à-vis a reluctant but managerial Home Office and the bureaucratic justice initiative in Canada. To be successful—that is, to gain new advantages or a rule change—strategic social mobilization is likely to orient its actions and demands in ways that are relatively compatible with a state's predominant political institutions, even as that movement may seek to change those institutions and public policies.[21] In the United States, for example, we tend to see grassroots protest oriented around legal and political "rights" rather than around the demands for economic redistribution and social equality. This kind of strategy tends to fit better with the liberal political tradition of the United States but may be out of sync with a more social democratic system, such as those of the Nordic countries where the concept of individual rights itself is underdeveloped.

This set of configurations also has consequences for and helps explain cross-cultural differences in public policies, including differences in criminal law and penal sanctioning. In his comparative research on imprisonment patterns in the United States and Germany, Joachim Savelsberg found that Germany's highly insulated bureaucracy and centralized political authority enabled state elites to resist public demands for tough crime control measures and keep imprisonment rates rather low. By contrast, the popular sovereignty and decentralization of the United States made state officials not only more vulnerable but more responsive to public demands for harsh justice.

Collective Agency

An institutionalist view of the democratic process is incomplete. Institutions are created and reproduced through repeated and patterned human interaction. Given this conceptualization, various forms of human agency are incorporated into the democratic process. Specifically, the forms and functions of collective agency, an undertheorized factor in the sociology of punishment, are given central importance. Collective agency captures how people take action in the political field. It refers to how ordinary people get involved in the public sphere and interact with state actors, especially through local, state, and national politics, elections, and policy making, to realize "mutual benefits" of collective life.[22] This concept seeks to go beyond the conventional use of public opinion in punishment studies by differentiating the activities and interactions of political actors in the political field.

Social mobilization can take on a range of deep and shallow forms, including voting in national elections, signing a petition, attending a rally, speaking at a community board meeting, or running for city council. It can be grounded in grassroots protest or take the shape of a formal social movement organization or special interest lobby. These diverse forms and practices vary spatially and temporally, meaning that they do not look the same in different times and places within the United States or cross-nationally. Moreover, collective agency varies dramatically in its effectiveness. Sometimes it can bring about new legislation, create new identities, or overturn traditional social hierarchies. Sometimes it can solidify the status quo, continuing to exclude certain social groups from the benefits of full citizenship. Sometimes collective agency can accomplish nothing. Students of social movements, such as William Gamson, have shown that under certain historical conditions, violent protest is an incredibly effective tool to bring about change but useless under others.

Like the institutional configurations of the state, collective agency significantly shapes the possibilities of action in the political field, and it shapes how people understand the very possibilities of action, how they make and realize meaning in the political field. As the late Charles Tilly explains, forms of social mobilization or popular contention in his terms, "is deeply cultural." It is cultural "in the sense that it relies on and transforms shared understandings concerning what forms and ends of action are desirable, feasible, and efficacious; collective learning and memory strongly limit the claims that people make and how they make them."[23]

The way ordinary people and protest groups interact with state agents and politicians through various forms of collective agency seriously impacts the nature of political conflict and its transformative potential. The character of collective agency can range from more or less contentious forms, some alleviating political disagreements and others aggravating clashes over needs, interests, and available resources. The character of collective agency varies temporally and spatially and includes multiple and overlapping forms, such as public protest, town hall meetings, expert commissions, parliamentary and other legislative hearings and committees, ombudsmen or liaison between state agents and public, and litigation.

Some forms of collective agency under certain conditions tend to inhibit the shared resolution of political conflicts. Disputes and disagreements tend to be repetitive, polarizing, and only temporarily resolved as individuals and various formal and informal organizations (e.g., political parties, interest groups, grassroots movements) continuously struggle over limited material, symbolic resources, and competing visions of a "good society." For example, the use of litigation as a political strategy by the U.S. civil rights movement and abortion rights activists has not really resolved fundamental questions about racial or gender equality. Instead, it has created ongoing and bitter political struggles, generating resentment and righteousness among winners and losers over piecemeal and symbolic decisions, decisions, moreover, that are not grounded in a democratic process.

By contrast, the character of collective agency can take on a more conciliatory or compromising quality. Here conflict over resources tends to be negotiated in such a way to satisfy or appease most if not all the relevant actors. For example, in social democratic countries such as Sweden, collective agency tends to be based on compromise, negotiation, and a sense of the collective good rather than private self-interest.[24] As such, it has helped create the country's inclusive and generous social welfare policies. At the same time, however, in this context conflict can also be ignored, avoided, or suppressed to promote an apparent rather than real consensus. In Sweden, the social pressure to agree with one another[25] can leave contentious policy issues, such as immigration and integration or race and crime, off the political agenda. Policy issues concerning ethnic and racial classification are extremely sensitive topics in Sweden, especially given the success of the eugenics movement and forced sterilization[26] and the country's neutrality during World War II.[27] The Ministry of Justice, for example, does not collect or publish data on the race of criminal offenders in part to protect minority offenders from social bias and racial prejudice.[28] Rather than document the extent of minority crime or discuss the possible causes of such social pathologies, government officials have basically buried the issue to preserve the notion of a fair and just criminal justice system and, by extension, a tolerant and open society, despite a more complex reality.

To make systematic comparisons across cases and localities, it may be helpful to consider a more restricted notion of collective agency. I turn to the work of Robert Putnam and others who have conceptualized the character and efficacy of collective agency in terms of "social capital." In *Making Democracy Work*, Robert Putnam uses the concept of "social capital" to capture how well people connect and cooperate with one another through civic engagement in order to bring about common goods.[29] In societies with a high degree of social capital, Putnam explains, people tend to be active in politics and community life, creating both dense and loose networks of social ties that can then increase cooperation, social cohesion, and mutual trust. In his comparative study on Italian regional governments, Putnam found that locales with a higher degree of social capital tended toward higher economic prosperity, more generous and efficient social policies, and less coercive social control.

Like state institutions, collective agency can significantly shape the substance and trajectory of public policies. In terms of crime and punishment, I hypothesize that in political contexts with a higher degree of civic engagement and social capital, we might expect to see more restorative crime victim policies and less punitive penal policies, policies dependent on a sense of mutual trust and social reciprocity. A restorative approach recognizes the harm done to victims and holds criminals responsible for the pain and suffering of victims and the emotional and economic costs to communities but does so without resorting to the coercive use of state power.[30] In political contexts in which people share a sense of civic duty, responsibility for self-governance, and social connectedness, they may be less willing to inflict on one another the violence of penal sanctioning.[31] In contrast, in contexts with a low degree of civic engagement and high degree of social polarization, we may be likely to see a more retributive approach to criminal victimization. Here polity members' antipathy toward one another, especially toward marginalized social groups, such as criminal offenders, can be easily expressed through penal sanctioning without much concern for the social reintegration of offenders.

Modes of Democratic Governance and Penal Regimes

One of the central claims of this book is that the character and intensity of penal regimes are deeply rooted in the specific structure of the democratic process. This argument is based in part on my understanding of the state, as fleshed out here, and in part by my understanding of punishment and political orders as loosely coupled social institutions.[32] That is, punishment and political orders tend to be mutually constitutive and highly interdependent social institutions, and under certain conditions they tend to be bound together by a shared historical trajectory and logic of action. Yet under other conditions, political orders and punishment practices depart from a shared logic, acting independently and autonomously. Prior work in the sociology of punishment has established this relationship, particularly the structuring role of penal sanctions in the production and reproduction of political authority and the conditions of citizenship.[33] I build on these important advances but focus my attention on the role of the democratic process, particularly their localized variants, in shaping the character and intensity of penal regimes. Specifically, I explore the how different modes of governance resolve the contradictory task of restraining and exerting brutal force to protect individual liberty and provide public safety. In the pages that follow, I show how and why certain forms of collective agency and political structures make it more likely that political actors will intensify penal sanctioning, especially at the expense of marginalized social groups, while others seek to impose limits on state coercion.

The case studies focus on subnational variants of political structures and collective agency, in part because nearly all criminal justice policy is formulated and implemented on the subnational rather than federal level. I also focus on subnational polities, the American states, because penal regime change, continuity, and difference are significantly shaped by localized institutional configurations in addition to national and global trends. Crime and punishment tend to be experienced and made meaningful on a more immediate level even as these institutions are subject to and agents of broad social and cultural changes. People tend to take action with the tools, schemas, and resources that are available to them in their particular contexts. So although we can identify a common upward trend in American penal sanctioning, we also see substantial differences in the character of penal regimes in the states, differences that were meaningful to the actors who created them out of familiar cultural goods.

This last section offers a brief overview of the democratic process and penal regimes in the case studies. Table 2.1 summarizes the key dimen-

TABLE 2.1. Political Structures and Collective Agency by Case Study

	CA	WA	NY
Political structures: degree of centralization[a]	Low	Low	High
Collective agency: degree of civic engagement[b]	Low	High	Low

[a] The Index of Governors' Institutional Powers is a useful indicator of the degree of centralization because it measures the degree to which governors control budgets, legislation, appointments, political parties, the strength of veto power, and the length of tenure, including the presence or absence of term limits. The stronger the governors' powers, the more centralized political authority, and vice versa. Both decentralized California and Washington (3.2) score below the national average (3.5) in terms of governors' powers and well below more centralized states like New York, scoring 4.1 out of 5 (Beyle 2004: 212–213). I also include the presence or absence of direct democracy measures as another indicator of decentralization: both California and Washington allow for citizen initiatives, New York does not.

[b] The degree of civic engagement is indicated by voter participation in state and national elections and by Putnam's composite index of "social capital," which includes how often people attend local town meetings, participate in local and state politics, and how much people trust one another. California ranks forty-fifth in the nation in voter turnout; Washington ranks thirteenth; New York ranks thirty-ninth (Gray and Hanson 2004: 93). In terms of social capital, California ranks twenty-eighth, scoring –0.18; Washington ranks tenth, scoring 0.65; New York ranks thirty-fourth, scoring –0.36 (Putnam 2000).

sions of the democratic process in each case: political structures and collective agency.

California: Polarized Populism and the Rise of Retribution

With its low degree of centralized political structures, California is an open polity, meaning that ordinary people and grassroots movements can influence the policy-making process through multiple access points. However, what is somewhat paradoxical is the state's relatively low rate of civic engagement: few people actually turn out to vote or participate in local affairs. California politics, elections and volunteerism, is dominated by the affluent white, a relatively small pool of the population.[34] Without a lively public sphere, Californians miss key opportunities to build social ties and develop norms of reciprocity across social groups, factors central to maintaining a mutual sense of trust and social cohesion in diverse societies. As such, these conditions can increase social polarization. Social polarization is then exacerbated by and expressed through California's acrimonious mode of collective agency, including but not limited to the initiative process. As a form of winner-take-all politics, the initiative process poses complex policy questions in simplistic "yes" or "no" formulations, thereby eliminating middle ground or compromising policy positions. It is also undermines standard democratic procedures because there are no requirements to consider input from other citizens, civic groups, or any other interested party before drafting legislation, and no one can be voted out of office or held accountable if the measure fails to deliver its stated goals.[35] Initially created to undercut corrupt politicians and express distrust of state elites, the initiative process has also been used to legislate intolerance toward minority racial and ethnic groups since its inception.[36]

These institutional configurations can lead to more coercive social controls as a disconnected and divided polity readily calls on the state's power to punish to solve complex policy problems, especially those involving socially marginalized groups such as criminal offenders and racial minorities. These factors are particularly salient when public policy is legislated through the initiative as occurred in the Victims' Bill of Rights in 1982, the Crime Victim Justice Reform Act in 1990, and the Three Strikes and You're Out initiative in 1993. In this context, California's penal regime has emphasized retribution, seeking to punish criminals and restrict offenders' liberties in the name of victim rights and public safety.

Washington: Deliberative Democracy and the Principle of Parsimony

Although the political structures in Washington State are decentralized and allow for the initiative process like California, the character of collective agency can under certain conditions create a more *deliberative* kind of democratic process. Washington's open political system is rooted in a more progressive-style populism based on the farmers' cooperative movement for self-governance, which depended on collaboration among various social groups and between the state and civil society.[37] Civic engagement has been relatively robust in Washington, generating a relatively high degree of social capital and social trust. Norms of reciprocity, crucial to maintaining social ties across diverse social groups, are further expressed through Washington's use of town hall meetings and hybrid state-citizen commissions, mechanisms deployed since the mid-1960s to pose and solve policy problems including but not limited to crime and victimization (e.g., Washington State Citizens Council on Crime 1966, Washington State Commission on the Causes and Prevention of Citizen Unrest 1968, Washington State Sentencing Guidelines Commission 1981–1983).

Small-scale public meetings can promote open discussion among state officials, ordinary citizens, civic leaders, grassroots movements, and special interest groups. In these settings, participants are encouraged to listen to a range of different viewpoints and work through dialogue and negotiation to reach a compromise, if not consensus.[38] Hybrid state-citizen commissions, made up of citizen representatives, civic leaders, and state officials, can open up a space for dialogue between civil society organizations and state actors, a space not available through conventional electoral politics, and can potentially generate trust among the participants.[39] Both forms of collective agency provide for a more inclusive mode of decision-making where various social groups and political actors can get the sense that their opinions matter to state elites and their interests may be incorporated into legislative proposals. Both promote the idea of self-governance, practices that are central to legitimate democratic rule. Of course, state elites can co-opt public opinion, defuse troublesome grassroots movements, and bury contentious issues through these very same practices and do so in the name of consensus politics. The outcome of which must be determined empirically.

The institutions and collective agency that make up Washington's democratic process make polity members reluctant but not unwilling to employ repressive forms of state power against one another. Penal sanctioning, especially the widespread use of imprisonment, the infringement of liberty, can intensify social divisions, break social trust, and undermine notions of self-rule as it simultaneously expresses and expands the state's power over civil society—all features that would seem to weaken if not contradict the basic principles of a deliberative political process rooted in intensive civic engagement, self-governance, and mutual cooperation. As a result, Washington's penal regime emphasizes the principle of parsimony, the reliance on the least repressive sanction possible, a move that has kept the state's imprisonment rate relatively low for over thirty years.

New York: Pragmatic Elitism and Managerialism

New York tends to follow a pragmatic but elitist mode of governance. Governance is highly centralized and dominated by just a few state elites, yet under certain conditions, it relies heavily on expert knowledge and scientific inquiry (rather than private self-interest) to guide its decision-making and public policy processes. This kind of political context tends to create technical and managerial approaches to policy problems. In this context, the pragmatic state shrewdly calculates the degree of responsiveness and compromise necessary to maintain legitimacy. In other words, the pragmatic state seeks to use state power efficiently and deliberately. Because of this, the state is less likely to overindulge in democratic participation and repressive exercises of state force. Because the state does not pursue democracy for its own sake, the state must show itself to be useful to maintain legitimacy. The pragmatic state seeks to intervene in and respond to crime and other perceived problems of order with technical rather than crude or vulgar responses. The state prides itself on its expertise and scientific engagement with social problems and is therefore less likely to pursue strictly punitive responses, considered crass and unscientific. As a result, we see a highly differentiated response to crime and differentiated penal sanctions.

In contrast to mass imprisonment, an indiscriminate use of state power, New York's differentiated use of confinement is a highly disciplined use of state power. The removal of violent and drug offenders from the community is an immediate display of state action and competence. The state moves quickly to remove contagious threats from communities. Violent and drug offenders are quarantined (but not cured) to maintain the health and viability of surrounding communities. Rather than invest in long-term social engineering, rehabilitation, or even crime prevention, imprisonment is a visible and quite dramatic expression of state action. Without delay, the state tells its citizens that it takes its duties and obligations seriously. Differentiated imprisonment efficiently provides internal security, reinforcing the legitimacy of the state.

3

The Case of California

Neopopulism and Retribution

Throughout the postwar period, California maintained one of
the most advanced correctionalist penal regimes in the country. The
Department of Corrections practiced many of the core tenets of
the rehabilitative ideal: indeterminate sentencing, individualized
diagnosis and treatment, reliance on criminological expertise, and
attempts to reintegrate offenders back into the community,
especially through work.[1] Yet in 1967, the California state legislature
passed and Governor Ronald Reagan signed Senate Bill 85–87, the
Reagan-Deukmejian "penalty package." SB 85–87 substantially
increased penal sanctions for any offender who inflicted "great bodily
harm" on a victim while committing another crime such as burglary,
robbery, or rape.[2] This legislation introduced the pain and suffering
of crime victims as a new rationale for increasing penal sanctions and
punishing offenders. By legislating and dramatizing the suffering
of victims, the penalty package changed the moral calculus of
justice in California. It introduced a more emotive, passionate, and
punitive approach to crime control, challenging the state's dominant
clinical, therapeutic approach. It made crime victims' pain central to
the justification, legitimation, and authority of criminal law and
penal sanctioning. The law not only opened up the acceptable range of

penal sanctions, it transformed what was possible in crime policy. It changed what was imaginable in the penal regime of California.

The Reagan-Deukmejian penalty package underpinned the eventual rejection of rehabilitation and presaged the rise of retribution in California. Retribution as the main goal and purpose of punishment came to dominate California's penal regimes throughout 1970s and 1980s, and it continues today. The retributive movement to make offenders pay back the harm done to victims and the public through the infliction of some kind of pain, such as loss of liberty or even loss of life, eventually superseded the movement to correct, repair, rehabilitate, or even simply manage offenders. As might be expected, this penal regime shift took time and necessitated multiple and overlapping pieces of legislation, budgetary and penal practices, as well as public support. For example, Death Penalty Proposition 17 (1972), Murder Penalty Proposition 7 (1977), Uniform Determinate Sentencing Law (1976), "Victims Bill of Rights" Proposition 8 (1981), "Crime Victim Justice Reform Act" Proposition 115 (1989), Sentence Enhancement or "Three Strikes and You Are Out" Proposition 184 (1993), Juvenile Crime Proposition 21 (1998), along with many other much more mundane changes in the California state penal code, all embody, express, and realize the force of retribution, mandating and stiffening penal sanctions. Many were citizen ballot initiatives seeking to avenge victims' pain and suffering through punishment.

Together, these pieces of legislation have intensified the criminal law and penal sanctioning, bringing more people under the coercive powers of the state. Over time and collectively, they have all increased the state's prison population, making imprisonment a policy priority and a harsh reality for thousands of Californians, particularly African Americans and Latinos, who now make up about 66 percent of the prison population but 40 percent of the state population.[3] Today, California has one of the largest prison populations in the country and an imprisonment rate of 471 inmates per 100,000 population, just above the national average.[4]

Why did this happen? Why this dramatic shift in penal regimes in one of the most unlikely places, California?

Some may point to the rise in crime or the backlash against civil rights. Others may point to the charismatic leadership of Ronald Reagan and the subsequent rise of social conservatism across the United States. In a sense, they would all be correct. But in another sense, they would all be partial and incomplete, missing the key dynamic that put this transformation in motion. As I argue in the following pages, the emergence of a neopopulist political order in California not only made penal regime change possible but gave it a retributive expression. In the 1960s, a major grassroots movement jolted California out its pragmatic and welfarist approach to governing and ushered in a neoconservative variant of the state's populist past. This movement would go on to challenge and eventually change the basic governing relationship between state and citizen, intensifying the state's repressive powers and diminishing social welfarism. It would go on to weaken social trust and solidarity between social groups in civil society. The resurgence of populism was not a top-down transformation or diffusion of a national trend but rather a political development that emerged from below, from the collective agency and experience of Californians living in the postwar period. It was firmly rooted in the local experience of changing social conditions and relied extensively on local products, local institutions, and cultural resources to create a new variant of American democracy.

The local experience and historical legacy of populism provided the institutional tools and resources, cultural schemas, and legitimating authority necessary to bring about such a major shift in the state's power to punish. Populism helped Californians make sense of the complex social changes associated with late modernity, translating rising crime, unruly youth culture, and racial unrest as signs of moral depravity necessitating strict discipline and authoritarian responses. Populism helped politicians like Ronald Reagan, public figures such as Paul Gann, and ordinary citizens like Mrs. Mays and Treena Davis take action against an unwanted cultural transformation. It helped ground the legitimacy of coercive state responses to crime in the name of "the people" and common sense. It gave "the people," ordinary citizens, grassroots organizations, and crime victims movements the tools—the initiative process itself—to legislate their own crime control policies, bypassing state elites and criminological expertise, perceived to be out of touch with the lived experience of plain folk. Many of the voter initiatives were driven in part by deeply felt emotions, moral outrage, and a firm belief that criminal offenders were not worthy of the rights and protections of full citizenship, emotional undercurrents resonant with populist intolerance for those perceived to be outsiders or freeloaders.

Populism: The Effects of Contentious Politics, Structure, and Collective Agency in Action

Populism locates and legitimates sovereignty, the right to rule, in "the people," the plain folk, the ordinary citizen as opposed to centralized government or political elites. With its low degree of centralization, California is an open polity, meaning that ordinary people and grassroots movements can influence the policy-making process through multiple access points. However, what is somewhat paradoxical is the state's relatively low rate of civic engagement: few people actually turn out to vote or participate in local affairs. California politics, elections and volunteerism, is dominated by the affluent white, a relatively small portion of the population.[5] Depressed civic engagement among African Americans and Latinos decreases the possibility that their opinions, ideas, and demands will be included in political negotiations and reflected in public policies. Moreover, without a lively public sphere, Californians miss key opportunities to build social ties and develop norms of reciprocity across social groups, factors central to maintaining a mutual sense of trust and social cohesion in diverse societies. As such, these conditions can increase social polarization.

Social polarization is then exacerbated by and expressed through California's contentious forms of collective agency, including (but not limited to) the initiative process.[6] As an enactment of popular sovereignty, direct democracy measures such as the initiative, referendum, and recall are all mechanisms by which ordinary people—that is, citizens, nonelected officials—can create legally binding legislation through the ballot box (voting). As a form of winner-take-all politics, the initiative process poses complex policy questions in simplistic "yes" or "no" formulations, thereby eliminating middle ground or compromising policy positions. It also undermines standard democratic procedures because there are no requirements to consider input from other citizens, civic groups, or any other interested party before drafting legislation, and no one can be voted out of office or held accountable if the measure fails to deliver its stated goals.[7] Initially created to undercut corrupt politicians and express distrust of state elites, the initiative process has also been used to legislate intolerance toward minority racial and ethnic groups since its inception.[8]

In this volatile political environment, crime is perceived to be especially threatening to social order. Crimes such as burglary or those causing great bodily harm are particularly insulting because they violate privacy, undermining the security of the home and integrity of the person. In a political culture that tends to value and emphasize individual freedom, personal autonomy, and private rather than communal life, crime is perceived as a moral failing of individual responsibility rather than a result of poor schooling, bad parenting, unfair labor markets, or other forms of social inequality. Criminal offenders are deemed "freeloaders" for failing to pull their own weight and "getting something for nothing," draining precious resources. Criminal offenders ruin the populist myth of self-governance and self-sufficiency and are condemned for this transgression. In this context, the prison and retribution make moral sense.

I suggest that these institutional configurations, taken together, can lead to more coercive social controls as a disconnected and divided polity readily calls on the state's power to punish to solve complex policy problems, especially those involving socially marginalized groups, such as criminal offenders and racial minorities.

Populism: Historical Roots

Populism is deeply rooted in the political development of California. Because past practices and institutional configurations create certain kinds of path dependencies, cultural supplies, and ideological frameworks for understanding political and social relations and resources for taking action in the political field, a few key moments are considered here.

In the late 1890s, populist activists initiated a grassroots reform effort that eventually transformed the political structures and political practices of the state. Though the agrarian-based populist movement itself did not survive into the twentieth century, populist political reforms, particularly direct democracy measures, had long-lasting effects on the substance and trajectory of public policy into the twenty-first century.

In 1890, 30,000 local farmers joined the Southern Farmers' Alliance and its associated cooperative to protect themselves and their family farms from economic ruin.[9] For nearly two decades, the monopolistic Southern Pacific Railroad, known as the Octopus, had routinely overcharged farmers to ship their goods to and from agricultural markets.[10] In Octopus, novelist Frank Norris vividly captured how central valley farmers viewed the Southern Pacific Railroad as an omnipresent and negative force in their daily lives. Describing an approaching train, he wrote:

> the galloping monster, the terror of steel and steam, with its single eye, cyclopean, red, shooting from horizon to horizon ... the symbol of a vast power, huge, terrible, flinging the echo of its thunder over all the reaches of the valley, leaving blood and destruction in its path; the leviathan, with tentacles of steel clutching into the soil, the soulless Force, the iron-hearted Power, the monster, the Colossus, the Octopus.[11]

By 1890, big commercial farmers had gained control over the fertile central valley and began to dominate the more lucrative fruit and vegetable markets. At the same time, wheat prices collapsed. Local farmers could not compete with big business. Swathed in a political culture of "producerism," local farmers and ranchers were further outraged that the railroads—that is, the nonproductive elements of society, big business with "special privileges"—had so much control over their economic well-being.[12] Farmers and ranchers viewed themselves as producers: farmers were workers, and because labor was considered a value in itself, farmers deserved the material rewards of their own labor.[13] The Southern Pacific Railroad was perceived to have nearly crushed farmers' economic viability and the promise of California, the dream of self-sufficiency, and economic opportunity. Farmers joined the Southern Farmers' Alliance for economic survival, but they quickly transformed this voluntary association into a broader political movement.

The Southern Farmers' Alliance eventually turned to politics as a way to pursue their economic demands.[14] Local farmers wanted the government to break up the monopolistic and price-gouging railroad industry so that they could compete in a fair market.[15] Yet the Southern Pacific Railroad, also known as the "absolute dictatorship," not only controlled the transportation routes and shipping fees, it exerted extensive control over California politics and state government.[16] As a consequence, neither the Democratic nor Republican Parties were especially responsive to demands for increased government control over the railroads and demands for economic self-sufficiency. Nor were the courts any help. The California Supreme Court consistently ruled in favor of the Southern Pacific between 1895 and 1910.[17]

Resilient rather than demoralized, the Southern Farmers' Alliance joined the third-party political movement, a movement that swept across America's heartland and into the West in the late nineteenth century. California farmers and ranchers joined the populist party, the People's Party. By doing so, they planned to bypass conventional party politics and elect their own candidates to statewide office. Throughout the 1890s, grassroots activists elected the People's Party candidates to the California State Legislature.[18] Populists and the People's Party advocated more government control over greedy, "nonproductive" big business and wanted the people or common folks to control government.[19] Following farmers' success with third-party politics, urban socialists and some labor unions joined the People's Party. Allied with the United Labor Party, the People's Party, now made up of independent farmers and urban laborers, again successfully elected third-party candidates to the California State Legislature. Third-party candidates promised to fight the economic exploitation of the railroad and fight for public ownership of utilities.[20] Despite these electoral successes, by the turn of the century farmer-populists had not gained government control over the railroads and were still struggling to maintain their economic viability and their dignity as producers.

By 1902, a bit weary of party politics, populists turned their attention to the structure of California's politics. Influenced by democratic reforms in Switzerland, California populists introduced the initiative, referendum, and recall into the political field.[21] With these direct democracy measures, populists wanted to cut through the party system. They wanted to override the Southern Pacific Railroad, unresponsive state elites, and sell-out politicians. With the initiative, referendum, and recall, populists wanted to write their own legislation and bypass representative democracy.

In 1902, an issue-oriented coalition made up of populists, the Socialist Party, labor unions, local farmers, suffragettes, the Municipal League, the Episcopalian Union Reform League, and John Randolph Haynes's Direct Democracy League pressed for and won a state constitutional amendment that established direct democracy at the local level.[22] By 1904, Haynes's Direct Democracy League successfully mobilized the citizens of Los Angeles to recall California's first public official, a city councilor.[23] Seeking to go beyond city politics, this conglomeration of disaffected associations pressed the California State Legislature for state-level direct democracy measures. The California State Legislature, obviously threatened by such measures, and with many of its lawmakers bought off by the Southern Pacific Railroad, rejected direct democracy in 1903, 1905, 1907, and 1909.

Only by forming an alliance with middle- and upper-middle-class progressive reformers, did populists and their allies finally see direct democracy measures institutionalized.[24] In 1910, gubernatorial candidate Hiram Johnson campaigned on a progressive platform, attacked patronage politics, and supported direct democracy. In California, progressives tended to support direct democracy because they believed that increased political participation could undermine the insularity and corruption of patronage politics. To progressives, direct democracy also had the potential to expand the state's role in the provision of social goods and services.[25] It could expand the state's dependence on progressives and the growing professional middle classes. On the campaign trail, Johnson characterized the election as: "a contest for freedom ... from William F. Herrin and the Southern Pacific Company, who have debauched, polluted and corrupted our state."[26] Johnson denounced the Southern

Pacific political machine as the "Shame of California."[27] Squeaking into office, Governor-Elect Johnson nevertheless took on major political reforms. He traveled around the state to drum up support for direct democracy. Again on the campaign trail for political reform, he described direct democracy as protection "against corporation greed, corporation control or political domination."[28]

In *The Initiative and Referendum in California*, V. O. Key and Winston Crouch note how local newspapers tended to support direct democracy. One such paper, the *Los Angeles Express*, frequently described the initiative and referendum as a way to protect citizens against political corruption. The *Express* explained how direct democracy could defeat corruption—that is, the initiative and referendum could protect citizens against "Every discredited politician who has lost his 'pull,' every corporation that was formerly in politics for revenue . . . every man who held a bribe and every man whose vote was for sale."[29]

After nearly twenty years of political struggle, an issue-oriented coalition made up of farmers, labor unions, suffragettes, progressive reformers, and urban socialists fundamentally transformed the structure of politics in California. By 1911, Governor Johnson, his progressive allies, socialists, populists, suffragettes, and labor unions successfully pressured the California State Legislature to institutionalize the initiative, referendum, and recall along with several constitutional amendments that included a Railroad Commission, workers compensation, and women's suffrage. Direct democracy became a reality in California. United in their opposition against the Southern Railroad and patronage politics, the diverse coalition radicalized democracy. The coalition's push for direct democracy measures opened up decision-making power to the people—it democratized state governance. The initiative, referendum, and recall enabled citizens—assuming they could mobilize sufficient numbers—to make their own legislative decisions, rewrite the state constitution, levy taxes, mandate certain social services, and eliminate others. Citizens could now outmaneuver unresponsive political representatives and special interests. By institutionalizing citizen participation in decision-making, grassroots activists hoped to deploy direct democracy measures to expose and challenge what they perceived to be abuses of power, corrupt politicians, and unfair public policies.

By 1918, Californians had already voted on ninety-nine ballot measures. They legislated an eight-hour working day, outlawed prostitution, supported nativists' oriented Prohibition, and tried to decrease taxes.[30] Despite their initial intent to bypass state elites and corporate corruption, direct democracy measures also enabled citizens and dominant social groups to turn on margin-alized social groups because it allowed the majority to legislate its own intoler-ance toward minority groups. Direct democracy did not provide mechanisms to protect minority groups from the majority's intolerance. Though progres-sives supported expanded democratization, these middle-class social refor-mers were especially hostile toward Asian groups in California, particularly the Japanese.[31] Progressives, like the Democratic and Republic Parties, sup-ported an Asiatic exclusion and an alien land law.[32] The main progressive paper, the *California Weekly*, advocated legislation that would limit Japanese property ownership to small parcels of land because they thought "a white population and a brown population, regardless of nationality or ideals, can never occupy the same soil together with advantage to either."[33] Since its inception, Californians have used the initiative process to legislate racial and ethnic intolerance.[34]

The initiative and referendum radicalized political participation, but these measures did not democratize public policy or private property. The initiative and referendum did not lead to a radical redistribution of state resources, nor a more equitable tax system, nor increased state regulation of private industry or redistribution of private property.[35] Instead, special interest groups such as bankers and financiers used the initiative process to promote their own interests, rather than the general welfare.[36] In addition, moral protestors such as prohibitionists, the Anti-Saloon League, anti–prize fighting and anti–horse racing groups, Bible reading groups, and animal rights groups all turned to the initiative process to press their own parochial concerns on the electorate and defeat their opposition.[37]

Direct democracy changed the structure of political authority in California. Over time, it changed the intensity and character of collective agency. By decentralizing decision-making power and by weakening political parties, direct democracy measures facilitated issue-oriented politics. As John Alls-wang and Elisabeth Clemens both note, the coalition that brought about direct democracy did not share a unified or common political platform. Socialists, suffragettes, and farmers were determined to bypass the clutches of the Southern Pacific Railroad and patronage politics for their own reasons and their own political agendas. In other words, challengers pursued political reform to promote their own political and economic opportunity rather than pursue a shared vision of equality of outcome. The fragile coalition held up over a number of years and achieved unprecedented political reforms. Yet they did not institutionalize this alliance by creating a new political party, nor did they throw their support behind an already existing party or create a more permanent political association.[38] There was no guarantee that any of these allies would be there for the next round. Issue-oriented politics both depended on and generated temporary alliances. Issue-oriented politics, as the name suggests, depended on momentary citizen engagement with single issues, rather than with coherent political platforms or centralized political parties.

These early moments of populist-inspired reform with its emphasis on direct democracy gave rise to a specific tradition of collective action in California. Direct democracy led to a more issue-oriented politics based on temporary alliances rather than institutionalized collaboration between the state and civil society. It also created institutionalized mechanisms that legitimated racial and ethnic intolerance in the name of the people or common good.

Populism Interrupted: Pragmatism and Social Welfarism

California's political history is complicated by its dialectical relationship with progressive welfarism—a relationship that had lingering effects on the substance and trajectory of public policy in California. Again, we need to take another look at progressive reform in California. Although progressive reformers supported direct democracy, increased political participation, and open primaries, measures that weakened political parties and undermined patronage politics,[39] they did not dismantle the state itself. Instead, progressives, especially middle-class club women, capitalized on California's open and decentralized political structures to introduce a more welfarist style state.[40] California progressives sought to expand the state's role in the provision of goods and services, and they were remarkably successful at doing so. Once the political machines and party bosses had been weakened by campaign finance reform, civil service reform, direct primaries, and direct election of politicians, progressives mobilized state capacities and resources to intervene in the ill effects of rapid industrialization and urbanization.[41] In California, progressive welfarism was oriented around the idea that a professional, educated, middle-class, and nonpartisan civil service, equipped with expert knowledge, could inform governmental decision making in ways that would improve social life. Propelled by a sense of their own efficacy to change the world around them, progressives turned to the state to help them realize their own fantasies of the American dream.

Rather than use state resources to benefit state insiders, big business, or private interests, the Women's Legislative Council of California, for example, pressed legislators to mobilize resources to improve the daily lives and political rights of women. To do so, we should note here, the council and other activists did not turn to the initiative process to press their demands; instead, they appealed directly to legislators. Bruised by the campaign to discredit state elites and patronage politics, California readily complied with these new demands. By doing so, the state could quickly regain its legitimacy and ensure the compliance of an already agitated and reform-oriented civil society. By the 1920s, California's nascent activist state had passed a slate of legislation that expanded women's and children's political and economic rights and social services and expanded the state's role in safeguarding these rights and services. California passed laws on women's minimum wage, child labor, access to public education, teachers' pensions, increased school funds, women's rights to guardianship, child support, and jury duty, among many others.[42]

By the 1930s, the Great Depression crippled California's economy and left thousands unemployed and impoverished. As farmers watched their crops rot and laborers organized widespread strikes across the state, the budding welfarist state could not muster a coherent relief policy. Pressed by the political force of the Workers' Alliance and gubernatorial candidate Upton Sinclair's "End Poverty in California" socialist platform, California had to respond in some way to the state's staggering economic conditions and growing political and social unrest. The state adopted old-age pensions but took on a stingier and more restrictive program than Sinclair had advocated under his "Ham and Eggs" campaign.[43]

As President Franklin Roosevelt's New Deal swept across the country, California also adopted a work relief program. Again, the state provided less wages and less coverage than almost all of its Western neighbors and New York.[44] In addition, California adopted the New Deal's Aid to Dependent Children. Yet it used one of the nation's stingiest versions of Aid to Dependent Children in spite if its earlier efforts to assist women and children.[45] While California's emergent welfarist state tried to respond in some productive way to the depression, the state adopted a tentative rather than generous social policy. Rather than develop a coherent or full-scale New Deal program, California responded to immediate pressures and the fiercest pressure group—in this case, the strength of the Workers' Alliance and its demands for old-age pensions. Throughout the 1930s, California maintained its progressive tendencies, but the state did not fully develop, institutionalize, or routinize big government associated with New Deal welfarism.

Populism Regained

In the postwar era, midwestern and other white middle-class professionals flocked to southern California, lured by the prosperous defense industry, cheap land, and federally subsidized suburban housing. Although the middle classes flourished, the reality of cold war politics infused their daily lives and heightened their atomized suburban living—conditions that brewed feelings of insecurity and paranoia.[46] In response, as Lisa McGirr explains in *Suburban Warriors: The Origins of the New American Right*, these "suburban warriors," defense industry professionals, small business and real estate entrepreneurs, created a new form of American populism. They went on to create a variant of populism that blended fervent antistatism and anticollectivism with social conservatism.[47]

McGirr shows how Orange County social conservatives, inspired by Robert Nisbet's *The Quest for Community*, blamed the state, especially centralized government, for their own atomized and isolated suburban living conditions—conditions, they argued, that led to the breakdown of family values, familial authority, and community. By hooking up with disgruntled libertarians who considered economic freedom and property rights as preconditions for political and personal freedom, social conservatives transformed the legacy of nineteenth-century agrarian populism into a decidedly antistatist but procapitalist political movement, a movement deeply distrustful of state elites and concentrated power. In the words of one of Orange County's influential grassroots activist, J. D. Collier, "a centralized government, that if we allow to be completely centralized will destroy every freedom we have"—that is to say, "too much centralized power is not good for a man or a government."[48]

By the mid-1960s, these "suburban warriors"—resentful of taxation they considered socialist, the expansion of social welfare to the "nonproductive" elements of society, growing "social permissiveness," the audacity of student protestors at the state's elite universities, and fearful of crime—propelled the conservative populist politics of Barry Goldwater and Ronald Reagan forward into contemporary California. While populists watched their man Goldwater falter in the 1964 presidential election, their relentless mobilization had sparked a new political movement that once again transformed California politics and governance.

By the mid-1960s, these neopopulists promoted self-governance or "self-reliance" and limited government. They reclaimed the initiative process and its inherent challenge to representative democracy and state elites, a form of collective agency that had fallen out of favor in the 1940s and 1950s.[49] Between 1940 and 1968, for example, Californians proposed and voted on 38 propositions, a figure far less than the 160 propositions of the years between 1920 and 1938.[50] By 1964, California had reinstated direct democracy with its explicit check on state power and fierce criticism of state legislators. In 1964, Californians passed Proposition 14 by a two-to-one margin, shocking state elites and Governor Pat Brown.[51] Proposition 14, a citizen initiative, repealed the Rumford Fair Housing Act. By passing it, Californians, particularly white voters across economic groups, soundly rejected antidiscrimination laws that would have protected African Americans from poor housing conditions associated with residential segregation. Afraid that racial integration would decrease property values and increase crime in suburban neighborhoods, advocates of Proposition 14 framed the campaign as a fight for individual freedom rather than an explicit assault on civil rights.[52] As Matthew Dallek explains in *The Right Moment*, fliers and other campaign materials, symbolically wrapped in the American flag, denounced Governor Brown's opposition to the initiative as an infringement on personal liberty and an attack on American freedom. One such flyer stated: "Governor Brown Opposes Freedom of Choice."[53]

Two years later, in 1966, Californians elected Ronald Reagan governor. Running as a "citizen politician," this former Goldwater supporter crushed the elder statesman, Pat Brown, by nearly a million votes, a historic landslide.[54] Reagan's victory, buoyed by neopopulists, posed a serious challenge to the pragmatism and social welfarism of an earlier generation. In the postwar period, three-term Governor Earl Warren and two-term Governor Pat Brown expanded the state's role in the provision of goods and services. Under Warren's strong leadership and the decline of direct democracy, California had rapidly expanded its centralized capacities and responsibilities to provide social welfare, public services, and realize a New Deal vision of the common good. Warren had increased social welfare provision, workers' compensation, mental and prison reform, state water works projects, and public education.[55] Governor Brown continued this tradition into the mid-1960s, until his failed reelection campaign.

Governor Reagan, although his own administration blended aspects of pragmatism and populism, tended to advocate limited government in public discourse. In a speech delivered at the Fifty-Ninth Annual Governors'

Conference in 1967, Reagan challenged social welfarism with his explicitly antistatist views of government. He explained:

> We are faced with a choice; either we go back to this collective "we" as the supreme power with the "state" its agent—supremely powerful and unlimited in its authority; Or we continue on the high road accepting man as a unique individual [with] a creature of the spirit with abilities and capacities God given master not of servant of his own creation the state. The time has come to reclaim our rights, our inalienable rights to human dignity, self respect, self-reliance to once again be the kind of people who once made this [Nation] great.[56]

In a speech to the Merchants and Manufacturers Association in Los Angeles and the Republican State Convention in Anaheim, Reagan reiterated his support for limited government. He stated:

> It makes one wonder how good business would be, just how much more industry and agriculture would be produced if they weren't hindered and hampered at every turn, if they weren't overburdened with regressive taxes, swamped with government-ordered paper work and threatened by thousands of rules and regulations promulgated by hundreds of unrelated, uncoordinated agencies at every level of government. It makes one wonder how much better off we would be as individuals if government weren't prying and poking into every nook and corner of our daily lives.[57]

While Reagan advocated self-reliance and limited state intervention, he could not undo the preceding decades of New Deal pragmatism with its associated social welfare provisions and expansive state intervention into social relations. In fact, while he successfully limited the growth of state government, he also initiated the biggest tax increase in the state's history. By doing so, he found a practical way to balance the budget and still maintain bargaining relations with the California State Legislature, dominated by Democrats.[58] Yet growing social unrest, student protests, contentious racial politics, and rising crime all fed into the momentum of grassroots populism, its challenge to New Deal social welfarism, and its particular vision of social order and collective goods. By the early 1970s, the unresolved tension between these two competing variants of American democracy gave way to populism.

Neopopulism and Crime Control

In the 1960s, across the fifty states, crime rates reached unprecedented levels. In California, crime seemed unstoppable. By 1966, California's crime index rate reached over 4,500 known crimes per 100,000 population, a figure well above the national rate of nearly 2,700 known crimes per 100,000 population and above California's rate in 1960 of nearly 3,500 known crimes per 100,000.[59] The crime rate in California continued to rise throughout the 1960s and 1970s until it peaked in 1980.[60]

At the same time in the mid-1960s, a youth culture and free speech movement gained control over the Berkeley campus and racial unrest exploded in south central Los Angeles.

In the fall of 1964, the free speech movement stormed the University of California (UC) Berkeley campus. Barred from distributing political pamphlets on campus, free speech advocates and students, inspired by the civil rights movement, organized large-scale sit-ins, rallies, and demonstrations.[61] In December, students took over Sproul Hall to protest the UC administration's restrictive speech policy, singing "We Shall Overcome" with folk singer Joan Baez.[62] An advocate for students' rights, Governor Pat Brown tried to negotiate with the students and asked them to disperse. Rebuffed, Brown sent in the California Highway Patrol to remove the protestors. By the end of the confrontation, the Highway Patrol had arrested nearly 800 students. The next month, January 1965, Republican State Senator Jack Schrade opened the California State Legislature session with a proposal to "expel all students arrested and convicted of a crime in connection with the recent campus 'free speech' activities."[63] In the aftermath, UC President Clark Kerr was fired for his purported permissiveness with student groups and failed leadership.[64]

In the summer of 1965, brewing racial conflicts bubbled up onto the streets of south central Los Angeles. Sparked by the Los Angeles Police Department's roughshod arrest of young African American drunk driver, thousands of African Americans spilled out onto the streets, protesting poor housing conditions, high rates of unemployment, economic deprivation, and overall neglect by city officials.[65] A year after the predominantly white electorate passed Proposition 14, rejecting the Rumford Fair Housing Act and antidiscrimination law in housing, black residents loudly and violently responded. Watts was on fire. African Americans protested life in the ghettos, ghettos created and solidified by institutionalized residential segregation. After five consecutive days of protest, looting, violence, and near chaos, 35 people were dead and nearly 4,000 people were arrested.[66]

In the following days, the *New York Times* reported the "bitterness and acrimony" on all sides as law enforcement, black civic leaders, poor black residents, middle-class African Americans, and white nonresidents blamed one another and the state for its failure to intervene.[67] Representative Augustus Hawkins, an African American legislator, explained the riots as a result of state neglect: "The trouble is that nothing has ever been done to solve the long-range underlying problems."[68] By contrast, one white Angeleno captured a typical divisive and dismissive sentiment: "This is no special concern of mine. All it proves is what I've known for a long time. The Negroes hate me and I hate the Negroes."[69] Shortly after, Latinos voiced their resentment over the private and public funds pledged to the black community instead of their own dilapidated barrios.[70] A few weeks later, civic leaders and state agencies concluded that "community alienation from the mainstream of life," rather than strictly material deprivation, had sparked the riots.[71] Many Californians blamed Governor Brown for failed leadership, especially for his delayed call for assistance from the National Guard.[72] In the aftermath, the Kerner Commission summed up Watts and its impact on future race relations: "Our nation is moving toward two societies, one black, one white—separate but unequal."[73]

In this social context, over 3.7 million Californians elected Ronald Reagan, the "citizen politician," governor of California, thoroughly defeating Pat Brown. Throughout his gubernatorial campaign and during his administration, Reagan characterized crime as a consequence of a morality gap and breakdown of common decency. Rather than marking it as a result of social or economic deprivation, Reagan successfully linked raging political and economic protest with social disorder and over time with street crime. He criminalized political protest and characterized street crime as a major threat to internal order and national security. To concretize this discursive move, he tapped into grassroots support and mobilized the support of many law enforcement officials and law enforcement associations, such as the California District Attorneys Association, the California Council of Criminal Justice, the attorney general, other conservative politicians. The state's longtime rehabilitative approach to crime and punishment began to be replaced by a more retributive penal regimes. Simple but mandatory penal sanctioning began to replace correctionalism, a regime based on individualized diagnosis and treatment, indeterminate sentencing, criminological expertise, and social deprivation theories of crime causation.

Although Reagan's actions emerged out of a populist political context (that is, his own agency was rooted in a specific political institutional environment), I want to highlight his political discourse on crime control because it is not only riveting, it is illustrative of the themes central to California's crime control and penal regime and was underpinned by key social support.

Morality Gaps, Indecency, and Communist Threats to American Democracy

Governor Reagan characterized the free speech movement not as a political protest upholding deeply cherished American values but as an orgy of sex and drugs somehow linked to the communist threat. In a 1966 speech, "The Morality Gap at Berkeley," Reagan derided the student protests as a result of society's moral breakdown and as a threat to America's democratic political order. He explained:

> There has been a leadership gap and a morality and decency gap at
> the University of California at Berkeley where a small minority
> of beatniks, radicals, and filthy speech advocates have brought
> such shame to and such a loss of confidence in a great
> University . . . You have read about the report of the Senate
> Subcommittee on Un-American Activities—it charges that the
> campus has become a rallying point for Communists and a center
> of sexual misconduct. Some incidents are so bad, so contrary to our
> standards of decent human behavior that I cannot recite them to
> you in detail.[74]

Reagan went on to detail the various acts of indecency because, as he explained, the people "who pay the taxes that support the University also have a right to know" about the charges.[75]

He then made an unflinching link between the students' political protest with violent crime and anarchy. He asked: "What in Heaven's name does academic freedom have to do with rioting, with anarchy, with attempts to destroy the primary purpose of the University which is to educate our young people?"[76]

Reagan's unapologetic connection between political protest and violent anarchy was not part of a uniform response or inevitable characterization of America's emergent counterculture. Consider, for a moment, a contrasting case. Consider how Reagan's contemporary Governor Daniel Evans, a

Republican, of Washington State characterized violent antiwar protests. Rather than criminalize protestors, Evans tried to understand and then explain students' actions. In a statewide television address, he explained how students were frustrated with the "disintegration of the order they have known—a disintegration of the national involvement, the national movement, the national morale."[77] In a politically generous move, he went on to translate destructive student protests against the Vietnam War into civic virtue. By doing so, he turned a potentially divisive protest movement into a fight for the common good—a "free society"—something that everyone, young and old, wanted in Washington. Embedded in a more deliberative political context, Evans looked for ways to bring the people together rather than pull them apart. He explained:

> I think by and large all students, law enforcement officers, and older citizens in our society look for essentially the same thing—an ability to live a life of their personal choice, to make it a rewarding life and a full life, to live it in a nation that has free society and a free system of government, a nation that is strong and vital, and a nation that has a real future. So we are really not so different in the ends we seek, but the differences that divide us today are deep.[78]

By contrast to Evans's conciliatory remarks, Reagan's more combative discourse was indicative of California's polarizing political context—practices that routinely set one group against another, highlighting group differences, mistrust, and potential sources of conflict. Reagan counterposed indecent and communist protestors against decent, law-abiding American taxpayers. He began to develop powerful discursive links between protest, violence, and crime and threats to common decency, social order, and even national security. Within a few years, he blurred the distinctions between these groups where one social pariah could stand in for another and stand against the decent taxpayer. Reagan, recently memorialized as the "great communicator," effortlessly made these disparate associations and made them make sense to a whole lot of people. In 1967, for example, Californians ranked his strong stance against student protestors as the third top reason for his strong approval rating, right alongside his upholding the law on capital punishment (ranked fourth) and right below his government expenditure cuts (ranked first).[79]

A few years later, Governor Reagan added race riots into the mix of student protests, violence, and anarchy, all threats to democratic order. In a rousing speech to the Joint Conference of California School Boards Association and California Association of School Administrations in 1968, he explained how American democracy itself was "under attack as it has never been before." Reagan explained how declining civic engagement could seriously undermine American democracy. Citizens' disengagement from the political field left the state vulnerable to attack. He stated: "When there is a lack of involvement and participation by too many citizens, the political and social stage in left undefended and the extremists take over. They have begun to do so on many of our campuses and in our so-called ghettos as well."[80] He then identified several extremist groups: "a coalition of coercive groups which seek total power or ruin—such groups as Students for a Democratic Society, Black Student Union, Progressive Labor, Castroites, Communists, Maoists, and some arrogant intellectuals bent on anarchy who view with contempt the average man."[81] Here Reagan not only ties political protest to anarchy once again, he adeptly severs any connection ordinary taxpayers might have with these groups. He links protestors with elitists and communists, social groups counterposed and threatening to common American folk, a move that increases the social distance between diverse social groups in civil society and decreases the possibility of mutual identification.

By the time Reagan was asked to testify on crime and violence at the Republican Platform Committee in August 1968, he had thoroughly intertwined crime, civil disorder, and race riots as a collective threat to democratic order. I quote his testimony at length because it vividly encapsulates his effortless discursive links between crime, civil disorder, and immorality. It also highlights his growing antistatist attack on the courts and his subsequent call for retributive rather than rehabilitative responses to problems of order. Reagan stated:

> Our nation is agitated by suspicion, hesitant out of fear and aimless from lack of leadership.
>
> We have seen the license allowed to the wicked and abuse heaped upon the decent and the innocent.
>
> Order has broken down in the streets.
>
> Organized rebellion has broken out on our campuses.
>
> The courts approve and often underwrite the very things our individual integrity rejects.
>
> The immorality of it all confounds the mind and exhausts the spirit and worst of all, it disenchants our young. . . .

Eight years ago terror did not stalk our streets and parks and schoolyards. Today it does. . . .

We must reject the permissive attitude which pervades too many homes, too many schools, too many courts.

We must reject the idea that every [time] a law is broken, society is guilty rather than the lawbreaker. It is time to restore the American precept that each individual is accountable for his actions.

The answer to poverty is jobs—not welfare, not handouts, but jobs. The walls of the ghetto are economic.[82]

He then explained that America needed equal enforcement of the law and equal protection of the law. Appearing on the same panel as Reagan and former Vice President Richard Nixon, New York City Mayor John Lindsay, somewhat overshadowed by Reagan and Nixon's more punitive stance, asked the Republican Party to stay away from "primitive solutions: clubs, guns, tanks" because the "root cause of the most crime and civil disorder is the poverty that grips over 30 millions of our citizens, black and white."[83] Embedded in a more pragmatic political context, the mayor called for a welfarist and state interventionist approach to social problems. In the summer of 1968, Mayor Lindsay, along with Governors Nelson Rockefeller, George Romney, Daniel Evans, among many other moderate or "progressive" Republicans, all stood by somewhat lamely as the Republican Party moved firmly and with certainty to the right.

The Rise of Retribution

Governor Reagan continued to characterize rising crime and civil disorder as a result of moral depravity and individual responsibility. Rejecting social causes of crime theories, derided as "pretentious double talk," Reagan explained on various occasions: "Let us have an end to the idea that society is responsible for each and every wrongdoer."[84] He went on to say, "There is no proof that righting the wrongs and satisfying the demands can stop riots and crime."[85] Instead, he advocated retribution: "We must return to a belief in every individual being responsible for his conduct and his misdeeds with punishment immediate and certain."[86] He explained, "Swift, unrelenting justice will take the fun out of lawlessness and cause juveniles to think twice before they let themselves go."[87]

Reagan continued to press his crime control package on the state legislature, a package that prioritized stiffer and certain penalties for a wide range of crimes. Swift and certain punishment, retribution, made sense because it logically tied penal sanctions to criminal offenses rather than to the criminal's social characteristics. Retribution made sense in a political context that favored self-governance and individual responsibility over state intervention and the kinds of social work ideas and elitist expert knowledge associated with rehabilitation and correctionalism. Retribution, an eye for an eye, is a commonsense approach to crime and punishment that the people can trust as their own. So, too, is the notion of harsh punishment as a deterrent to crime. By contrast to the various social programs, social spending, and taxes inherent in a rehabilitative model, tough punishment presents itself as a bare-bones, scaled-down, and potentially cheap way to restore justice.

Reagan pursued his retributive stance even though it had been previously and partially rejected by the California State Legislature. In 1967, the legislature had passed only a part of Reagan's crime control measures. As the art of political compromise began to break down in the legislature, Lou Cannon, in a Reagan biography, describes the emergence of a more reductionist-style debate on the central crime committee, the Assembly Criminal Procedure Committee. In Cannon's words, the committee became "a total exercise in law enforcement and civil libertarian rhetoric rather than in the legislative process."[88] Rather than hash out a compromise bill based on both positions, committee members became entrenched in their more partisan and ideological positions. Legislators rejected the punitive package proposed by Reagan's allies, George Deukmejian and Senators Grunsky and Lagomarsino. Specifically, legislators rejected Reagan's attempt to restrict the distribution and "peddling of smut...that poisons the minds of our youth,"[89] regulate sexual activity, and create a "straight life" prison term for robbery, rape, and burglary committed with a deadly weapon.[90]

Yet the California State Legislature eventually passed and Reagan signed Deukmejian's Senate Bill 85–87. The legislature and Reagan increased the penalties for violent crime and did so in the name of crime victims.

At this moment, we begin to see California turn toward mandatory prison penalties. The Reagan-Deukmejian penalty package, SB 85–87, increased the minimal penalty from five years to fifteen years to life imprisonment for offenders who inflicted "great bodily harm" on victims of rape, burglary, and robbery. As noted, this legislation fundamentally changed the rationale in penal sanctioning. It introduced the pain and suffering, great bodily harm,

of crime victims as a legitimate reason to increase penal sanctions. It emphasized the need to repair the harm done to victims by inflicting some kind of
pain, loss of liberty, on offenders. Rather than imprison offenders for their own
good, that is, to diagnose, treat, correct, normalize, and rehabilitate them,
offenders were punished to avenge victims. This move later underpinned
the state's rejection of rehabilitation as the primary purpose of imprisonment
in the mid-1970s, and it laid the groundwork for crime victims to become
principal players in criminal justice in the 1980s and 1990s. The penalty
package counterposed victims against offenders, right against wrong, and
did so in a way that simplified justice and bypassed "elitist" theories of crime
causation.

At first, the impact on the prison population was minimal. The new
penalties did not pull in additional offenders; instead, it sentenced those
already going to prison for longer terms. This shift toward retribution did
not automatically replace the core tenets of rehabilitation; this came a bit
later. Nor did it mandate prison terms across all crime categories. Noncustodial
sanctions were still possible and were supported by Reagan through the
Probation Subsidy Acts in 1966 and 1969, subsidies that local and city governments fiercely supported because they were dependent on state financial
assistance to cover the costs. What we need to pay attention to is the penal
package's gradual but certain impact on the prison population. What we notice
is a delayed but cumulative effect over time as the offenders originally sanctioned under the penalty stayed in prison for longer periods of time, stacking
up with new commitments, increasing the population. In the late 1960s,
California's prison population actually declined, a move that may have led
to increased social support for mandatory penal sanctions, especially among
those fed up with student protestors, urban riots, and other signs of disorder.
The penalty package began to change the justification and understanding
of penal sanctioning, a shift supported by key social groups and grassroots
movements.

Retribution Takes Hold

In 1976, the California State Legislature passed and Governor Jerry Brown
signed SB 42, the California Determinate Sentencing Law (DSL). By doing
so, legislators ended indeterminate sentencing, fixed criminal penalties, and
prioritized punishment over rehabilitation.[91] The DSL provided uniform and
fixed prison terms—a move that could reduce if not eliminate sentencing

disparities. The DSL also enabled judges to prolong prison terms with "enhancements." Any offender who committed a crime with a deadly weapon, used a firearm, intentionally caused great bodily injury, and caused "great loss of property" received longer prison terms.[92] The DSL increased prison terms for repeat violent offenders. We should note here that the legislature increased the penalties for burglary—a move that made this frequent nonviolent offense eligible for a prison term and enhanced prison terms if victims sustained great loss of property.

The state legislature fulfilled the anticrime strategy proposed by the California Council on Criminal Justice (CCCJ) in the early 1970s. The CCCJ, established in 1967 and made up primarily of state law enforcement officials, suggested that law enforcement go after burglars, car thieves, and petty thieves, because these common crimes had a "high public visibility."[93] By cracking down on burglars, the CCCJ argued, the state could produce visible results. The CCCJ characterized these nonviolent offenses as "controllable crime." By the 1980s, California imprisoned an increasing number of burglars, drug offenders, and other nonviolent offenders and began to return parole violators to prison at higher rates than ever before.[94] The DSL did not necessarily increase prison terms across the board, but it made it more likely that lower level offenders would go to prison.

Retribution and the Rise of the Crime Victims Movement

In 1982, California voters approved Proposition 8, the Victims' Bill of Rights, 56 percent to 44 percent. Proposition 8 changed the California State Constitution and penal code—it created crime victim rights, mandated restitution, increased penal sanctions for certain repeat offenders, limited plea bargaining and bail in certain cases, loosened the rules of evidence, and enabled victims and victim families to participate in sentencing and parole hearings. Recognizing crime victim rights, the California Constitution now reads:

> The People of the State of California find and declare that the
> enactment of comprehensive provisions and laws ensuring a bill of
> rights for victims of crime, including safeguards in the criminal
> justice system to fully protect those rights, is a matter of grave
> statewide concern. The rights of victims pervade the criminal justice
> system, encompassing not only the right to restitution from the
> wrongdoers for financial losses suffered as a result of criminal acts,

but also the more basic expectation that persons who commit
felonious acts causing injury to innocent victims will be appropriately
detained in custody, tried by the courts, and sufficiently punished
so that the public safety is protected and encouraged as a goal of
highest importance.[95]

Proposition 8 changed the state constitution and penal code in ways that
altered the meaning and practice of criminal justice. Crime victim rights
were now officially sanctioned by law and officially incorporated into criminal
case processing.

To explain this outcome, I suggest that crime victims' moral protest gave
Proposition 8 its emotional tenor, resonating with voters. Yet despite the power
of anger, indignation, and raw emotion, crime victims and their representatives had to mobilize this righteousness in ways that were compatible with
California's political institutions and do so in ways that might lead to a policy
change. To accomplish this task, victim groups took advantage of the state's
open political system through its direct democracy measures (the initiative)
and capitalized on the pervasive sense of conflict and distrust among social
groups in civil society.

In 1981, Paul Gann, the initiative's chief sponsor, and his Citizens
Committee to Stop Crime quickly gathered the half a million signatures
needed to qualify the Victims' Bill of Rights for the June 1982 ballot.[96]
Grassroots activists volunteered to collect signatures and campaign for the
initiative. As one volunteer explained, "[I'm] willing to spend Saturdays stand-
ing outside of Albertson's, Safeway, and schools (on weekdays) passing out
petitions."[97] Another wrote to Gann: "Since our legislature does not do what
the electorate wants, we will again have to legislate."[98]

This particular campaign chose not to rely on state elites or the legislature
to respond to their demands despite their close ties to conservative politicians.
Although prominent conservative lawmakers were involved in the victim rights
campaign, Proposition 8 was nevertheless a ballot measure that depended
on the public's participation rather than on the exclusive actions of the legislature.[99] Skeptics might argue that the public and grassroots activists were
merely used, coopted, and duped by elites. Although this argument
may have some validity in specific instances, it presumes that ordinary
people were either virtuous or disinterested until they were manipulated by
elites. Instead, I suggest we take a serious look at just how hostile crime
victim groups and their representatives were toward criminal offenders as

this antipathy found expression in and was simultaneously deepened by California's populist political roots.

In the 1970s and early 1980s, the discourse, actions and public policies of Governor Edmund G. "Jerry" Brown's administration dramatically illustrate the salient features of California's political environment, an environment that facilitated the movement for victim rights. In his inauguration address, the ritualistic display of political power, Brown described his contemporary era as an "era of limits" and asked Californians to lower their expectations concerning the provisions of public goods and social services. The state would provide less. The next year he explained that difficult governing conditions, namely, slow economic growth, high unemployment, and "increasing social instability," forced the state to reorganize itself: "it is now a question of reordering priorities and choosing one program over another."[100] Anticrime measures were one of three government priorities, along with technological innovation and environmentalism.

At the same time, in terms of crime control, the Brown administration curtailed its responsibility to address the underlying causes of crime perceived as multiple, overlapping and diffuse: unemployment, bad parenting, social disorganization, violence on television, contentious race relations, and family breakdown. The state turned program priorities away from crime prevention even as crime rates continued to increase into the late 1970s and despite the administration's routine portrayal of crime as an epidemic. In 1980, the Los Angeles police chief concurred: "The people of this city are frightened— they have reason to be."[101] The administration pursued crime control by prioritizing punishment, which included a $94 million proposal to expand the state prison system. By the end of 1981, the California State Legislature passed and the governor signed over 100 anticrime measures designed to stiffen penalties and quicken punishment.

Although the Brown administration and California state legislature passed numerous anticrime measures and stiffened criminal penalties, citizens, elected representatives, and newspapers criticized the state for failing to "do something" about crime—a move that both illustrates and reinforces distrust and disconnectedness among polity members. By 1981, the California Field Poll found that 40 percent of Californians thought Governor Brown was doing a "poor" or "very poor" job; and 51 percent thought he "does not work well with the legislature."[102] In this polarized and fragmented political context, citizens and social groups in civil society neither saw nor acknowledged, nor trusted for that matter, how the state responded to crime.

Lieutenant Governor Mike Curb, a Republican and elected separately from the governor, did not help matters much for the state. On California State letterhead, Curb sent out a mass mailing to fellow supporters describing California's dire crime statistics. He explained that "violent crime is completely out of control" and warned citizens that "there is roughly a 50 percent chance that you or a close friend or family member will be the victim of a serious crime within the next 14 months."[103] I quote the lieutenant governor at length here because his statement nicely illustrates his inflammatory remarks on crime that stir up fear and insecurity rather than detached analysis.

> Today, thousands of honest and decent people are afraid to leave their homes for a few days or even a few hours for fear juvenile vandals will rip apart their homes and personal property. Or that professional burglars will loot their homes of their life savings and cherished possessions.
>
> Unfortunately, there is *no way* you can isolate yourself or your family from this virtual tidal wave of crime.
>
> You can't move away from it. Not any anymore. You can't escape it. . . .
>
> *In many cases, the habitual offender is turned loose to commit more violent crimes even before his last victim is out of the hospital.*[104]

In the media, the *San Francisco Chronicle* described how the administration and legislature's "startling bad decisions, prevailing legislative indifference, and inability to act" led to a "great deal of justified citizen frustration" in response to crime.[105] Joining the fray, Carol Hallett, the California Assembly Republican Leader, explained, "the Legislature has failed the people of this state in its refusal to enact the stringent anticrime measures we so desperately need."[106] Robert Agnew, a Paul Gann supporter, summed up a common sentiment at the time: "The very foundation of our society is threatened by the universal indifference of an effete body politic toward a crime-beleaguered public . . . swift and violent punishment is the only possible crime deterrent."[107] Another Gann supporter described her own sense of feeling belittled and neglected by state government after she wrote a letter to the governor complaining about crime: "I feel if I had been somebody important I would probably have an answer by now."[108]

The structure of California's political system, such as its decentralized political authority, contributed to the perception of government inaction on crime, a condition that I argue can undermine trust between the state and civil society. In this situation, citizens may have been more likely to turn to the initiative, a dramatic embodiment of California's decentralized decision making and distrust of state elites, to try to solve their own problems, especially given deteriorating social conditions of the 1970s. Between 1970 and 1980, for example, Californians voted on eighty-four qualifying initiatives, a figure double that voted on between 1940 and 1969.[109] As already noted, the use of citizen initiatives can be a problematic way to resolve political disputes because it tends to increase rather than alleviate conflict, and it counterintuitively undermines aspects of the democratic process: it limits the public's input and, as I suggest, it can dampen public participation. In April 1982, two months prior to the vote on Proposition 8, most of the public had not even heard of the initiative. According to a public opinion survey conducted by the California Field Poll, 84 percent had "not seen or heard" of Proposition 8.[110] Likewise, most of the public, 76 percent, had not seen or heard of Proposition 1, a prison construction initiative on the same June 1982 ballot.[111] These low figures suggest a disengaged public from the policy-making process, a situation, according to the California Field Poll, which can lead to "large portions of the public relying more on their superficial impressions rather than carefully formed judgments when they go to the polls."[112] Alternatively, this situation can lead to a relatively small pool of the population making legally binding decisions for the rest of the public. Neither situation is especially reflective of a vibrant civil society carrying out its civic duty.

Moreover, a recent survey conducted by the Public Policy Institute of California (PPIC) found that Californians who voted in a special election on initiatives expressed dissatisfaction with the process itself: 38 percent said that the special election made them "feel worse about California politics," compared to 21 percent who said they felt better; 55 percent said the wording was "complicated and confusing"; 77 percent favor mandatory televised debates between proponents and opponents; and although 50 percent expressed confidence in their fellow voters, 49 percent expressed no confidence in other voters.[113]

In addition, the initiative process can, under certain conditions, lead to rather blunt policy instruments rather than coherent or long-term policies and programs. For example, voters may face competing initiatives on the same ballot, measures that are incompatible with one another, making confused and convoluted policy (e.g., multiple fiscal bond measures on the March 2004 ballot). In California, voters can only vote "yes" or "no" on initiatives, a formulation that cuts short discussion on complex issues and I suggest undermines compromise. Initiatives ask either/or policy questions: are you in favor of victim rights? Yes or no? Consider some of the published arguments in favor of and opposed to Proposition 8.

Arguments in Favor of Proposition 8:

> While criminals murder, rape, rob and steal, victims must install new locks, bolts, bars and alarm systems in their homes and businesses. Many buy tear gas and guns for self protection. FREE PEOPLE SHOULD NOT HAVE TO LIVE IN FEAR . . . THERE IS ABSOLUTELY NO QUESTION THAT THE PASSAGE OF THIS PROPOSITION WILL RESULT IN MORE CRIMINAL CONVICTIONS, MORE CRIMINALS BEING SENTENCED TO STATE PRISON, AND MORE PROTECTION FOR THE LAW-ABIDING CITIZENRY. IF YOU FAVOR INCREASED PUBLIC SAFETY, VOTE YES ON PROPOSITION 8.[114]

Arguments Against Proposition 8:

> You're afraid of crime—and you have the right to be. If Proposition 8 would end crime, we would be the first to urge you to vote for it. But Proposition 8 is a hoax . . . It will not reduce crime, help victims, or get dangerous criminals off the streets . . . [It] TAKES CONVICTED KILLERS OFF DEATH ROW . . . It makes it harder to convict criminals, will lead to endless appeals, and will create chaos in the legal system. It may be good politics, but it is bad law. PLEASE, VOTE NO ON PROPOSITION 8.[115]

Yet voters' policy preferences may lie somewhere in the middle. As indicated by the PPIC survey, 83 percent favored changing the current procedures to give the sponsor and legislature a chance to "forge a compromise" rather than put winner-take-all proposals on the ballot.[116] The dichotomy of yes-or-no voting can exaggerate and reify opposition and disagreement: if you oppose victims' rights, for example, then you must favor criminals and "senseless violence." If you favor victims' rights, then you must support stiff penalties and life imprisonment.

During the Proposition 8 campaign, crime victim groups engaged in a type of collective agency and moral protest that fit into the dichotomy of the initiative process and took advantage of the polity's social polarization. Gann and his Citizens Committee to Stop Crime counterposed the worthiness of one group against another, necessitating and justifying the punishment of the unworthy. We might think of this as an absolutist, zero-sum moral protest. It is a type of protest based on the righteousness of one set of moral principles to the exclusion of others, often backed up by a zealousness about the truth of the moral principles at stake.

Gann routinely posed the worthiness of crime victims and the victimized public against the unworthiness of offenders: "it makes me shudder when I think about the fact that the criminal is entitled to more protection than the victim."[117] He warned: "Crime in California reached the epidemic stage and is still growing. Law-abiding citizens put bars on their windows to keep criminals out. Streets and schoolyards have turned into jungles with human animals attacking the innocent."[118] Like Gann, activists posed the worthy, "hurt" and "innocent victims" against the unworthy, "drug-crazed," "killers and gang-sters," "escapee sex offenders," "convicted killers and rapists and robbers" who "are freed to kill again." One such activist conveyed a common sentiment in a letter to Gann: "It seems like the victim is forgotten and not much is ever said about them at all."[119] Another counterposed the liberty of criminal offen-ders with the forced imprisonment of citizens: "so long as criminals are turned loose by judges, parole boards and by technicalities, the criminal citizen is now in prison."[120] According to this logic, when criminal offenders are free, citizens become imprisoned. Another wrote about his frustration with prisoners' rights advocates: "Prisoners rights groups use their liberties as a license to abuse the rights of other people."[121] Similarly, one activist wrote, "Brown and his bleeding hearts would probably cry out in horror against such cruel treatment of these lawbreakers. . . . First consider the lawabiding [sic] taxpayer."[122] Anoth-er wrote, "Take care of the good people and there will be a great reduction in the bad."[123]

As these statements help illustrate, this type of moral protest is based on dichotomous logic, posing one set of values—in this case, the public's sense of safety—against another set of values—in this case, any sense of the humanity or rights of criminal offenders. I argue that the logic of this type of protest made it increasingly difficult for Proposition 8 supporters to reconcile the rights of criminal offenders with the rights of victims—the two were logically incompatible and emotionally unfeasible. To challengers, because criminal defendants brought harm to the worthy, this further insult made offenders unworthy of the rights of full citizenship. As such, supporters could justify the retraction of due process protections. In the words of one activist: "If you really want to get tough on crime—cut off this free lawyer bit."[124] Proposition 8 sped up case processing and as result, loosened rules of evidence and standards of proof, which eroded defendants' full legal protections against state power.[125]

To garner additional support for Proposition 8, challengers counterposed "decent law-abiding citizens" against "killers and gangsters," posed hard-working "taxpayers" against freeloading "public wards," posed "the good" against "the bad." Challengers interchanged the categories of worthiness so that one could stand in for the other and vice versa. In this moral calculus, taxpayers became victims, welfare recipients became criminals, and criminals brought harm to taxpayers. In the words of one activist:

> [There] never seems to be a lack of funds to pacify the demands
> of angry welfare recipients or pay for the expensive extra fuel
> required to bus children ... put jails to work ... In all justice, it is
> not right that public wards should have voting rights. Would love
> to see a law suspend the voting rights of any able-bodied, able-
> minded welfare recipient until one year after his or her removal
> from the dole roll.[126]

This letter links civil penalties for convicted felons with welfare recipients. In the words of another: "Taxpayers don't mind at all to take care of the disabled, but there are the able, who wouldn't have a job at any price. This is the group that [is] committing about or more each 10 major crimes [sic]."[127]

Challengers' associations of worthiness and unworthiness tapped into a subtext of race and crime where concerns about "crime" were legitimate ways to express perhaps a deeper anxiety about race and animosity toward poor and socially marginalized groups, particularly African Americans. As noted earlier, the initiative process has been an effective way for special interest groups to legislate their own parochial needs, including racial and ethnic prejudices, as illustrated in the recent past by the approval of Proposition 187, which barred illegal aliens from public services in 1994, and Proposition 209, which banned affirmative action or "preferential treatment by state and other public entities" in 1996.[128] In their analysis of California's three strikes initiative, Tom Tyler and Robert Broekmann found that voters' support for the punitive measure tended to be associated with anxiety about declining moral cohesion and increasing diversity.[129] Moreover, the themes of crime, insecurity, and law and order also have been effective political resources in the backlash against civil rights. As Katherine Beckett explains, conservative politicians since Barry Goldwater and Richard Nixon have used the public's concern about crime as a way to express resentment over growing racial equality and an expanding welfare state.[130] During the Proposition 8 campaign, supporters referred to criminals as freeloaders, "nonproductive elements" who drained limited resources and were "getting something for nothing" while "decent law-abiding" citizens wasted their tax dollars to support them.

I suggest that this dichotomous logic, counterposing the worthy against the unworthy, is indicative of a political context with low social trust and low social connectedness. The letters to Gann in support of victims' rights are striking because they contain little sense of mutual obligation or norms of reciprocity, features that may be necessary to sustain policies rooted in the broad public interest. Instead, the letters express much animosity, bitterness, insularity, and a sense of embattlement from an imposing but ineffective government and from a dependent but threatening criminal class. To repeat Gann's own words: "Streets and schoolyards have turned into jungles with human animals attacking the innocent."[131] These are hardly the words and sentiments of a civic leader willing to compromise or bring about more inclusive and less coercive public policies.

In this case, a contentious form of collective agency capitalized on California's neopopulist political structures to mobilize grassroots support for what appears to be a rather vindictive crime victims campaign. Proposition 8, the Victims' Bill of Rights, granted victims new rights, restitution, and participation in parole and sentencing hearings, but these were interlinked with the retraction of the rights and liberties of criminal offenders as the new legislation limited plea bargaining, restricted bail, loosened rules of evidence in favor of prosecutors, and stiffened penalties for repeat offenders.

Neopopulism and Retribution Repeated

In November 1994, Californians approved Proposition 184, the Sentencing Enhancement Repeat Offenders initiative, known as "Three Strikes and You Are Out," with 71.85 percent of the vote.[132] The legislation mandated and lengthened prison terms for repeat felony offenders. It eliminated probation for repeat offenders, substantially increased prison terms for second-time felony offenders, and mandated twenty-five years to life imprisonment for offenders convicted of a third felony, including nonviolent offenses.[133] The campaign for Three Strikes mobilized grassroots support and moral outrage around the brutal shooting of a young woman during a robbery and the kidnapping, sexual assault, and murder of a young white girl from Petaluma, a fairly affluent part of northern California, by a repeat sex offender. Like the campaign for the Victims Bill of Rights, the Three Strikes campaign counterposed the worthiness of crime victims against the unworthiness of criminal

offenders, seeking to diminish offenders' claims to the liberties and protections of full citizenship. Like Proposition 8, Proposition 184 dramatized the
pain and suffering of crime victims to justify the intensification of the criminal
law and penal sanctioning. Proposition 184 also favored retribution to repair
the harm done to victims. Unlike every other three strikes legislation in other
states, in California actually it has had a major impact on the state's prison
population, driving imprisonment rates up gradually over time.[134]

Despite popular and scholarly attention paid to the Three Strikes initiative,
this legislation did not transform California's penal regime overnight or by
itself. What I have tried to show in this chapter is how California's retributive
penal regime emerged slowly and cumulatively over time. It was not created by
one piece of legislation, a dramatic moment, or by a crisis in governance. The
introduction of great bodily harm penal sanctioning in 1967, determinate
sentencing in 1976, crime victims' rights in 1982, three strikes in 1994,
along with minor changes in the penal code and budgetary priorities, high
rates of parole revocation, and incremental and numerous state legislature
bills, all helped achieve this shift. All contributed to the unraveling of California's rehabilitative approach to crime control and solidified retribution as the
main purpose of punishment, which has been legitimated and justified in the
name of crime victims' pain and suffering.

Recent Reforms: Return to Pragmatism?

That said, recent reform efforts may indicate a shift or at least a challenge to
California's dominant penal regime and its associated high imprisonment
rates. In 2004, grassroots activists led an initiative campaign, Proposition
66, to amend and restrict California's Three Strikes laws. In 2003, newly
elected Governor Arnold Schwarzenegger created the Independent Review
Panel to analyze and overall California's prison system. In the spring of
2007, the California State Legislature passed and Schwarzenegger signed the
Prison Reform Act, a nearly $8 billion piece of legislation intended to reduce
prison overcrowding and reemphasize rehabilitation or "reentry" as a legitimate and effective way to reduce recidivism and the state's prison population.
Between 1999 and 2002, California's imprisonment rate declined for the first
time since the brief dip in the early 1970s. To a certain degree, these shifts
may indicate a return to pragmatic governance. The historical and dialectical
tension between pragmatism and populism has not been fully resolved in

California, creating an inherent tension that enables change. A more compromising, expert-driven, activist mode of governance concerned with the general welfare may be resurfacing.

With the recall of Governor Gray Davis and the election of Schwarzenegger in 2003, California may have been jolted out of its habits and routines. In his swearing-in remarks, Schwarzenegger testified to his desire to change California governance. He stated, "To those who have no power . . . to those who've dropped out—too weary or disappointed with politics as usual—I took this oath to serve *you*."[135] I quote his remarks at length as they bring together many of the political themes that make up California's political tradition discussed throughout this chapter. He continued:

> Today is a NEW day in California. I did not seek this office to do things the way they've ALWAYS been done. What I care about is restoring your TRUST in your government . . . Californians have lost CONFIDENCE. They've felt that the actions of their government did NOT represent the will of the people . . .
>
> Everywhere I went during my campaign, I could feel the public hunger for our elected officials to work TOGETHER, to work OPENLY, and to work for the greater GOOD. . . . So I've appointed to my cabinet Republicans, Democrats, Independents—because I want people to know that my administration is NOT about politics. It is about saving California.
>
> The State of California is in crisis . . .
>
> For millions of people around the world, California has ALWAYS glimmered with hope and glowed with opportunity. Millions of people around the world send their dreams to California with the hope that their lives will follow.
>
> My fellow citizens.
>
> I have taken the oath to uphold the Constitution of California. Now, with your help and God's, I will ALSO uphold the DREAM that is California.[136]

Prison Reform Act 2007

The 2007 Prison Reform Act (PRA), generated in part by Schwarzenegger's reform-oriented approach to governance, passed by a bipartisan compromise, guided in part by leading penal experts such as Professor Joan Petersilia, and supported by Department of Corrections and Rehabilitation officials, law enforcement officials, and over 60 percent of the public,[137] suggests a major change in California's penal politics. The PRA represents an effort to restrain the crass rationale of retribution, unbounded and limitless, that motivated much of California's sentencing and penal policy for the past thirty years. Although the policy is based on the expansion of prison capacity with 53,000 new beds, it ties any new prison construction to rehabilitation services and increases rehabilitation services in existing prisons.[138] To support this shift, the PRA authorizes the creation of smaller community-based centers (16,000 beds) responsible for the reentry of offenders back into their home communities. Rather than release and return offenders to prison, as evidenced by the state's 70 percent recidivism rate, a figure much higher than the 40 percent national average, the Department of Corrections is suppose to provide increased and improved job training, mental health and substance abuse counseling, and housing placement to ease the difficult transition from prison to public life, keeping ex-offenders out of prison and potentially reducing the prison population over time.[139] Echoing Schwarzenegger's swearing-in remarks, the PRA suggests a more hopeful vision of California's prison system, one that can reform rather than simply punish.[140]

At the same time, however, the PRA does not represent a clean break from the past; in many ways, it reiterates past policies and past justifications for punishment. Although the PRA emphasizes rehabilitation, it does so in the name of public safety and crime victims rather than in the name of offenders. As Schwarzenegger's Ask the Experts panel on the PRA explain: "more rehabilitation, fewer victims."[141] In other words, the emphasis on reentry is justified as a way to protect the public and decrease criminal victimization rather than a way to reform, correct, and normalize offenders as the rehabilitative ideal once promised. In addition, as other commentators and prison reform advocates have pointed out, the PRA's main reform program expands prison capacity. Although this move can reduce overcrowding and improve prison conditions, it also creates new institutions to house even more inmates. The PRA basically creates more prison space for more punishment. States can reduce their prison populations by incarcerating fewer people, increasing early release, and tying sentencing schemes to prison capacity, as Washington State does. California does not seem to be pursuing these alternatives but plans to build more prisons. Furthermore, some of the other provisions (e.g., the creation of a sentencing commission, alternative sanctions for parole violators, and the decarceration of low-risk female offenders), provisions that may have reduced the prison population, were excluded from the final bill.[142] We should also note that California was under tremendous pressure to reduce prison overcrowding because the federal courts threatened to limit the state's prison population.[143] Given these circumstances, the reform package most likely reflects the growing tension between conflicting political regimes and a response to immediate political pressures rather than an indicator of deep-seated change.

Proposition 66: Limitations on Three Strikes

Moreover, just three years prior to the PRA in 2004, California voters rejected Proposition 66, a grassroots initiative intended to reform the state's relatively harsh Three Strikes law. According to several leading criminologists, California's Three Strikes laws are indeed out of line with the rest of the nation's versions, imposing long sentences on relatively minor crimes.[144] Proposition 66 would have limited the strikes to new violent or serious felonies, narrowed the kinds of felonies considered violent or serious, required separate trials per strike, and resentenced offenders currently serving life terms who had been convicted of a nonviolent or nonserious offense.[145]

Grassroots activists argued that Proposition 66 would restore Three Strikes to its original purpose—that is, to punish repeat, serious, and violent offenders rather than imprison large numbers of nonviolent, petty offenders. Working in collaboration with the American Civil Liberties Union of Southern California, activists such as Citizens Against Violent Crime (a victims rights group led by Joe Klaas, grandfather of Polly Klaas, whose kidnapping and murder sparked the original Three Strikes initiative), Families to Amend Three Strikes (a prisoners' advocacy group), California Church Impact (a coalition of twenty-four denominations), the Violence Research Foundation, and the National Black Police Association voiced much frustration with the Three Strikes law because it was perceived to be unjust and misleading, resulting in the mass imprisonment of numerous nonviolent offenders for life and at quite a cost. As illustrative of this critique, TV commercials advertised $1 million baby formula, suggesting that the petty theft of baby formula would cost the state of California $1 million.[146] Some of the official arguments posted on the ballot in favor of Proposition 66 stated: "After ten years, Three Strikes has stuck California taxpayers with a $6 billion bill to punish videotape and T-shirt thieves, and other nonviolent petty offenders"; "*Voting yes on Proposition 66 will save taxpayers billions of dollars* over the next decade by doing what makes sense—ensuring that only truly dangerous or violent repeat criminals, such as murderers and kidnappers, spend the rest of their lives in prison"; "PROPOSITION 66 IS NOT ABOUT GETTING SOFT ON CRIME, IT's ABOUT GETTING SMART ON CRIME."[147]

In their literature, the Families to Amend Three Strikes (FACTS) highlighted the devastating impact of Three Strikes on the lives of inmates and their families, cataloging "150 Stories of Inmates" on their Web site, including the stories of Rene Landa for stealing a spare tire, Mark Bishop for possession of a controlled substance, and Johnny Quirino for petty theft of razor blades.[148] The ACLU of Southern California emphasized the public's growing awareness of the "excesses and injustices of the law" and the strong public support for reform.[149] Throughout the spring and well into the fall, Proposition 66 did in fact enjoy strong public support. According to three statewide surveys conducted by the California Field Poll from May into October 2004, a large majority favored Proposition 66, including self-identified Democrats, Republicans, nonpartisans, conservatives, middle-of-the-road, and liberal voters.[150]

Yet Proposition 66 failed. Forty-seven percent voted in favor with about 53 percent opposed.[151] By the time of the election, opponents successfully mobilized resonant themes in California's long history of penal populism, themes that countered proponents' discourse on injustice, betrayal, cost-effectiveness, and rational crime control. Crime Victims United of California (CVUC), a political action committee made up of crime victims groups, law enforcement organizations, and high-profile state officials such as the governor and attorney general led a campaign against Proposition 66 based on fear and loathing. They tapped into the public's fear of random violence, its sense of victimization and insecurity about crime, moral outrage about child molesters and sex offenders, and emphasized the unworthiness of criminal offenders, deemed "hardcore criminals who've worked hard to be in prison."[152]

In one of his first public policy campaigns, Governor Schwarzenegger vigorously opposed the initiative, characterizing the reform as a "legal loophole" for criminals and claiming it would "flood our streets with thousands of dangerous felons, including rapists, child molesters, and murderers."[153] In their official Arguments against Proposition 66, Schwarzenegger, Attorney General Bill Lockyer, and Harriet Salarno, CVUC chair, counterposed the brutal acts of convicted three strikers against the pain and suffering of crime victims, warning that crime would increase if the reform passed.[154] Arguments against Proposition 66 included an inflammatory but authoritative statement by Wayne Quint Jr., president of the California Coalition of Law Enforcement

Associations: "Crime will go up and innocent people will be hurt or killed if Proposition 66 passes. This is a very dangerous initiative."[155] Reiterating these themes in the aftermath of the vote, Mike Reynolds, author of the original 1994 Three Strikes initiative, characterized the defeat as the "difference between greater public safety and certain murder and mayhem."[156]

I suggest that Proposition 66's failure indicates the strength and persistence of California's populist political traditions and the longevity of its retributive penal regime rather than the emergence of a sustainable reform movement. Today, California's imprisonment rate continues to climb, hovering above the national average despite a brief period of decline between 1999 and 2002.

Conclusion

What I have tried to show in this chapter is the centrality of neopopulism, the emergence of a more conservative and antistatist variant, to California's penal regime change. Neopopulism provided the institutional and cultural resources that social actors, state elites like Governors Reagan and Brown and grassroots organizations like the crime victims' movement, used to remake their political order. California's retributive penal regime was made up of local goods and services and made sense to the locals steeped in narratives of self-governance, common sense, and intolerance to those perceived to be outsiders or morally depraved. The prison, a comparatively blunt policy instrument of incapacitation and exclusion, provides an intuitive form of justice and emotional release. It makes the most sense to those who resent social scientific expertise, social theories of crime causation, and precious resources spent on offenders, practices linked to the rehabilitative ideal.

I suggest that what Californians have created over the years is a relatively "thin democracy," to use Benjamin Barber's terminology. Out of the raw material of California's past politics, they have created a variant of American democracy that prioritizes private and parochial interests rather than a common purpose. They have created a variant that downplays compromise and negotiation in favor of winner-take-all politics and irreconcilable moral positions. As such, neopopulism tends to undercut the norms and practices of social trust and social reciprocity, practices that are necessary to keep a highly complex and diverse political community together.

In this context, crime and punishment provide a pivotal resource for state elites as well as grassroots activists to couch their particular vision of the good society in the greater good, public safety, and internal security at the expense of those most socially marginalized. Crime and punishment provided the tools through which a neopopulist movement changed the basic governing relationship between state and citizen and changed mutual obligations between social groups in civil society. In this context, social actors have not only failed to keep a check on state repression, they often have demanded it and demanded that it be used against others. Rather than limiting state power as an infringement on personal autonomy and individual liberty, social actors have expanded the range and capacity of the state's power to punish. Because this coercive power has been internally directed, against its own members, against its own vulnerable members, California's retributive penal regime has essentially undermined the social obligations across social groups. Given these developments, retributive penal sanctioning has contributed to the changing the conditions of citizenship, creating a political community based on the exclusion of others.

4

Washington State Deliberates

From Fortress Prison to De-Escalation

After thirty years of thinking about crime and trying to avoid it, we may no longer be able to appreciate the real shock that many experienced in the late 1960s as crime rates reached unprecedented levels. The rapid escalation of crime shocked many Americans who were just settling into the comforts of affluence, brought about by the Cold War and its associated industrial and economic growth. High crime rates left many people feeling unsettled and shaken because the new prosperity and the old New Deal social programs should have solved the crime problem. High crime rates stung as they pierced the legitimacy and authority of state governments and strained group relations and the social solidarity necessary to connect an increasingly complex society of the postwar period.

Despite what appears to have been a uniform and coordinated response to crime—that is to say, increased imprisonment—at the time, most American states struggled to make sense of the new crime experience and scrambled what were mostly ad hoc and piecemeal responses together. Throughout the 1960s and 1970s, state governments were much less organized and less professional than they are today.[1] Many criminal justice departments were also less organized and less technologically advanced. In the early 1970s, many law enforcement officials still relied on outdated radio equipment, which impeded communication between patrol cars and headquarters.[2] Although President Lyndon Johnson established a new federal agency in 1968, the Law Enforcement Administration Agency, to subsidize state-level crime control, state governments maintained the authority, discretion, and jurisdiction over crime control policy. Many state governments were simply overwhelmed and uncertain about what to do. Some took initiative, taking inventory of current practices, keeping the ones that seemed to work, and discarding the ones that did not. State officials in Washington and New York, among other places, discovered that the correctional or rehabilitative programs thought to be in place since the early twentieth century were never fully implemented and were never funded properly.[3] In the late 1960s and early 1970s, most state prisons, with the possible exception of California, were ill equipped, understaffed, and underfunded to carry out the great ambitions of the rehabilitative ideal.

In these frantic moments, state officials in Washington realized or at least admitted publicly that their "correctional" facilities were merely custodial institutions. In one of his many public addresses on the subject, Governor Daniel Evans, a nearly lifelong elected official and moderate republican, de- nounced the state's prisons as "warehouses of territorial days."[4] He explained how "we have simply come to the end of the line in terms of what we can achieve through rehabilitation in our existing, large fortress prisons."[5] Washington's prisons had become imposing, large-scale holding tanks with minimal services available to an undifferentiated mass of criminal offenders, penal practices that undermined the individualized diagnosis and treatment so central to the rehabilitative ideal.

Rather than fix or reform correctionalism or simply embrace incapacitation, state officials pursued a radically different kind of penal regime: de-escalation and the principle of parsimony.

De-Escalation and the Principle of Parsimony

In the late 1960s and early 1970s, officials in Washington State began a long-term project to divert offenders away from prison. By limiting commitments to prison, decriminalizing certain offenses, rejecting mandatory prison terms, and shortening prison terms, the state began an unofficial policy of decarcera- tion, effectively reducing the state prison population within a few short years.[6] By sanctioning offenders to probation rather than prison, increasing probation subsidies, introducing first-time offender waivers, expanding work release, and relying heavily on community supervision, state officials prioritized noncus-todial sanctions over imprisonment for many offenders, especially but not exclusively nonviolent and first-time offenders.[7] In these transformative mo-ments, Washington created a kind of penal sanctioning based on the principle of parsimony.

According to Norval Morris, the principle of parsimony requires that state authorities punish lawbreakers with the "least restrictive (punitive) sanction" possible to maintain public safety.[8] The principle of parsimony economizes penal sanctioning; it rations stiff penalties, reserving them for the most serious offenses. It depresses the upper limits of what is possible in punishment, especially for minor criminal offenses. A prison term, for example, becomes too restrictive, too punitive, the upper limit unimaginable for many first-time and nonviolent offenses. The prison becomes an institution to be avoided, a penal practice of the last resort. In Washington, state officials actively pursued policies to divert offenders away from prison and release inmates early and in large volume through good time credits, parole, and work release. Officials also restricted parole revocation, that is, they limited the return of parole violators back to prison for technical violations or new crimes.[9] This cluster of practices stands in opposition to California, which has tended to lavish the prison on all kinds of criminal offenders, parole violators, first-time offenders, nonviolent offenders, along with repeat and violent offenders. As discussed in chapter 3, California's retributive penal regime seeks to punish offenders for inflicting harm on others, and it does so by invoking crime victims' pain to justify, legitimate, and support the authority of the criminal law and penal sanction-ing. Criminal justice in California embodies and invokes the infliction of pain to restore order. By contrast, criminal justice in Washington to a certain degree invokes and protects offenders' liberty. In this penal regime, the preservation of civil liberty and individual freedom become central to the maintenance of social order. Doing so challenges conventional and classical notions of justice that require punishment to be harmful, painful, or humiliating.[10]

Initiated in the 1960s, the principle of parsimony continued to inform Washington's penal regime through the 1980s. In 1983, Washington passed the nation's first sentencing guidelines legislation with the Sentencing Reform Act. The state's sentencing guidelines prioritized proportionality and commen-surate sanctions, linked penal sanctions to available but limited prison capaci-ty, and encouraged the use of alternatives to incarceration.[11] By the late 1980s, the imprisonment rate in Washington had dropped substantially.[12] However, in the early 1990s, the principle of parsimony was seriously challenged by a powerful and effective crime victims movement demanding that justice recognize their pain and suffering by inflicting harm on offenders, demanding more custody to protect the public. With the subsequent passage of the Community Protection Act in 1990, the principle of parsimony survived, but it had been compromised. Although Washington continues to maintain one of the lowest imprisonment rates in the nation, 273 inmates per 100,000 population, ranking forty-first in the United States, the imprisonment rate has steadily increased over time, and diversion through first-time offender waivers has declined.[13] Of course, in comparative perspective, Washington maintains a much higher imprisonment rate than many democratic nations, such as the Netherlands, Sweden, Germany, and France, among others,[14] reminding us to think about the principle of parsimony in relative and more localized (rather than absolute or universal) terms. What is more, we should note that both de-escalation and the principle of parsimony, the privileging of noncustodial sanctions, coincided with the rise in the overall imprisonment rate over time. Washington was not immune to the secular trend towards increased imprisonment. Although the state processed more offenders over time, it continued to send a lower percentage of them to prison and has continued to make efforts to keep the prison population down.

Washington maintains one of the lowest imprisonment rates in the nation by shifting the site of punishment away from state and toward civil society. That is, Washington diverts offenders away from prison and toward probation, noncustodial sanctions, and community supervision. It has the highest percentage of its overall correctional population under community supervision in the nation.[15] State officials have limited to a certain degree restrictive and punitive sanctions, the deprivation of liberty; they have done so not by decreasing punishment but by increasing reliance on community sanctions.

A critical interpretation of this shift, as informed by Michel Foucault, might interpret this penal regime as subjecting offenders to more insidious forms of power and control: the normalizing power of the community and the disciplining power of work. Critical readers might also interpret this penal regime as a colonizing form of state power, that is, a kind of state power that is dispersed and diffuse, spreading itself into civil society and other nongovernmental fields of action, and thereby increasing its capacity to regulate, manage, and discipline the population beyond the prison walls. Other readers may interpret Washington's principle of parsimony as the result of a more homogenous, less violent population. Others may simply doubt that the state's penal regime is really any different than the penal regimes of California or any other American state because the overall imprisonment rate has increased over time, linking it the general trend in the nation.

These interpretations point to some of the key dynamics of punishment: crime control, state power, racial threat. Yet as explanations of penal regime change, continuity and difference, they are incomplete; under certain conditions, they are inaccurate, unsupported by empirical evidence. They cannot explain why Washington changed its penal regime in the late 1960s, why state officials moved away from fortress prisons to the principle of parsimony. It is not clear why a less violent or more homogenous population would reject correctionalism, the long-standing penal ideology based to some extent on social solidarity and social stability. Nor is it clear why Washington began to divert criminal offenders away from prison at the same time it experienced intense racial unrest as well as significant shifts in the racial composition of urban areas. Instead, I suggest we investigate and try to appreciate how the people of Washington—state officials and social groups of civil society alike—experienced and made sense of rising crime and contentious racial politics. We can try to understand how these people made sense of the social world within which they lived and how they took action. To do so, we need to look beyond the ominous functions of state power, demographic patterns, and essentialized characterizations of American punitiveness. Taking cues from Stuart Scheingold, we need to examine how ordinary people made sense of crime and punishment and how they took action within a localized context to account for the de-escalation of punishment at a most unlikely time.

Democratized Deliberation and Less Coercive Penal Sanctioning

As I argue in the pages that follow, the emergence of a more deliberative democratic process in Washington State helped defuse growing social conflict and suppress reactionary moves toward repression. It did so in large part through democratization and communicative action. That is to say, the emergence of a more deliberative process expanded citizen participation in decision making, increased power-sharing arrangements between the state and civil society, and emphasized the significance of open discussion, dialogue, debate, and negotiation in politics and policy making. As a set of political structures and collective agency, the rise of a more deliberative process provided the raw material, cultural resources, and legitimating authority necessary to sustain the principle of parsimony and depress state reliance on confinement, relationships I develop shortly.

Amidst the upheaval, doubt, and aggression of the 1960s, political leaders in Washington democratized political power and reinvigorated deliberative forms of collective agency. By calling on the state's mythic and real past, Governor Daniel Evans valorized and sought to reestablish the practices of self-governance, cooperative movements, volunteerism, and a "producerist" work ethic. By doing so, he lent cultural weight to the subsequent shifts in the state's political organization, changes that would transform to a certain extent the state's governing relationship with its citizens as citizens became "partners in the unfolding task of government."[16] The state began to move away from what had become a relatively closed period of governance in the postwar era and reestablished its more open, democratized institutions of the progressive era. As Governor Evans explained: "We are not a private club down here and we cannot make our way in secrecy. We need to adopt the principles of 'open decisions' openly arrived at."[17] The state gave up a certain degree of political power and control to social groups in civil society, asking ordinary people to do more for themselves and others, asking regular citizens to get involved in the political process, engage and discuss policy issues, negotiate solutions, and take on more responsibility of self-governance. Evans explained: "When we collectively get off the sidelines ... and put our own time, talent, and determination to work ... we will finally find success."[18] Ordinary people, social movements, and various social science experts and legal professionals increased their access and influence over key policy-making decisions, especially in the areas of criminal law and penal sanctioning, as indicated by the creation of new state-citizen commissions, new organizations for volunteering, and continued recognition by the governor for their efforts.[19]

Civic engagement in Washington has been relatively robust. People consistently turn out to vote in elections, regularly attend local community meetings, volunteer, and belong to a range of social and civic associations.[20] This intensity has been key to supporting relatively high rates of social capital and social trust. Washington ranks tenth in the nation in terms of Robert Putnam's social capital index. A high rate of social capital suggests that people are relatively well connected to each other and have well-developed norms of reciprocity. Reciprocity, that is to say, the mutual exchange of support, gifts, favors or even goods and services, goes beyond the exchange of contractual obligations with its threat of force. Reciprocity indicates a desire to maintain and build rather than break down social ties and willingness to take a chance on others. It suggests a willingness to trust other people and engage others with mutual respect.

Under certain conditions, these social practices can bring about a more conciliatory mode of governance, a mode that I argue is less likely to pursue coercive public policies.[21] In this context, crime is perceived to be a common feature of modern social life, rather than the result of morally depraved criminals, and criminals are considered to be part of the political community rather than fully excluded from it. As such, polity members are reluctant but not unwilling to inflict the violence of penal sanctioning on one another.[22] Moreover, heavy reliance on imprisonment, the infringement of individual liberty by the state, may fail to resonate, to find the necessary emotional and political support, in a civic culture based on a belief in and practices of self-governance, mutual cooperation, and the power and efficacy of civil society. In this context, sanctioning "wayward" offenders in the community makes much more moral and political sense.

A Note on the Countertrend

This chapter provides a glimpse into an important but understudied trend in American punishment: the countervailing principle of parsimony and de-escalation. This focus may provide some insight into alternative modes of penal sanctioning, especially at a time when many U.S. state governments and grassroots organizations are seriously questioning and challenging the massive prison build-up over the past thirty years. In recent years, researchers effectively have shown that imprisonment tends to exacerbate rather than alleviate social and political inequalities.[23] Researchers have also documented the extraordinary obstacles prisoners face with "reentry" as they leave the prison and return home, obstacles that tend to increase recidivism.[24] Aware of the rising economic and social costs of mass incarceration, some state governments are reconsidering the widespread and quick reliance on the prison to solve complex social and economic problems. The case of Washington may provide useful tools to rethink the intensity and character of penal sanctioning in the American states. At the same time, it may provide a different way to think about the political process and the importance of citizen participation in the policy-making process. By contrast to the exclusively negative and punitive effects of electoral politics on penal policies, the research here shows that citizen involvement can actually restrain the repressive powers of the state. Civic engagement in penal policy making may be essential to any significant reform because the citizens, after all, are the ones who give the moral authority and emotional resonance to state punishment.

Democratized Deliberation: The Historical Legacy of Progressive Populism

Progressive populism rooted in farmers' cooperative movements of the late nineteenth century has played a structuring role in the political development of Washington State. Progressive populism sought to promote social welfare but without building up the capacities of the state[25] to control, regulate, or discipline civil society. It sought to advance social welfarism through voluntary associations, mutual cooperation, and self-governance. The success of this movement established more democratic political institutions, decentralizing political authority, and it helped legitimate the role of civil society organizations in the provision of public goods. The legacy of this transformation created institutional memories, path dependencies, and cultural resources for understanding the recent past and present politics of Washington. A few key moments in Washington's political development are considered below.

Progressive Populism

In the 1890s, Washington became a major site of populist protest and progressive politics, politics that would go on to remake the political order of the expansive American West.[26] In *The Populist Moment*, Lawrence Goodwyn explains how American populism emerged out of an agrarian protest against widespread economic exploitation and institutionalized debt. To avoid what were perceived to be unfair banking practices of most commercial financial institutions, activist farmers created the Farmers' Alliance in 1873. This organization was designed to provide members with mutual economic support and financial independence. As the alliance grew, populists challenged dependency on big banks, railroad corporations, state elites, and state representatives, often thought to be unresponsive, self-interested, and corrupt. As populists turned more and more to institutionalized politics, creating third parties such as the People's Party, populism became a much broader political movement. By fighting for increased political participation, populists sought to undo the social hierarchies of the United States.[27] Specifically, they pushed for the redistribution of resources as they wanted to maintain the independence of "plain people," farmers and laborers. In the words of Washington Governor John Rogers: "the great plain people...are to unite against the organized aggression of the privileged few."[28] In some contexts, populists wielded considerable influence on the structure and substance of American politics. In some contexts, they successfully challenged their own economic exploitation and introduced more socialist organizing principles into American political and economic life.

In Washington, populism was strong and quite successful.[29] Throughout the 1890s, voters consistently supported populist political candidates. In 1896, for example, the People's Party made up the majority of the Washington state legislature.[30] By 1910, Washington's population had reached 1 million people, a threefold increase within twenty years. The population explosion made up of migrant farmers, loggers, and other populist-leaning laborers soon overwhelmed the state's nascent government, recently established in 1889. By 1911, populist reformers such as the Direct Legislation League, the Grange, the Farmers' Union, and the State Federation of Labor successfully pressured the Washington legislature into changing the state constitution to codify direct democracy measures.[31] Washington amended its state constitution to codify the initiative, referendum, and recall. In 1911, the new constitution stated: "the people reserve to themselves the power to propose bills, laws, and to enact or reject the same at the polls, independent of the legislature," and "reserve power, at their own option, to approve or reject at the polls any act, item, Section or part of any bill, act or law passed by the legislature."[32] Citizens were now empowered to write their own legislation and vote on it through the electoral process, which allowed ordinary people, unelected citizens, to make new laws, circumventing elected representatives in the state legislature. After twenty years of movement activity, populists had successfully transformed the political structures of Washington.

In *The People's Lobby*, Elisabeth Clemens explains how Washington's populist revolt took a particularly progressive form. Populists sought to advance progressive reforms without building up the state. Specifically, they sought to expand social welfarism without expanding the capacities of the state. Instead, they wanted to rely more on civil society organizations and mutual aid. They stressed the more consensus-based politics and collaborative practices of earlier farmers' cooperatives, such as the Grange (formed in 1873) and other "producerist" associations. In Washington, "producers," such as farmers, laborers, small merchants, and other workers had formed various kinds of cooperatives to support each other. They collectively pooled and shared their resources to protect each other against what were perceived to be unfair business practices of the banking industry.[33] To maintain their independence without financial ruin, the Grange and other cooperatives emphasized the values of work, productivity, cooperation, mutual aid, and self-governance. These associations regularly challenged state elites to redistribute resources to protect farmers and workers.

According to Clemens, progressive populists helped create and expand public services and protect the working classes from some forms of economic exploitation, but they did so on the condition that voluntary associations rather than the state would play the lead role in the provision of goods and services. From 1890 to 1915, Washington's farmer–labor alliances challenged state property taxes, pressed for more protective labor legislation, demanded state-funded education, and supported the temperance movement.[34] By 1915, Washington ran six employment agencies in collaboration with organized labor but had neither passed a law establishing these public services nor codified this cooperative arrangement.[35]

Expanding Social Welfare, Constraining the State

Like earlier generations of Christian exiles who colonized the Atlantic Seaboard, Washington farmers and loggers dreamed that they, too, could build a new and better society in the West. They believed in and helped perpetuate the myth of the Western frontier—that is, the myth of the American West as the unspoiled land of opportunity where independent and self-sufficient pioneers could flourish, free from the clutches of East Coast financiers, perceived to be corrupt and self-serving politicians.[36] These and other utopian visions, essential to the America fantasy of building a "city on a hill," underpin the development of social welfarism in Washington.

In Washington, social welfarism, the provision of goods and services for the collective welfare, depends to some extent on citizens' sense of their own efficacy, a belief in the power to change the social world around them. It depends on the belief in the capacity to fix social problems, challenge social inequalities, and even change undesirable social conditions.[37] Governor Daniel Evans captured this sentiment: "While we cannot escape history, we can within reasonable limitations, be active makers of history rather than its helpless victims."[38] Of course, we should note that this sense of efficacy is not a universal or ahistorical phenomenon. It is deeply embedded in and varies across cultural and political contexts.[39] In Washington, this sense of efficacy is particularly tied to the capacity of civil society organizations and the self-governance of ordinary people, rather than the state itself. This construct influenced the development of social welfare in the state, a development that continued to shape the provision of goods and services throughout the twentieth century, including crime control and penal sanctioning.

In the 1930s, the Great Depression nearly crippled the state of Washington along with many other American states and the federal government. With the near collapse of financial, agricultural, and other industries, millions of people lost their jobs and livelihood, many became impoverished, and some starved. State governments struggled daily to avoid growing social unrest, provide meager support, and prevent large-scale rioting. In Washington, organized labor, such as the Unemployed Citizens' League of Seattle, rallied workers together, marched in the streets, challenged capitalist exploitation, and demanded social and economic equality. Sometimes they did so with violence.[40]

Throughout the 1930s, other civil society organizations joined this mass protest. The Grange, the Townsendites, the Washington Old Age Pension Union, the Washington Commonwealth Federation, the General Welfare Clubs, the Workers Alliance, McGroarty Clubs, the Democratic Party, and civil rights advocates all pressed for and won the expansion of social welfare in Washington.[41] By the end of the 1930s, the state was one of the first to adopt President Franklin Roosevelt's New Deal. Washington began to expand social welfarism.[42] Pressured by staggering economic conditions and large-scale social mobilization, Washington turned more and more to a social welfare state that would and should intervene in the ill effects of market economies. By adopting the tenets of the New Deal, work relief programs, unemployment compensation, Old Age Assistance and Aid to Dependent Children, Washington expanded and liberalized public assistance.[43] By 1940, the state ranked ninth in the nation for its generous wages under the Works Progress Administration.[44]

At the same time, social welfarism maintained a populist tinge in the state of Washington. The state never fully embraced big government and centralized power—elements feared, resented, and distrusted by populists who prioritized self-governance and direct democracy. Despite its relative welfare generosity throughout the twentieth century,[45] for example, Washington has never passed a state income tax to generate a steady source of revenue to pay for these and other governmental insurance programs. We should also note that in the 1930s, Washington prioritized and was much more generous with the

New Deal's work relief program, the Works Progress Administration, than its other social welfare programs.

In *Bold Relief*, Edwin Amenta explains how the Works Progress Administration (WPA) created an unprecedented system of public employment in the United States. The WPA put 3.5 million skilled and unskilled workers to work on labor-intensive public projects across the nation throughout the era.[46] In Washington, WPA workers built the massive Grand Coulee Dam in the central part of the state.[47] Given the legacy of the cooperative movements, it makes sense that work relief dominated public provision in Washington. During the formation of farmers' cooperatives, farmers and laborers valued work, self-sufficiency, and the ability to contribute to public goods. The legacy of producerism gave the WPA and other work-oriented programs much-needed structural support and legitimation during a critical time of social unrest and social reordering.

In Washington, from the late nineteenth century onward, the social mobilization of civil society organizations has played a key role in constraining governmental power and bureaucratic capacity and done so even during the great state building effort of the New Deal. State officials have tended to concede power during moments of political conflict rather than react with repression. Political development in Washington has tended to follow a long-term pattern of democratization, that is to say, the expansion of citizen participation in the political process with its associated restraints on state power.

The Structure and Agency of Deliberative Democracy in Washington

In Washington, political authority is highly democratized and collective agency is based on intensive but deliberative forms of civic engagement. Political authority is not only decentralized and shared across the branches of government,[48] but ordinary people, citizens, social movements, and social groups in civil society have a relatively high degree of access to decision making. Citizens can participate in governance through voting, statewide community meetings, public hearings, volunteer programs, citizen councils, citizen advisory boards, and state-citizen commissions. Nonstate actors can influence legislation and even create laws through various direct democracy measures, such as the initiative and referendum, although they have been used much less frequently and less aggressively than in California.[49]

Government officials frequently organize citizen councils and what I think of as a type of hybrid state-citizen commission to bring in nonstate actors such as civic leaders, citizen representatives, or professional experts to discuss, debate, and often propose public policy reforms. To be sure, these commissions are not made up of ordinary people randomly selected through a lottery, but neither are they governmental agencies made up exclusively of bureaucrats, technocrats, or elected officials, which is often in the case in other polities, such as New York (discussed in more detail in chapter 5). Instead they represent a distinctive mix of nongovernmental actors and interests. One such committee, the Committee of Law and Justice, established in 1968, included a city council member and law enforcement officials and also a sociology professor, private attorney, schoolteacher, mental health worker, civic leaders, a citizens' anticrime organization, and a representative of Indian tribal judges, among others. Similar organizations such as the Citizens Committee on Crime, Washington Citizens Council on Crime and Delinquency, Washington State Commission on the Causes and Prevention of Civil Unrest, and the Council on Urban Affairs played key roles in the development of crime control and penal policy through the 1960s, 1970s, and 1980s.

By making this effort to include nonstate actors, the state routinely creates institutional mechanisms to increase the voices, opinions, and expertise of those in civil society. By doing so, it establishes more frequent and less formal interaction between state actors and the public. These structures can encourage debate and dialogue about pressing policy concerns in ways that electoral campaigns tend to cut short, reduce to sound bites, and easily caricature.

Social groups in civil society can also influence the substance and trajectory of legislation and public policies through participation in statewide community meetings by giving oral or written testimony on various topics and specific policy proposals. Local community meetings, sometimes referred to more quaintly as town hall meetings, are typically hosted at community centers, public schools, recreation centers, and other public locations by state officials and representatives. Some meetings are organized around a specific topic, and others are open forums for discussion. One recent announcement states:

Give us a piece of your mind.
    Senator Debbie Regala, and State Representatives Jeannie
Darneille and Dennis Flannigan invite you to "talk Olympia" at the
fourth 27th District town hall meetings.

The state faces a $2 billion dollar budget shortfall. Find out how the economic downturn could affect schools, higher education, health care, human services, and the environment—and what you can do about it.... See you there.[50]

Another posting invited citizens to attend an open forum to discuss state government. The eighth district state legislators announced:

Citizens with questions, comments, concerns or ideas about state government are invited to attend upcoming town hall meetings hosted by Sen. Pat Hale, R-Kennewick, Rep. Shirley Hankins and Rep. Jerome Delvin, both R-Richland.

Three meetings have been scheduled for Saturday, Feb. 21. They will be held in an open forum format to allow the public to speak and ask questions about issues under consideration in the Washington Legislature.[51]

In addition, state officials tend to encourage attendance to these public meetings with various welcoming messages, such as, "You're all invited, please come!" and "I hope we have a good turnout because the more people communicate with us, the better we can represent them here in Olympia."[52]

Community meetings are created by a highly democratized political structure, but they also represent a particular form of collective agency. They can help bring about what Habermas conceptualized as communicative action and they can promote more deliberative forms of collective agency.[53] Deliberation is a specific kind of collective agency that allows for an open exchange of ideas among citizens and between citizens and the state; deliberation can give "voice" to individuals rather than organized special interests; it can encourage the expression of different points of view and push these differences toward compromise. In his analysis of deliberative forums in Britain, criminologist David Green found that participants were likely to express more "liberalizing" views of crime and punishment and decrease their demands for custodial sanctions and retribution after discussing the issues with other people.[54] He suggests that given the opportunity and resources, ordinary people can indeed make informed decisions about crime control policy and do so in ways that are not inherently punitive. Similarly, Gerry Johnstone argues that through participation, citizens can learn more about the negative effects of penal sanctioning and quite possibly develop a broader sense of the public interest.[55] Deliberation can give participants, particularly ordinary people, a sense that their ideas, interests, and needs are taken seriously by state officials and politicians. Open deliberation can also promote a more positive view of government since citizens can speak directly to representatives. In this kind of forum, the state is held accountable directly to individuals and social groups in civil society, rather than exclusively to special interests that dominate politics.[56] It can also increase the public's sense of connection and commitment to a shared political community.

Of course, there is also the possibility that this dialogue and accountability are more apparent than real. Community meetings can be stage-managed and controlled. Individuals who speak up have their own special interests, and the dialogue may not actually lead to any concrete results. In other words, community meetings can be all talk and no action. Public testimony can also be coopted by state officials and used in ways counter to the intent of the citizen speakers. Politicians can advance their own agendas while pacifying the public's demands for inclusion. Officials can use community meetings to defuse potential conflict without necessarily responding to its underlying sources. The degree to which deliberative forums are effective participatory mechanisms or instruments of state control is an empirical question and most likely varies spatially and temporally. We need to ask who shows up, what the culture of the debate is like, how it is kept civil, how the results get filtered into the policy process, and how reasonable voices may prevail or when angry ones dominate.

Deliberative Democracy and Crime Control

In this section, I map out how deliberative democracy shaped the development of crime control and penal sanctioning in Washington from the 1960s through the early 1990s.

The Commonplace of Crime

By the mid-1960s, Washington's "war babies" had grown up, bringing with them an unfamiliar youth culture based on teenage leisure and angst. They also brought juvenile delinquency, higher crime rates, and apparent idleness not well received in civic culture based in part on a producerist work ethic. This mass of teenagers had "too little to do and too few job opportunities and too much abuse of drugs."[57]

At the same time, the state's vast green space lost ground to city life and rapid urbanization, bringing an unfamiliar experience of congestion, an "environmental backlash," and the emergence of black ghettos. Throughout the postwar period, African Americans migrated west, doubling and tripling their numbers in cities such as Seattle. Although their absolute numbers remained relatively small, by the late 1960s, Seattle's black population had increased nearly seven times.[58] Like earlier generations of pioneers, farmers, and loggers, black families moved west to make a better life for themselves. Once there, black migrants faced housing and employment discrimination. As Quintard Taylor explains, many Southern black families such as the Garners moved into cramped apartments in run-down neighborhoods and ended up in the low-paying service industry rather than in the more lucrative union jobs at the Boeing factories.[59] By the late 1960s, high crime rates made life even more difficult for poor and black neighborhoods, particularly in the Central District of Seattle.

Across Washington, crime rates increased through the 1960s. Between 1960 and 1965, the violent crime rate, including murder, assault, and rape, doubled.[60] It doubled again by 1970.[61] Although the absolute levels of violence were much lower in Washington than in other states (such as New York), the rapid escalation of such crimes was experienced as a major problem for the state's overloaded criminal justice system. Additionally, the overall crime rate, the index crimes, increased rapidly and surpassed the national average.[62] Drug crimes—drug possession, drug dealing, and crimes committed to support drug habits such as petty theft, burglaries, robberies, and violent crimes stemming from the drug trade—although not recorded in the official crime rate were nevertheless a growing concern to state officials.[63]

During these tense moments, national leaders portrayed increasing crime as a major threat to social order. J. Edgar Hoover, director of the Federal Bureau of Investigation, vividly captures the perceived rapaciousness of crime:

> We have on the loose in our country today a Predatory Monster called
> crime. It is growing in size and volume. Its far reaching forages
> threaten every city and hamlet in the nation and it strikes fear in the
> hearts and minds of law abiding public. IT IS RIPPING AWAY
> THE VERY FIBER OF OUR SOCIETY AND OUR SYSTEM OF
> GOVERNMENT.[64]

In his 1968 presidential campaign, Richard Nixon blamed poor discipline and poor self-control for rising crime, the "insufficient curbs on the appetites or impulses that naturally impel individuals towards criminal activities."[65] California governor Ronald Reagan linked rising crime with indecency, immorality, and social disorder. In his address to the Republican Platform Committee in 1968, he explained:

> We have seen the license allowed to the wicked and abuse heaped
> upon the decent and innocent.... We must reject the permissive
> attitude which pervades too many homes, too many schools, too many
> courts.... We must reject the idea that every [time] a law is broken,
> society is guilty rather than the lawbreaker.[66]

Localized Crime Control

In Washington, political leaders, civic leaders, and criminal justice officials rejected more conservative characterizations of crime and rejected a quick turn to more coercive forms of crime control. Rather than view crime as a result of moral indecency or poor discipline, key actors tended to portray it as the result of a modern life growing more complex, populous, impersonal, and unequal. As such, they tended to propose crime control policies that tried to alter the environment and improve social conditions, rather than transform individuals or simply punish lawbreakers. They asked citizens to take more responsibility to protect themselves against crime, and they also introduced policies and practices intended to alleviate social inequalities, especially through employment, repeating dominant themes of work, mutual cooperation, and self-governance. The mixed set of crime control policies tended to share the unifying theme of parsimony. That is, they tended to express what I see as movement to restrain the capacities of the state to control, regulate, and discipline it citizens, constraining the repressive powers of the state to limit individual freedom and autonomy. At the same time, social groups and the institutions of civil society assumed more responsibility, obligation, and moral authority to sanction offenders in the community.

For example, in 1966, the Washington Citizens Council on Crime and Delinquency, a citizen advisory board made up of community leaders and criminal justice professionals, proposed enhanced street lighting as a cost-effective way to prevent crime.[67] In 1970, the Committee of Law and Justice, a hybrid state-citizen commission, stressed the importance of citizen responsibility to prevent crime, take precautions, and govern themselves.[68] These early proposals and eventual policies prefigured what criminologists now refer to as "situational crime prevention" and what David Garland characterizes as the "criminologies of everyday life." They prefigured an understanding of crime as commonplace, a normal part of every life, and an understanding of crime prevention as requiring shifts in the daily habits of the public rather than the large-scale mobilization of public resources, law enforcement, or even social scientific knowledge.[69] They relied more on the efficacy of civil society to self-organize and self-govern rather than on the state to punish.

In response to growing urban unrest and rising crime in poor black neighborhoods, social groups in civil society turned away from criminal justice solutions and tried to improve the conditions of black city life. For example, black families, white suburban homeowners, and civil rights organizations worked with the Kirkland Fair Housing Organization and Operation Equity to challenge residential segregation and demand equal protection in housing.[70] By 1968, these organizations led a successful campaign for open housing, resulting in new legal protections against racial discrimination in housing.[71] We should briefly note here that around the same time in California, voters mobilized around Proposition 14, an initiative to block fair housing, a move that upheld residential segregation in the name of personal freedom and, I suggest, subsequently contributed to growing social polarization in the state, evident in the Watts riot and beyond.

In 1968, the Urban Affairs Council, a gubernatorial advisory board, established the Washington State Commission on the Causes and Prevention of Civil Unrest to further investigate and analyze the causes of urban conflict or "black disorders" in Washington. According to A. Ludlow Kramer, the commission's chair, the panel issued its report with the hope that it would "improve understanding between various racial and ethnic groups" in Washington.[72] In the report, "Race and Violence in Washington State," the commission explained how black migration, residential segregation, and economic marginality had created the "ghettoization" of the state's black population, conditions conducive to crime and increased violence. Rather than criminalize poverty or blame African Americans for their situation, the commission proposed ways to protect minorities in the labor market.

By the early 1970s, Governor Evans and state officials institutionalized the commission's Employment Security Initiative with the creation of a job security package. Organized around "multiservice centers" in local communities, city governments and civil society organizations would provide "outreach, counseling, basic education, vocational and job training, and job placement" to black residents in poor neighborhoods.[73] The Work Incentive

Program, Operation Job, Employment Supplement Program, Jobs for Veterans, and Public Service Careers programs soon followed with the intention of increasing labor participation among the state's more marginalized members. Similarly, the Department of Personnel, the Department of General Services, and the Department of Employment Security's "Operation Impact" worked toward increasing black labor market participation, public awareness about race discrimination in employment, and increasing minority contracts with the state.[74]

These formative steps toward black political and economic integration moderated how the state responded to crime in general and specifically in black neighborhoods. Civil society organizations, state officials, and state-citizen commissions sought ways to improve the living conditions of black and other minority communities rather than criminalize poverty. Rather than call on law enforcement or turn to more repressive means to subdue potential urban unrest and contentious racial politics, these groups, through debate, discussion, and cooperation, helped institutionalize civil rights. This process of democratization, the full and equal political participation of African Americans, provided a long-lasting buffer against the use of imprisonment as a crude instrument of racial social control.

De-Escalation: Community Sanctions and the Discipline of Work

From the late 1960s onward, state officials, supported and pushed by civil society organizations, moved away from fortress prisons and increasingly came to rely on community sanctions. Washington created the Juvenile and Adult Probation Subsidy Programs to divert young offenders and adult offenders, especially but not exclusively first-time offenders, away from prison, and subsidized local community efforts to develop and implement alternatives to incarceration.[75] According to the Law and Justice Planning Office, a state-citizen hybrid commission, the state should "avoid removing offenders from the community" and "disrupting the ties they have to society, especially employment and family financial support and relationships."[76]

By 1978, the Law and Justice Planning Office offered a more detailed strategy to reduce the prison population and presented it to the state legislature. In written testimony to the state house of representatives' Institutions Committee, William Henry, a Statistical Center researcher for the Law and Justice Planning Office, warned against prison overcrowding, rising crime, and an overloaded criminal justice system. To regulate the prison population, he suggested the state could gain more control over both input and output mechanisms by decreasing prison commitments and increasing prison releases.[77] To do so, Henry drew on similar reforms in Oregon and Minnesota and advised:

> Increase community based sentencing alternatives for convicted felons;
> Increase preconviction diversion programs;
> Change the sentencing statutes to selectively reduce the types of offenses and conditions under which imprisonment is used as a sentence;
> Reduce the number of parolees returned to prison for technical violations of parole;
> Increase the bedspace capacity of the prison system by capital construction;
> Increase the use of work release;
> Increase the volume of persons released to parole.[78]

Many of these proposals eventually became institutionalized in the state's penal policies. Washington has maintained a relatively low imprisonment rate by relying extensively on noncustodial sanctions.

Although the state has de-emphasized but certainly not eliminated imprisonment, it has prioritized work for all kinds of criminal offenders. In 1966, for example, the Washington Citizens' Council on Crime and Delinquency made work release, the development of state prison industries, and postinstitutional employment central to the state's penal regime.[79] By 1967, Governor Evans and the state legislature had passed a "work and training release" program. This program allowed inmates to leave the prison for part of the day to work at some state-approved site with the expectation that inmates would continue to work at these sites after their release from prison. Likewise, the Law and Justice Planning Office prioritized community-based programs that facilitated employment and educational services. The Law and Justice Planning Office also sought ways to expand the "correctional volunteer" program so that newly released inmates would be matched with a "responsible person within the community, in order to assist the offender to readjust when released from the institution."[80] In the mid-1980s, the state formalized its Community Service Program, allowing convicted felons to work on various public service projects instead of serving prison or jail terms.[81]

Today, the Department of Corrections runs various off-site work crews that use prison labor to assist a range of community associations such as the

Chinook Trails Association, McNeil Island Bicycle Project, and community baseball fields; religious groups, such as the Church of Our Savior, Central Christian Church, and New Horizon Christian Church; and multiple state and city departments, such as the Department of Ecology, Amboy Territorial Days Park, Grant County Public Works, Lincoln County Department of Public Works, and the Coyote Ridge Corrections Center Pheasant Farm, among many others.[82]

To be sure, the use of prison labor and community service always involves a degree of coercion and control, subjecting inmates to unfree choices and the discipline of work. It also provides the state a mechanism to intervene in the labor market. In Washington, we can also understand the emphasis on work and reliance on community sanctions as expressive of a particular kind of morality and collective agency. It reflects the legacy of producerism with its associated practices and values of self-sufficiency, mutual cooperation, and contributing to public goods. It delegates power to civil society organizations providing them with the authority to manage and resocialize offenders, subjecting them to the normalizing grip of the community.

Sentencing Guidelines: Formalizing the Principle of Parsimony

In the early 1980s, after nearly ten years of debate and deliberation on sentencing reform, the Washington state legislature passed and Governor John Spellman signed the Sentencing Reform Act (SRA), introducing sentencing guidelines and formalizing the principle of parsimony. The SRA replaced the state's indeterminate sentencing structure, deemed "unjust," "dishonest," uncertain, unfair, and discriminatory against racial and ethnic minorities by reformers. The SRA introduced a commensurate and proportional determinate sentencing grid to guide penal sanctioning. The sentencing guidelines provided judges with a presumptive range of sentences that intensified penal sanctioning by the seriousness of the offense and offender's prior record. The sentencing grid reserved the harshest penalties for the most serious offenses, relying on the "least restrictive" sanctions whenever possible. For example, mandatory prison terms were limited to three violent crimes in the first degree: murder, assault, and rape.[83] The guidelines also provided sentencing alternatives, including first-time offender waivers and noncustodial sanctions such as community supervision, community service, and restitution for a wide range of lower level offenders.[84] The guidelines tried to impose a degree of uniformity on sentences, proposing similar sanctions for similar kinds of offenses by justifying sanctions with legal factors rather than extralegal concerns about offenders' future dangerousness or past unemployment.[85] Yet at the same time, the grid preserved a certain degree of judicial discretion, enabling judges to sanction offenders above or below the standard range with departures subject to review.

The SRA also linked the available range of penal sanctioning with the state's prison capacity, a move that placed structural limits on an unfettered use of imprisonment. With the injunction to "make frugal use of the state's resources," the generous use of good time credits and work release, the SRA provided state officials a legitimate mechanism to regulate the prison population by depressing commitments to prison and increasing release from prison. By the end of the 1980s, imprisonment rates had fallen nearly 20 percent as the sentencing guidelines had enabled judges and corrections officials to divert offenders, particularly nonviolent ones, away from prison.[86]

The emergence of sentencing guidelines in Washington was not the result of a dramatic moment, a political crisis of legitimacy, the successful scheming of newly elected politicians, nor a function of racial social control. Instead, it was the result of an ongoing reform process that began in the late 1960s and intensified in the 1970s with the movement away from fortress prisons toward de-escalation. It was neither a top-down directive from the governor's office, nor the brainchild of correctional officers, nor a moral protest from the grassroots. Instead, it was the result of a collective enterprise, which was put into motion and made meaningful by a wide range of state actors and civil society organizations working within the state's democratized political structures and deliberative forums. Decentralized decision making, power sharing, and structural integration of citizen participation through hybrid commissions provided the institutional mechanisms that enabled a diverse set of reformers to discuss, debate, and eventually reach a compromise on sentencing reform and penal sanctioning without resorting to unilateral decisions, crude policy instruments, or mechanical responses to either to public opinion or special interest groups.

The relatively democratized political structures helped facilitate a more deliberative policy process based on a willingness to consider, debate, and even respect opposing points of view.[87] By doing so, the deliberative process may have helped defuse potential conflict, deflect grievance, and avoid to a certain extent dogmatic policy positions. Simultaneously, the state's democratized deliberation provided the cultural resources to make sense of crime and justify penal responses in meaningful ways. Specifically, it enabled reformers to mobilize the capacity and authority of civil society to restrain the repressive powers of the state and promote self-governance.

As illustrated but not commented on in the preceding sections on crime control, the policy making process in Washington often incorporates the governor, state legislatures, and criminal justice professionals as well as hybrid state-citizen commissions, citizen councils, citizen representatives, and grassroots organizations. During the debate about sentencing reform, these organizations vocalized and pressed varying views and proposals on crime control and penal sanctioning. The Washington State Association of Prosecuting Attorneys, for example, played a lead role in promoting determinate sentencing from the mid-1970s onward. In their policy proposals, members severely criticized Washington's sentencing scheme as ineffective, dishonest, and unmanageable.[88] To increase public accountability and confidence in the criminal justice system, they created and agreed to follow a set of guidelines that limited their discretion.[89] Christopher Bayley, an influential county prosecutor from Seattle, championed determinate sentencing as "more humane and less dangerous to individual liberty" than indeterminate sentencing.[90] He sought ways to introduce "just deserts," to exact retribution, without stiffening penalties and institutionalized personal and public vengeance.

The Washington state representatives' Institutions Committee created their own Task Force on Sentencing, which mixed together concerns for public safety and retribution along with earlier penal welfarist concerns about criminal offenders' social deprivation.[91] The task force included divergent organizations such as the American Civil Liberties Union Prisoners' Rights Committee, Families and Friends of Missing Persons and Violent Crime Victims, and the Board of Prison Terms and Paroles. The Families and Friends of Missing Persons and Violent Crime Victims, a victims' advocacy organization, prioritized public safety, opposed what they perceived as the "excessive use of probation," supported restitution and victims' participation in prosecution, and wanted penal sanctions, including community service, to be perceived as punishment rather than rehabilitation, which they argued treated criminal offenders as victims.

The Sentencing Guidelines Commission, an advisory board established by the state legislature to oversee sentencing reform and made up of criminal justice representatives, citizens' representatives, professional experts, and state officials, held statewide public hearings to further debate sentencing reform. At these public meetings, ordinary people, citizens, voters, and representatives of civil society and professional associations expressed a range of views on crime control and penal sanctioning. Some witnesses thought the sentencing guidelines were too lenient and argued for more punitive sanctioning, while others supported and pushed for community sanctions and other alternatives to incarceration. It is important to note that in Washington, ordinary people unaffiliated with either an interest group or professional organization are strongly encouraged to participate in public meetings, a tradition of the underlying political culture.

Public support for alternatives to incarceration was not a uniform response, but it was certainly widespread. A few telling statements are illustrated here and stand in contrast to the conventional portrayal of the public as simply and uniformly punitive, thoughtless, and merciless.

Consider the testimony of Jean T. Hueston, president of the Unitarian Universalist Service Committee of Washington State:

> We wish to commend the Sentencing Guidelines Commission for their in-depth work on sentencing guidelines. We hope serious efforts will be made to establish meaningful alternative sentences for the first offenders and even habitual offenders of non-violent crimes. The very term "habitual" implies that incarceration is not a real deterrent for repeaters. Both public safety and frugal use of resources require that alternatives to total imprisonment be available to offenders statewide.[92]

Tina Peterson, listed as a citizen in the public hearings testimony, echoed this sentiment when she argued that the "state can't afford to imprison all offenders," and so "alternatives are needed."[93]

In a letter to the Sentencing Guidelines Commission, Maria Lindsey expressed her opposition to lengthy prison terms. She wrote:

> As a concerned citizen, I have tried to familiarize myself with the proposed sentencing guidelines. . . . In my estimation these guidelines suffer from some shortcomings. The one which most concerns me is that one effect of these guidelines will be to lengthen prison terms and further overcrowd facilities which are already under severe strain. . . . I can hardly imagine any better way to foster and re-create all the negative conditions we have come to associate with the state penitentiary at Walla Walla than to plan for ever-larger, ever more overcrowded facilities and then to fail to provide any adequate educations or rehabilitation programs.[94]

Jonathan C. Nelson, a Lutheran pastor of the Campus Christian Ministry at the University of Washington, testified at length about his opposition to the prison. Nelson had served a short prison term for civil disobedience, and he explained his position:

> The ultimate consideration in any scheme of dealing with criminal behavior has to be the health of the whole society. . . . From all my experience with prisons and jails, I have come to realize they are a vile septic system in our communities. We send a-social people there and we mix them in that fearsome acid that prison represents, and in almost every instance they are poured out into society a much greater risk to the safety of the community.[95]

Mary Ann Connelly of the League of Women Voters, Janet Rice of the King County Public Defenders, Bart Haggin (a citizen), defense attorney Mark Vovos, Gerard Sheehan of the American Civil Liberties Union, Margaret Casey of the Washington State Catholic Conference, Lamont Smith (a criminologist), former public defender Mark Muenster, and members of the Catholic Prison Jail Ministry and Unitarian Universalist Service Committee all testified in favor of alternatives to incarceration and community sanctions.[96]

The Sentencing Guidelines Commission eventually produced ten working papers and a proposal that reflected a pluralist, compromised position on sentencing reform and penal sanctioning. The sentencing guidelines established a determinate but not punitive sentencing structure based on proportionality and commensurate sentences that facilitated the diversion of first-time and nonviolent offenders away from prison and the imprisonment of more seriously violent offenders.[97] Sentencing reform recognized and incorporated widespread social support for noncustodial sanctions, expressing a deep-rooted concern to restrain state coercion in favor of the authority and control of civil society.

The Principle of Parsimony Challenged

In the late 1980s, the rise of a powerful, vocal, and outraged crime victim movement seriously challenged the underlying logic of Washington's penal regime. By demanding relatively stiff penal sanctions and increased state regulation over offenders, the movement rejected the principle of parsimony in favor of harsh retribution and repressive social control. The movement was not entirely successful, but it made a serious impact in penal sanctioning, to a certain extent reconfiguring the governing relationship between state and citizen.

With this example, I suggest that Washington's democratized deliberation played an important structuring role in crime victims' protests and a structuring role in restraining state power. The deliberative process may have had a dampening effect on victims' anger and righteousness as it exposed them to other people's experience and concerns in public forums. As a more conciliatory kind of politics, the deliberative process can, under certain conditions, facilitate compromise (if not reconciliation) between opposing views and pacify the needs and interests of a broad range of social groups. By doing so, a deliberative process potentially can defuse social conflict, downplaying resentments and hostilities. Instead, it can encourage empathy among participants, tapping into their sense of mutual obligation and social connectedness, features that tend to be associated with more inclusive and less coercive public policies.[98] The resulting legislation, the Community Protection Act (CPA; 1990), represents a collective attempt, however flawed, to reconcile the rights of crime victims with the rights and liberties of criminal offenders.

Community Protection Act

In 1989, the sexual mutilation of a young boy from Tacoma sparked a statewide campaign against sex crimes. In the days and weeks following the crime, graphic details of the assault dominated news coverage, as did details of the assailant's prior convictions. People from all over the state raised nearly $600,000 and sent hundreds of teddy bears to the boy, recovering in a local hospital.[99] Governor Booth Gardner as well as seasoned state senators responded just as quickly, calling for public hearings to debate new sex offender legislation. Four days later, crime victim groups marched on the state capitol, demanding life imprisonment for repeat sex offenders. By the end of the year, the legislature passed and governor signed the CPA.

The CPA increased penal sanctions for most sex crimes, provided treatment for many sex offenders, introduced sex offender registration, created a new government bureau, the Office of Crime Victim Advocacy, and created the highly controversial civil commitment provision for "sexual predators."[100]

I suggest that the controversial civil commitment provision can be better understood as a pragmatic response to a mixed set of demands and a desire to avoid increasing penal sanctions across all crime categories. The task force responsible for the CPA did not want to introduce life imprisonment for sexual predators. To do so would have undermined the principles of proportionality that inform the state's sentencing guidelines, a reform enacted just five years prior to the sex offender debate.[101] It would have also undermined the rights and liberties of all other criminal offenders because it would have required increasing penal sanctions across all crime categories. The civil commitment provision was drawn quite narrowly. Today, less than 1 percent of convicted sex offenders have been subject to civil commitment.[102] Between 2000 and 2004, for example, Washington processed over 5,000 sex offender cases, and only 226 were subject to commitment.[103] Civil commitment is not a mandatory penalty, and most convicted repeat sex offenders are sentenced to and released from prison. Washington also introduced the Special Sex Offender Sentencing Alternative (SSOSA), a noncustodial and treatment-oriented sanction.[104] Currently, there are over four times as many sex offenders in the SSOSA program than are subject to civil commitment.[105] These provisions mitigate the most coercive aspects of the civil commitment, a sanction that has not been widely used in practice.

By focusing our attention exclusively on the controversial aspects of the civil commitment provisions, we may miss some of the restorative and democratizing aspects of the CPA. The CPA changed the exercise of state power to incorporate crime victims into governance. It institutionalized crime victim advocacy at the level of state government. Crime victims gained institutionalized access to government resources and decision-making power. By working with crime victims and local communities, the Office of Crime Victim Advocacy continues to develop victim-oriented legislation and community programs that are oriented toward crime reduction and victim services rather than the punishment of criminal offenders.[106] We should note here that in her analysis of crime control policies in Washington, Lisa Miller found a similar dynamic. Miller found that community participation in the federal government's "Weed and Seed" program actually transformed the substance and trajectory of the program away from its punitive and risk management goals toward quality of life, education, and job-based programs.[107]

By expanding victim services and victim participation in governance, the CPA was not an outcome based exclusively on the state's power to punish. We should take care to note, Washington rejected mandatory life imprisonment for repeat felonies and rejected some of the most coercive forms of state power: execution and castration. During the Senate Law and Justice Committee public hearings on the proposed legislation, some witnesses called for the death penalty for repeat offenders, and several state senators asked why the task force had not included provisions for the castration of sex offenders.[108] None of these provisions made it into the CPA. The CPA was an attempt to reconcile the rights of crime victims with the rights and liberties of criminal offenders.

Crime victims' moral protest, angry and vengeful at times, softened some of its most vitriolic aspects through Washington's political process. In its assessment of blameworthiness and justice, crime victims recognized the pain and suffering of other victims, and they did so in a way that did not necessitate the absolute condemnation of criminal offenders. Unlike the campaign for victims' rights in California in the early 1980s (discussed in chapter 3), crime victim advocates acknowledged the importance of the rights and liberties of offenders. Some went as far as to invoke Robert Cover's description of the criminal justice system as an "organized practice of social violence" to warn against lingering impulses toward vengeance.[109] Cover called attention to the brutality and violence inherent in the use of state power against its citizens. David Boerner, a law professor who participated in the debate, recalled the influence of Cover's warnings against "the intentional infliction of harm to fellow human beings" on the substance and trajectory of the CPA.[110]

In Washington, widespread public participation significantly shaped the tone of the debate and substance of the proposed sex offender legislation. Within two days of the trigger event, Governor Gardner and key state senators called for statewide public hearings. Both the executive and legislative branches refrained from the opportunity to seize control over sex offender legislation and refused to draft hasty laws fueled by the initial shock and anger of the sensational crime. Instead, the state took steps to ensure a long-term process that incorporated a wide range of citizens, crime victims, victims' advocates, state officials, and various professionals. As the Senate majority leader explained: "You don't rush out there and do anything without careful consideration."[111] State elites opened up decision-making to citizen participation through public hearings and with the creation of the Governor's Task Force on Community Protection.

Despite crime victims' angry protest at the state capitol, grassroots activists decided to work with state officials to develop public policy rather than continue to oppose criminal justice policies. Governor Gardner created a Task Force on Community Protection to lead the state's response to sex offenders. The task force was made up of a mix of citizen representatives, political representatives, criminal justice personnel (including the secretary of the

Department of Corrections), the president of the Washington Association of Sheriffs and Police Chiefs, a legal aid lawyer, a judge and law professor, social workers, and crime victim advocates, including the chair of the Rights of Crime Victims organization, and three prominent crime victims activists: Helen Harlow, leader of the Tennis Shoe Brigade and mother of the maimed Tacoma boy; Ida Ballasiotes, leader of Friends of Diane, whose daughter was killed by a convicted sex offender; and Trish Tobias, leader of Family and Friends of Missing Persons and Violent Crime Victims.

Norm Maleng, King County prosecutor and longtime public figure in Washington state politics and chair of the task force, described the impact of the crime victim advocates on the task force:

> In addition to the excellent professional members, we were greatly
> assisted by our citizen representatives who are personally acquainted
> with the tragic consequences of criminal violence. These members
> served as our conscience, charting our course toward changes which
> will make real differences in people's lives. Despite the daily
> reminders of their pain and their losses, they were our most active
> participants, sustained by the determination that their experiences
> must not be repeated.[112]

By participating on the task force, crime victim advocates gained significant access to state government, gained decision-making power, and increased their influence over the substance of anticrime public policy.

General citizen participation at the public hearings also played an important role in shaping the substance and trajectory of the CPA. In his report, "Governor's Task Force on Community Protection Report November 28," Maleng described the impact of the public testimony:

> This effort was distinguished by the personal courage of citizens who
> testified at the twelve hearings held across the state. We asked people
> to tell us how the system should be changed, and over and over again,
> people accepted this invitation. Typically, those testifying at public
> hearings represent professional or civic organizations, and their
> comments conform to the group's official position. In contrast, our
> hearings were attended by men and women whose lives were deeply
> scarred following crimes committed by strangers as well as family
> members. People who had never before testified in public stood before
> us and described the pain they had endured.[113]

Exposed to other people's experience and concerns in public forums, the deliberative process may have had cooling effect on crime victims' righteousness. As a conciliatory mechanism, a deliberative process reflects but can also bring out a sense of mutual obligation and social trust among participants, encouraging empathy and norms of reciprocity. Not only did the prominent, vocal, and outraged crime victim representatives Ballasiotes and Harlow join the task force and cooperate with officials they initially blamed for the brutal crime, they participated in the public hearings. By doing so, they were exposed to a broader set of interests and demands of the public. For example, crime victims and their families testified at the same hearings as family members of convicted offenders, experts in crime victim services, and criminal justice officials. Kathy Taylor, one such family member of a convicted felon, expressed her own "distress" and worry about the negative effects of long-term incarceration; she personalized and humanized the idea of the convict by discussing how her husband yearned for a second chance and desperately wanted to be a "productive" member of society.[114] Several victim services advocates, such as Karen Bachelder, Joanne Dufelle, and Kurt Clevin of the Washington Association of Defense Attorneys, testified about the vicious cycle of abuse and revictimization; they asked for more funding for treatment to prevent those who have been abused from becoming criminal offenders and the need for "primary prevention" to limit the amount of abuse in the first place.[115] The mother of a young offender who had been molested at a young age similarly testified; she explained "they're victims and they are not being helped and end up being offenders."[116]

The deliberative process not only allowed for a broad range of voices to be heard in public forums, it did so in ways that provided some official recognition of those diverse views. It allowed crime victims to express their own frustration, anger, and indignation in ways that were taken seriously and integrated by the task force. It allowed for the inclusion of a wide range of concerns and emotions, including disgust and compassion.

In some instances, victims tempered some of their more punitive positions, cooled some of their passions, and edged toward compromise. For example, although Ballasiotes supported the most punitive aspects of the CPA, she also expressed doubts about the community notification provision of the campaign as it infringed on the liberties of ex-offenders. Reflecting later on the provision, she explained:

It disturbs me when I see people, citizens, going around and
plastering pictures up of this guy and going from door to door and
saying "Hey, you know there's a sex offender in your neighborhood."
At that point, I don't know and they don't know that someone
hasn't gotten their life together. . . . I don't like the vigilante quality
that sometimes comes up.[117]

She also explained to the state senators debating the bill that the task force's
proposal was a "consensus piece of work" that not only reflected multiple
interests but left out some of the demands for more punitive policies' "stronger
things" in terms of sentencing.[118]

Also consider how Harlow, invested with authority to speak for victims,
expressed her indignation and demands for retribution: "I want the people out
there to know that they have every right to be angry about this. . . . That anger is
what's got to keep the public opinion of this situation alive until it's
actually dealt with, until in some way, not just this person is dealt justice,
but this loophole is plugged."[119] But Harlow also took care to find common
ground and empathy. She framed her son's victimization as a shared experience rather than as a highly individualized one. After the sexual mutilation
of her young son she declared: "My son is every child."[120] Rather than
frame victimization as an isolating experience or an attack on the integrity
of personhood—an attack that takes the violated and injured self outside
common experience[121]—Harlow reported her son's speedy recovery and desire
to return to the routine of everyday life. Similarly, in one of her many public
statements, Ballasiotes connected her own experience and the individual experiences of other crime victims with the broader public interest. Indicating
other crime victims, she declared, "We are the public."[122] Victims eventually
began to speak for other victims and the public in ways that went beyond their
immediate experiences.

Although Harlow channeled her anger and frustration toward criminal
offenders as in the California Proposition 8 campaign, she also insisted that
the state "find a solution" to sex crimes. She wanted to "help everyone focus the
different factions and ideas that will *help the system*."[123] In these telling moments, Harlow simultaneously implicated the state by pointing out its failure
to prevent her son's attack and offered a systematic rather than individualized
explanation of criminality. Later, during the Senate hearings, one senator
concurred with this view of systemwide failure: "The system has been failing
the people."[124] Describing the CPA, Harlow later explained: "The intent was

not to fire people up and get a vigilante mind-set.... It was to inform people, for safety purposes, so they could take precautions."[125]

Similarly, other crime victims, victims' advocates, and Governor Gardner put forward a broader view on the causes of sex crimes, linking them to social conditions. Two of Harlow's neighbors who found the boy became involved in the Pierce County Sexual Assault Center, running workshops to explain how the "roots of violence" are embedded in broader social conditions.[126] Governor Gardner referred to sex crimes as part of the "disease of violence" in contemporary society.[127] In his 1990 State of the State address, Gardner linked the need to protect crime victims with the need to respond to underlying causes of violence, poor social conditions:

> Let's all affirm right now that the victims of crime have a right to recovery, and to humane treatment that helps heal the wounds of fear and grief...chaos.... In the long term, ending the scourge of violence requires breaking the cycles of poverty, addiction and, family violence.... Protecting ourselves from the symptoms of poverty isn't enough; we must protect ourselves from the economic conditions that make poverty inevitable.[128]

From these illustrations, we can see that the way crime victims and their advocates constructed the problem of sex crimes influenced to a certain degree the way the state tried to solve the policy problem.

Moreover, according to task force chair Maleng's final report to the governor, crime victims and ordinary citizens' testimony shifted the task force's agenda away from its exclusive focus on sensational crimes toward a broader concern with sexual abuse, sexual assault, and family violence.[129] After the hearings, the task force changed its agenda from the confinement of repeat violent sex offenders to include the public's concern for crime prevention and treatment approaches to sex crimes, especially for young offenders who may have been caught in "cycles of violence."[130] The task force eventually proposed increased penalties for sex offenses, yet they also proposed a major expansion in the state's and local counties' victim services and the creation of a centralized crime victims bureau to give victims a "permanent voice in state government."

In Washington, crime victims' moral protest helped bring about sex offender legislation, legislation that probably would not have passed without their efforts. In many ways, crime victims challenged the underlying principle of parsimony by seeking stiffer penalties and more state regulation of sex offenders. However, as illustrated, Washington's deliberative political process had a major influence on the substance and trajectory of sex offender legislation. By encouraging citizen participation at all levels of the policy-making process, the state opened itself up to a broader set of demands than it had originally set out to address. Victims' participation shifted the state's original focus on the confinement of repeat violent sex offenders toward an expansive view of sexual assault and sex abuse. Intensive civic engagement forced the state to develop much broader public policies concerning crime victims at a much greater expense than it had originally considered, especially with the creation of the Office of Crime Victim Advocacy. The deliberative process allowed for victims and their representative to express their outrage, resentment, and remorse, and it did not entirely eliminate victims' demands for coercive control of offenders. But it may have weakened some of crime victims' impulses toward vengeance and punitive penal sanctions by recognizing the rights and liberties of criminal offenders. The state's relatively high level of social capital and social trust enabled polity members to express some sympathy for criminal offenders as they considered systemic (e.g., "cycles of violence," "symptoms of poverty") rather than individualized causes of crime. They may have felt some level of social connectedness even to those most socially marginalized, criminal offenders. Washington's political process undermined the full force and legal expression of crime victims' vengeance.

Summing Up

What I have tried to show in this chapter is how Washington's parsimonious penal regime emerged slowly and cumulatively over time through a series of small and large changes to penal practices, as well as through a series of mundane and dramatic legislative reforms. The use of first-time offender waivers, probation, work release, early release, and sentencing guidelines all shaped the state's rejection of indiscriminate mass imprisonment and kept the imprisonment rate relatively low for nearly thirty years. These practices emerged out of and supported a penal regime that values offenders' liberty and self-governance and tries to minimize the pain, suffering, and humiliation of punishment, an important countertrend in the United States, one that many reformers are beginning to take seriously.

Recent Reforms

Rise of Neopopulist Retribution

Recent high-profile reforms in Washington may have seriously undermined the state's dominant penal regime and its associated low imprisonment rates. In 1993, Washington passed the nation's first "three strikes" law, mandating stiffer penalties for repeat felony offenders, and did so through the highly charged initiative process. In 1995, the state legislature passed "Hard Time for Armed Crime," increasing penal sanctions for crimes committed with firearms, through an initiative to the legislature.[131] In 1997, the legislature passed and Governor Mike Lowry signed a major piece of juvenile justice reform that moved sixteen- to seventeen-year-old violent offenders to adult courts and increased penalties for repeated crimes. In 1998, Governor Gary Locke pressed for and won increased penalties for the manufacture of methamphetamine, described by state officials as an "epidemic." The governor followed up a year later with the Methamphetamine Response Team, a special police unit devoted to tracking and closing down meth labs. According to the Washington State Sentencing Guidelines Commission, these reforms and others have lengthened prison terms and increased the state's prison population over time.[132] To accommodate the state's growing prison population, in 2006 newly elected Governor Chris Gregoire allocated $50 million to expand the state's prison capacity. Like her predecessors, she and the state legislature have continued to stiffen penalties against sex offenders and methamphetamine drug offenders.

To a certain extent, these reforms may indicate a partial shift in governance in Washington, a shift toward neopopulism and away from deliberation and compromise. The state's own political history and open democratic political institutions coupled with the success of the crime victims' moral protest in the early 1990s not only enabled but probably encouraged this development. As discussed in the case of California, a neopopulist mode of governance quickly turns to criminal law and penal sanctioning—the repressive rather than productive powers of the state—to remake social order at the expense of marginalized social groups. This type of political regime depends on and facilitates more antagonistic social relations and winner-take-all politics, downplaying mutual respect and social reciprocity.

I pause here a moment to consider the 1995 Hard Time for Armed Crime legislation because it represents aspects of this shift toward neopopulism and retributive penal politics. Unlike the historic three strikes law, the armed crime legislation has had a much more substantial impact on the prison population. It has been described by the late Norm Maleng, longtime public figure and King County prosecutor, as "quietly becom[ing] the most significant criminal justice measure of the 1990s."[133] We should note here that although the federal government and twenty-two states passed three strikes laws in the early 1990s, California is the only state where the law has had a major impact on the prison population. It doubled the penalties for the second strike and mandated twenty-five years to life for the third strike, including nonviolent felonies. In other words, the California law incarcerates offenders who might not otherwise have been sentenced to prison and imprisons them longer.[134] By contrast, in Washington, three strikes legislation was drawn quite narrowly targeting offenders who were already being sent to prison under existing statutes. Unlike California's law, it tightly focused on repeat serious and violent offenses such as murder, armed robbery, rape, and kidnapping.[135] By contrast to Washington's three strikes, Hard Time for Armed Crime has reached many more offenders, increasing sentencing enhancements and lengthening prison terms.

Building on the momentum of the three strikes initiative, the same law and order entrepreneurs John Carlson and David LaCourse continued their public campaign for stiffer penal sanctioning. Carlson and LaCourse's Washington Citizens for Justice, a grassroots organization, led the reform movement and was supported by various law enforcement officials as well as by local and national associations, including the Washington State Council of Police Officers, the National Rifle Association, and the Washington Association of Prosecuting Attorneys. Like California's earlier campaign for victims' rights in 1982 (Proposition 8), advocates of Hard Time pursued a more dogmatic and visceral moral protest, counterposing crime victims' pain and suffering against the sheer brutality of criminal offenders. In a now familiar refrain, in their testimony to the Washington State Senate Committee on Ways and Means, supporters argued that "victims need more protection and violent criminals need more punishment," highlighting the public's basic fear of being attacked violently by strangers.[136] In a policy brief, author and advocate LaCourse detailed the heinous crimes of offenders targeted by Hard Time, cataloging the pistol-whipping, duct-taping, kidnapping, terrorizing, and violation of crime victims, some of which were too "traumatized" to "go out in public."[137] According to LaCourse, Hard Time would provide "tough lessons" to offenders.

Supporters' discourse on victimization worked to justify and legitimate stiffer penalties, and it contrasted sharply with opponents' less emotional and more pragmatic concerns about cost-effectiveness, fiscal impact, and over-worked courts.[138] Opponents, such as the Washington State Catholic Confer-ence, Washington Defenders Association, Washington Association of Criminal Defense Lawyers, Washington Protection and Advocacy System, and Families Against Mandatory Minimums, argued that "mandatory minimums do not reduce violent crime but do result in increased prison costs." Opponents argued that the proposal would increase workloads, expand the corrections budget, and would "inappropriately increase the number of offenders who would be classified as persistent offenders."[139] Although opponents raised concerns about increased penal sanctioning, they seemed to have displaced what were once resonant themes about offenders' rights and liberties and calls for a less retributive kind of justice.

In 1995, the Washington state legislature passed the Hard Time initiative, a criminal justice reform that continues to shape the state's penal regime and impact its prison population.

Recent Reforms Revisited: Defusing Retributive Penal Politics, Continued Moralizing

Despite the punitive outburst of Hard Time and similar legislation, Washing-ton has not experienced a fundamental change to its political character. Rather, the state's recent populist moment represents a dynamic political culture that is influenced by multiple and competing political traditions, tensions that are not fully resolved. The state's democratized deliberation and its less repres-sive penal politics are still rather strong and persistent. Consider, for example, John Carlson, leader of the three strikes and Hard Time initiatives, could not translate his rough and tough anticrime rhetoric into a successful guber-natorial campaign. In 2000, he lost miserably to Governor Gary Locke, the first Chinese American governor in the United States, 60 to 40 percent, providing a counterexample to the presumed effectiveness of law-and-order politicians. Additionally, by contrast to many characterizations of contemporary politics, the use of the initiative process has been rather limited in most states, except California. Between 1914 and 2006, Washington has only turned to the initiative process twice to legislate crime and punishment, three times if we include the Hard Time initiative to the legislature.[140] In California, voters used the initiative process three times to legislate crime and punishment just between 1982 and 1993.[141] Washington has continued its reliance on hybrid state-citizen commissions to analyze and propose crime control and penal reforms, a form of collective agency that tends to encourage debate, informed opinion, and compromise. The state's Sentencing Guidelines Commission is just one example.

At the same time that Carlson and LaCourse's Washington Citizens for Justice introduced a more polarizing discourse on crime and victimization, opponents of the get-tough movement as well as leading state officials, including the governor, continued the state's long-term tendency toward moderation, emphasizing systemic and structural causes of crime over moral depravity and brutality. For example, in his 1996 State of the State address, Governor Mike Lowry argued that punitive sanctions and increased imprisonment would not prevent crime. Instead, he argued that the state would have to stop the "cycle of violence" that propels abused and neglected children into crime. To give readers a sense of the tone and substance of his argument, I quote the address at some length:

> Today, we also face the challenge of keeping our children safe in a world that has already taken too many young lives and irreparably damaged countless others.
>
> The cycle of violence that is killing our children begins long before a child joins a gang or steals a weapon. It begins during the most impressionable time in his or her life, when a child is abused, or sees parents hitting each other.
>
> And until we deal with the root causes of violence, until we deal with child abuse and neglect, with domestic violence, and with fetal alcohol syndrome, we will continue to spend millions of dollars building new prisons, and our streets won't be one bit safer.
>
> Make no mistake—responsibility, accountability, and tough penalties for serious crimes are critical. But until we can stop a child from picking up a gun for the wrong purpose, we will have failed.[142]

In the penal realm, state officials revisited an earlier and enduring trend toward de-escalation, seeking to defuse pressures toward retributive punishment. Concerned with the rising costs of a growing prison population, the state legislature sought ways to "stabilize future prison populations." In 2005, the legislature directed its associated research team, the Washington State Institute for Public Policy, to investigate the fiscal impact of "prevention and intervention programs, sentencing alternatives, and the use of risk factors in sentencing" to contain prison growth.[143] A few years earlier, in 2002, the legislature introduced a series of drug reforms as a way to control growth and reform what were perceived to be disproportionate penal sanctions, reducing prison sentences for nonviolent drug offenders.[144] State funding for drug treatment and prevention has also substantially increased since 1997.[145] In 1999, the state legislature returned some discretion to judges as a way to reduce recidivism, giving judges more sentencing options for individual drug offenders.

That same year, Governor Locke and the legislature passed the Offender Accountability Act (OAA), a move which reemphasized aspects of the rehabilitative ideal, treatment, and reform. The OAA intensified Washington's ongoing and long-term tradition of community supervision and sought ways to reduce recidivism through offenders' risk assessment. Although the state has sought ways to keep offenders of prison, officials have done so through the normalizing and moralizing powers of civil society. The OAA imposed a series of restrictive conditions on offenders in the community, including "rehabilitative treatment,"[146] mandating drug treatment, for example. The OAA tried to dictate the norms and rhythms of everyday life for former felons, even setting guidelines about whom they could socialize with. According to Governor Locke, the OAA banned "ex-cons from hanging out with past associates or drinking or taking illegal drugs."[147] By doing so, the OAA sought to transform offenders rather than simply incarcerate or harshly punish them but do so in ways that were nevertheless coercive, "the gentle way of punishment" in Foucault's terms.[148] The OAA builds resonant themes of self-governance and the power of civil society to govern so central to Washington's penal politics.

Conclusion

What I have tried to show in this chapter is the affinity between a certain kind of political order and specific kind of penal regime. Specifically, I focused on how highly democratized political structures and more deliberative forms of collective agency tend to support less coercive penal policies. In Washington, a reinvigorated democratized deliberative process more fully realized from the mid-1960s onward seems to have mollified social conflict and depressed reactionary impulses toward repression. By democratizing decision-making through the structural integration of citizen participation and by emphasizing the communicative action of deliberation, debate, and negotiation, social actors used the state's local political products and their cultural weight and legitimating authority to support and sustain the principle of parsimony. They worked with a variant of American democracy that emphasizes negotiation and compromise instead of dogmatism and winner-take-all politics.

Deliberative democracy to a certain degree is based on and facilitates a sense of reciprocity and mutual respect. In Washington, polity members tend to be less willing to inflict imprisonment on one another out of a concern for others' well-being and autonomy. At the same time, I tried to show how a democratic process that is rooted in a more progressive form of populism with its narratives of mutual cooperation, public goods, and self-governance provides the institutional and cultural support to restrain the repressive powers of the state in favor of the authority and control of civil society organizations. Also, the legacy of cooperatives and self-governance provide the cultural and institutional support necessary for officials to pursue noncustodial community sanctions based primarily on the discipline of labor and the perceived virtues but coercive powers of civil society. Taken together, these policies and practices restrain state coercion, creating more inclusionary but normalizing conditions of citizenship.

5

New York

Elite Pragmatism and Managerialism

In 1973, the New York state legislature passed and Governor Nelson A. Rockefeller signed the Rockefeller drug laws, revising Chapter 276 of the Laws of New York. The laws mandated prison for all serious Class A, B, and C drug felonies, including fifteen years to life imprisonment for the sale of one ounce and possession of two ounces or more of heroin, opium, cocaine, amphetamines, and LSD.[1] The drug laws also increased prison terms for lower level Class D and E drug felonies.[2] Drug addicts convicted of a felony, once offered treatment, could now be subject to imprisonment or confinement by the Narcotics Addiction Control Commission.[3] The new approach was justified as a public health campaign: incapacitation would prevent the spread of a "contagious disease," "eradicate this dreaded cancer," and contain a deadly virus that threatened to consume the public itself.[4] Over time, the drug laws led to an unprecedented and one of the largest confinements of drug offenders in the United States.

During the same legislative session, lawmakers began to mandate prison for repeat felony offenders with the "second felony offender" provision.[5] They also institutionalized diversion and short (less than twelve months) terms for lower level felony offenders with the "alternate definite sentence."[6] A few years later, in 1978, the legislature introduced and Governor Hugh Carey signed the "persistent violent offender" law, which mandated and increased prison terms for repeat violent felony offenders.[7] This set of legislation formalized a two-tiered approach to penal sanctioning—prison for serious violent offenders, diversion for others. Conceptualized as a triage approach to controlling crime and managing the public's insecurities, state officials would begin to better differentiate, sort, and classify crime in terms of perceived threats to the public and allocate resources accordingly.[8] According to the expert commission that proposed the approach, "violent attacks by strangers" generated the most fear and insecurity among New Yorkers, so the state should concentrate its resources on the "relatively small number of cases that involve serious, unprovoked attacks on strangers committed by people who are chronic offenders."[9] Punishment in these cases was simply incapacitation because officials doubted the efficacy of rehabilitation for "any large portion of the violent offender group by means that are consistent with our standards of justice and humanity."[10] This triage approach was later augmented by parole practices based on "differentiated supervision," the intensive surveillance of the most serious cases, and a higher rate of release for nonviolent offenders, institutionalized in the Presumptive Release Initiative.[11]

By developing a rather calculated approach to penal sanctioning, state officials depressed the raw emotion embedded in retribution and undermined the morality of transformation linked to penal welfarism. Rather than seek retribution for the pain and suffering of crime victims or seek vengeance for the breach in public security or invest in the rehabilitation, reintegration, and correction of offenders, state officials developed a much more technocratic response: managerialism.[12] Specifically, New York's managerial penal regime entailed expert-driven policies and practices that sought to regulate and minimize collective risk in the most cost-effective way to preserve limited sources. With an epidemiological model of crime, state officials proposed and carried out policies designed to identify and classify the most threatening risks to public health and isolate and contain those risks. In the 1970s, drugs and violent crime were deemed especially threatening to public health because they were perceived to be contagious, spreading more crime, infecting entire communities. Simultaneously, low-level offenses, including lower level felonies, were perceived to be fairly innocuous, not deserving of the state's resources or emotional energy necessary to support such an effort. Unlike in Washington State, low-level offenders were not subject to community sanctions legitimated by the perceived virtues and normalizing powers of civil society. New York's relatively early adoption of a managerialist approach may have been a precursor to later developments across the United States, which Malcolm Feeley and Jonathan Simon have identified as the "new penology" and actuarial justice: the regulation of aggregate risk rather than the punishment or rehabilitation of individual offenders. Without dramatic ritual, New York officials pursued the quarantine of perceived risks in the name of public health, but they did not necessarily seek to cure criminals. Here, the conceptualization of justice and the rational for punishment is rooted in a sense of public security, rather than the individualized pain and suffering of crime victims as in California or concern for individual freedom as in Washington.

By the 1970s, managerialism helped transform New York's penal regime from an outdated custodial institution to a much more efficient, discriminating, and strategic penal apparatus, an approach that varied significantly from California's retributive justice and Washington's faith in civil society. Over time, this managerial regime has led to high rates of imprisonment for violent and drug offenders and lower rates for other offenders. Today, violent and drug offenders make up over 83 percent of New York's prison population, 53.4 percent and 30 percent, respectively, figures above the national average.[13] Yet this differentiated regime has also led to the state's surprisingly modest imprisonment rate: 322 inmates per 100,000 population, ranking thirty-seventh in the nation, below the national average of 440, and below the national average for much of the thirty years under study.[14]

Some readers may dispute the characterization of New York's penal regime as technocratic or managerial, pointing to the draconian drug laws as evidence of a harsh, punitive, and retributive regime responsible for the mass incarceration of young African American males. Some may also insist that the drug laws were passed for the sake of political expediency, that is, to bolster the presidential ambitions of Governor Rockefeller, who was perceived as far more liberal and lenient than the more socially conservative and rising star of the Republican Party, Ronald Reagan. These characterizations both touch on important social and political factors that have been crucial for understanding the character of American penal regimes: racial social control and electoral politics. That said, they do not actually explain the development of a managerial penal regime in New York. First, we cannot reduce New York's overall penal regime to its drug laws, which only capture part of the regime and sidestep the more mundane but just as central routine practices, which filter out many other kinds of offenders. Second, contentious racial politics certainly played a role in the drug laws but in much more complex and insidious ways: many African

Americans in urban areas supported the drug laws. Third, by focusing on the immediate events surrounding the drug laws such as a political campaign, we miss the long-term policy process that was well under way since the early 1960s. Finally, of course, we certainly miss the deep underlying structural factors and forms of collective agency that led to and supported New York's managerialist penal regime.

Pragmatism: The Effects of Elitist Management

As I argue in the following pages, New York's long-standing pragmatic app-roach to governance provided the raw material, cultural resources, and legit-imating authority necessary to develop and sustain a managerial penal regime. It did so by downplaying ideological conflicts, rationalizing crime, unloading some of its emotional weight, and without moralizing about punishment. It did so by strategically deploying the coercive powers of the state on a well-defined but limited target to produce immediate and visible results.

A pragmatic mode of governance is not primarily about the realization of ideological principles, political doctrines, or even the public will. Rather, it is geared toward effective management and adaptation to changing social condi-tions. It is informed by progressive sensibilities of efficiency and rationality. In New York, pragmatism is rooted in a reformist tradition that sought to create a more regulatory and interventionist state based on technical, expert-driven, and practical responses to emergent social problems. Yet unlike their counter-parts in the West, New York progressives sought to centralize and consolidate political power, rather than spreading it across the polity with direct democracy measures. Consequently, the state has been highly insulated from public participation, and it is surprisingly somewhat underdemocratized. It has very low rates of civic engagement and is now one of three non-Southern states under federal court order to improve voter participation, especially among minority voters.[15] Governed by powerful elites, the state maintains its legiti-macy not by appealing to the will of the people or the authority of civil society, but by appearing to be useful to the public. The state must appear to provide for the well-being its citizens, offering social welfare and public security. However, because the state is so centralized and insulated from the public's check on its power, at various times elites have taken advantage of this situation. They have become thoroughly enmeshed in their own power dynamics, closing them-selves off to public works and pursuing private self-interest. This kind of governance can solidify existing social hierarchies as elites simply look after their own, using state resources for their own benefit, and ignore the public welfare or social inequalities. Over time, this privatization of public goods can weaken the state's authority and impinge on its legitimacy, creating the conditions conducive to increased state repression.

In a political environment dominated by elite pragmatism, high crime rates and other visible signs of disorder are perceived to be especially threatening to the integrity of state authority. The state is defined and legitimated by its usefulness—its ability, capacity, and willingness to address emergent social problems and provide security for its citizens. As such, the presence and public experience of crime tends to reflect poorly on state officials as well as on criminals: they appear to have failed to do their job. Because crime often has been defined in the epidemiological terms of disease and contagion, it has been defined more as a technical than moral problem. As such, the task falls on the state to manage such risks rather than condemn criminals.

Consequently, state officials tend to act decisively to subdue potential threats. They may act quickly to remove signs of disorder by quarantining violent and drug offenders to protect the health and viability of the surrounding environment. The removal of violent and drug offenders from public space is an immediate display of state action. The state vividly illustrates that it is responding, making itself useful, protecting the public, acting competent, justifying its authority, and delaying if not suppressing challenges to its elitist character. A pragmatic mode of governance tends to manage rather than prevent crime through incapacitation. Because state officials try to avoid the kinds of programs that drain resources, are cumbersome, may come to depend on public participation, and simply do not produce immediate, tangible, or visible results, they are less willing to invest and develop long-term social engineering, rehabilitation, and programs designed to the address the underlying causes of crime. In addition, pragmatic officials prioritize efficiency and rationality, seeking to avoid the waste of resources and curtail the excesses of a nondiscriminating policy of mass incarceration. They value expertise and scientific engagement with social problems and are therefore less likely to pursue strictly punitive responses, which are considered crass and unscientific. When state officials are geared toward the provision of public goods rather than private self-interest, they may also make an effort to curtail the excesses of state coercion by restricting or differentiating imprisonment. They may try to avoid alienating the public by limiting indiscriminate and excessive displays of power and control. They must justify such action as strategic, useful, and goal-oriented. As such, differentiated incapacitation—prison for violent and drug offenders, diversion for others—makes practical sense in this context. By relying on a managerial penal regime, a pragmatic mode of governance maximizes its legitimacy while minimizing force and expenditure. It exercises a highly disciplined form of state power.

Pragmatism: Historical Legacies of Elitism

Like California and Washington, New York continues to be informed by its past. The political development of the state's political structures and collective agency have created certain kinds of path dependencies and cultural resources that continue to shape the policy process today. As such, they provide local actors with the local products for understanding and resolving political and social conflict, and they do so in ways that tend to make sense to those involved and provide those actions with a degree of legitimacy and authority. Consider a few key moments here.

Weighed down by its history of elitism and antidemocratic tendencies, New York has never escaped its patrician past. It continues to display its aristocratic pedigree. Established in the early seventeenth century, Dutch settlers organized New York's social and political system according to their own *patroon* system, institutionalizing a quasi-feudal system in which the landed elites dominated the economy and government.[16] Even in the colonial period, challenged by democratic fervor, state elites managed to retain power and depress democratization. In 1777, drafting its first constitution, elites centralized political authority in the executive branch, a move that all other colonies soundly rejected as an anachronistic and imperial political arrangement.[17] Drafters went on to limit the powers of local government, restrict voting rights to the propertied elite, and permit only the wealthiest men to vote for governor, moves that further consolidated political power in the hands of a few rather than the many.

Patronage

Through the nineteenth century and into the twentieth, antidemocratic tendencies flourished under patronage politics. Patronage politics, fully realized in New York, New York City, and much of the rest of the country at this time, entailed a type of political agency oriented toward the consolidation of political power for personal gain.[18] Under a patronage system, political parties, once in power, used a wide array of political connections and state resources to advance their own interests rather than public interests. In New York City, for example, "Boss Tweed," head of the Tammany Hall political machine, infiltrated local government to such an extent that the organization regularly dipped into city coffers, skimming as much as $75 million by 1870.[19] To maintain power and ward off challenges, patronage-oriented parties spread favors around, rewarding loyalists and favorite sons with public offices, bribing elected officials, advancing special interests, and getting out the vote for machine candidates. Tammany Hall regularly got out the vote. With its extensive reach into the Irish immigrant community and the city clerk's office, Tammany Hall transformed new arrivals into new citizens at extraordinary rates.[20] The machine wielded considerable electoral power, frequently electing its favored candidates to local and statewide offices.[21]

By the end of the nineteenth century, however, the patronage system could no longer sustain its control over local and state politics nor suppress growing demands for public services. Rapid industrialization, urbanization, the population explosion, and mass immigration strained public services. By 1910, for example, New York City alone housed nearly 2 million immigrants, up from 1 million in the previous decade.[22] Between 1890 and 1920, for example, New York State's population increased from nearly 6 million to over 10 million.[23] European immigrants faced the grim reality of American modernization: material deprivation, squalid living conditions, violence, ill health, culture clashes, and alienation, among many other social pathologies. State and local government could not keep up even in the most limited way, and local charities and benevolent associations were stretched thin.

Out West, in California and Washington, populists, farmers, ranchers, and urban socialists teamed up with progressive reformers to challenge the perceived corruption of the patronage system and business monopolies and loosen the grip of the Eastern financial establishment on local economic affairs. As discussed in chapters 3 and 4 Western reformers were fairly successful in reclaiming control over local affairs, undercutting the party system, and increasing state regulation over public utilities. In California and Washington, populists and progressives institutionalized direct democracy, a move that democratized political authority and transformed the very structure and practices of governance. In the more industrialized east, populist-farmers did not gain much traction at the beginning or end of the agrarian revolt.[24] Populist challengers faced many obstacles. The machines were tight, exerting control over political parties and potential allies, the immigrant working classes.[25] And New York was the bank—the Eastern financial establishment home to Cornelius Vanderbilt, John D. Rockefeller, and J. P. Morgan, home to rail, steel, and oil, respectively.

Progressive Pragmatism

Yet settlement house women in eastern and midwestern cities were able to harness the momentum of the progressive movement and turn it against the parties and limited laissez-faire state of the nineteenth century.[26] By doing so, these reform-minded women, entrenched in urban slums, spirited by Protestant evangelicalism, and propelled by their own fantasies of social engineering, not only tried to clean up the streets, they tried to clean up government. The settlement house movement, along with middle-class professionals and upper-class philanthropists—emboldened with their newly discovered social scientific knowledge, John Dewey's philosophy of pragmatism, and a belief in their own efficacy to change the world around them—pushed for and won major social and political reforms.[27] Progressive-era reforms would eventually transform the nature of governance across the American states. In *Building a New American State*, Stephen Skowronek explains how progressive reformers replaced the "spoils" system of patronage and the weak state of "courts and parties" with an extensive administrative state. The new American state was made up a professional and meritocractic civil service, rather than party loyalists, and oriented more toward public management than private pursuit.

In New York, progressives and reform-oriented mayors tried to rid the city of boss-led political machines and improve the everyday living conditions for city residents. Repulsed by the dingy city, progressives sought measures to improve sanitation services, housing conditions, and street lighting. Squeamish about child poverty and the proliferation of aggressive street urchins, progressives, following the lead of the New York Society for the Prevention of Cruelty to Children, eventually created the Bureau of Child Hygiene, the juvenile court, and a host of social services to manage "wayward children."[28] Undaunted by the long list of social and political ills, reformers took on the political machines, institutionalizing ways to undermine machine influence over city and state government. Progressives introduced a series of electoral reforms that included the creation of primary elections and nonpartisan city managers. Primary elections would allow voters, rather than the party bosses, to select the party's candidate for the general elections, and city managers would take charge of the administration of public services, decreasing the chances for graft and corruption. These and other progressive political reforms seriously undermined machine party politics. Yet the machines survived and lasted in a weakened condition through the 1970s in New York.[29] In keeping with their more elitist orientation, progressive New Yorkers did not propose or institute direct democracy measures such as the initiative process or recall like their contemporaries in California and Washington. Instead, they consolidated governmental power.

In 1899, New Yorkers elected Theodore Roosevelt, a wealthy Progressive (who became U.S. president within a year), to the governor's office. Roosevelt and his progressive-oriented successors, Governors Charles Evans Hughes, Alfred Smith, and Franklin D. Roosevelt, descendant of New York's Dutch aristocracy and future U.S. president, all continued to strengthen the political power of the executive. In New York, the executive branch, especially strong since colonial days, rapidly expanded its reach into all aspects of day-to-day governing. By consolidating over 187 boards and commissions, New York governors gained control over state administration, budget process, and the substance and trajectory of public policies.[30] During the progressive era, this set of governors mobilized their extraordinary powers and state resources to reorganize state government, realigning the goals and priorities of what constituted good governance. New York introduced a state income tax and unemployment insurance, created a professional civil service, expanded the state regulation of public utilities and business, stiffened labor laws, increased workers compensation, and the expanded the nation's first public school system.[31]

In a few short years between 1905 and 1915, progressive reformers changed the policies and politics in New York. They imagined a new kind of state. They imagined an interventionist state, a professionalized state, one that would prioritize social welfarism, protecting its citizens against the ill effects of the market economy. In New York, progressives realized many of their hopes for a new improved American government—one that was well organized, efficient, based on scientific knowledge, and brought technical solutions to bear on emergent social problems.[32] Progressives engineered their way out of nineteenth-century limited government, but they did so in a way that may have stunted democratization and dampened civic engagement. By narrowing public participation in the business of governing and by valorizing expert knowledge and technical solutions to governance, and establishing it in governmental offices and agencies, this managerial approach to governance not only discouraged but organized out mass civic participation.

This managerial approach to governance lent support to a particularly antidemocratic impulse, New York's own eugenics movement, including forced sterilization.[33] In his social history of American welfare, *In the Shadow of the Poorhouse*, Michael Katz explains how in 1911 New York created the Bureau of Analysis and Investigation to explore eugenics research. After its extensive research and analysis of the state's growing poor population, the Bureau of Analysis and Investigation concluded the state's "defective and hereditary paupers," its "subnormals of the human race," simply cost too much money to institutionalize. The bureau recommended forced sterilization because "the public welfare demands that degenerates shall be prevented from the reproduction of their kind."[34] By 1931, over 12,000 people had been sterilized nationally.[35] Moving on from paupers to immigrants, eugenicists sought to restrict immigration from eastern and southern Europe, a move they thought would decrease the number of "defective genes" in the population.[36]

Although New York abandoned its interest in eugenics, state officials' desire to control and regulate certain populations remained in the repertoire of public policy. That is, the state would continue to sort and classify possible contaminants and move to quarantine these perceived risks. By doing so, the state would claim that it protected the general population from perceived contagions, pollution, and other sources of harm.[37]

Social Welfarism

By the late 1920s and early 1930s, New York's pragmatic approach to governance was put into overdrive, lasting well into the twenty-first century. Faced with a staggering economic downturn, rising unemployment, and growing social unrest, Governor Franklin D. Roosevelt mobilized an unprecedented level of state resources to provide public relief. In keeping with the state's forms of collective agency, Roosevelt created a new administrative agency, the Temporary Emergency Relief Administration, to manage $20 million in relief.[38] By 1932, President-elect Franklin D. Roosevelt nationalized his early New York relief measures, ushering in some of the most generous social assistance programs in the nation's history.

Roosevelt's New Deal for America expanded preexisting veteran's benefits and state workers compensation laws; introduced grand-scale public works projects and public employment, which together put to work over 5 million unemployed; and established contributory social insurance programs, state-run public assistance, and a range of housing programs.[39] Throughout the Great Depression, New York continued to provide relief, outpacing many other states in welfare generosity. For example, by 1940, New York ranked sixth in Works Progress Administration wages and provided a generous $24.50 per child per month Aid to Dependent Children, almost double the $13 national average.[40] Throughout the 1940s and 1950s, New York consistently ranked in the top ten in welfare generosity for Aid to Dependent Children, Old Age Assistance, and Aid to the Blind.[41] By the 1960s, in its average payments per person, New York ranked second in Aid to Dependent Children, thirteenth in Old Age Assistance, seventh in Aid to the Blind, third in Aid to the Permanently and Totally Disabled, ninth in General Assistance, and tenth in unemployment insurance.[42] Today, New York still ranks high on various public policy indicators, ranking fifth in overall state expenditures.[43]

Though the progressive era has long since past, progressives' emphasis on expert knowledge, centralized state administration, and technical approaches to public policy have had long-lasting effects on collective action in New York. They helped create a professionalized state oriented toward the public welfare. They did so in part by insulating and centralizing political power, a move that contributed to the state's relatively underdemocratized and elitist collective action.

The Structure and Agency of Pragmatic Governance

In New York, political authority is highly centralized, and collective agency tends to be pragmatic, reliant on expertise, and oriented toward problem solving, but it also shows tendencies toward elitism and the pursuit of private self-interest. From the time of Dutch settlements, state officials have consolidated power, concentrating it in the executive branch, and to certain extent have restricted democratization. So what we see in New York is the continuity of elitism—that is, the elite dominance of political power—but discontinuity in collective action. Collection agency shifts from patronage politics and the pursuit of private gain and self-interest to the ideals of progressive pragmatism and the pursuit of public works, without making a clean break from either one.

The institutionalized powers of the governors are substantial and above average. On Thad Beyle's often cited index, New York scores well above the national average in terms of the "governors' institutional powers" to veto legislation, control the state budget, run for unlimited terms, control state agency appointments, and dominant his or her political party.[44] Controlling much of the state budget process, governors draft the budget, send it to the legislature, and then if they want, veto line by line any items the legislature may have added.[45] By requiring a special majority vote to override line item vetoes, New York is one of only four states that grant such budgetary power to governors.[46] Of course, gubernatorial power consolidation has not gone unchallenged by state legislators. They have often tried to exert their power over the budget, producing gridlock, delays, and backdoor, late-night negotiations. In California and Washington, by contrast, both decentralized polities, the legislature can change any aspect of the governor's budget, a move that decreases gubernatorial power and spreads political authority across government.[47] These apparently mundane rules of the game, the minutiae of the bottom line, have major repercussions on the substance and trajectory of policy making because they channel action in certain ways rather than others, empowering some actors more than others to control the direction of state resources. Consequently, governors in New York wield a considerable amount of control over all aspects of governmental decision making, as vividly illustrated by Governor Rockefeller's mass mobilization of state resources to modernize New York.[48]

New York does not allow for direct democracy, which limits public participation to voting for representatives and further concentrates power among elites. Because centralization routinely blocks citizens' access to elites and other key decision makers, citizens may become quiescent. Because their demands and protests are often met with advanced bureaucratic procedures and institutionalized channels of action, citizens may not be encouraged to develop a sense of their own efficacy in the political field. In this context, citizens may not develop a lively sense of civic responsibility, a responsibility to keep a check on state power. In New York, citizens tend to participate less often in public life, particularly in electoral politics, than many other states.

In the 1970s and 1980s, New York ranked thirty-sixth in voter turnout in state and national elections; California ranked thirty-first and Washington ranked fourteenth.[49] By the mid-1990s, New York ranked forty-fifth, California ranked forty-sixth, and Washington ranked seventeenth.[50] Between 1997 and 2002, only 35 percent of New York's voting age population voted for governor, a figure far lower than the nearly 44 percent of the national average.[51] In *New York Politics*, Edward Schneier and John Murtaugh point out that because New York has maintained fairly low voter participation rates since the 1920s and

1930s and has continued to do so well into the twenty-first century, the state is now one of three non-Southern states under federal court order to improve voter participation, especially among minority voters. Even the Voter Assistance Commission, charged with improving the democratic process, is made up almost entirely of elites, insiders, and high-ranking professionals.[52] We pause here to consider just how effective this strategy could be in mobilizing voter participation in the South Bronx, a district made up of less well-off nonwhite Latinos. We also note that Betsy Gotbaum, the New York City public advocate, is included on the Voter Assistance Commission. In New York City, voters elect a public advocate to serve as the people's representative on the City Council. The people's watchdog becomes fully embedded in the apparatus of government—she becomes part of the machine.

Given the chance to participate in nonelectoral forms of political and civic life, New Yorkers, upstate and downstate, opt out more often than not. Consider Robert Putnam's index of social capital and rates of civic engagement. New Yorkers attend fewer public meetings, join fewer social and civic associations, attend few club meetings, volunteer less often, serve on fewer local committees, and trust people less often.[53] For example, only 40 percent of New Yorkers agreed that "most people can trusted," whereas 59 percent of Vermonters and 63 percent of Minnesotans thought so.[54] Just 10 percent of New Yorkers reported that they attended a meeting on town or school affairs, whereas 21 percent said so in Washington; just 5 percent of New Yorkers served as an officer of a club, whereas 13 percent did so in Washington.[55] We can see that New Yorkers are rarely joiners. They are less engaged in civic and public affairs than many of their peers across the American states. As a consequence, New Yorkers not only leave many important decisions up to a smaller pool of citizen participants but readily yield decision making to elites—governors, state legislators, and other insiders who are certainly not shy about exercising state power.

Pragmatic Agency

Under these political conditions—that is, when citizens are less engaged in political and civic participation and political authority is highly centralized— we might expect state elites to hoard resources, divert them for personal gain, or abuse power since there are limited checks on state power. At times, this is exactly what we see in New York politics, as partly evidenced by the 2006 election of Governor Eliot Spitzer and his reform-oriented administration.

Yet more often than not, governance is New York has been oriented toward pragmatism, a technical and managerial approach to social and political conflict, even as it remains in tension with tendencies toward privatization and elitism.

Informed by progressive ideals about social improvement, New York has tended to orient government toward public goods in an attempt to improve the living conditions and economic well-being of its citizens. In his 1978 Annual Message, Governor Hugh Carey captures this sentiment: "We are New Yorkers, and for us, survival is not enough. We know that in the human condition, there has to be a better way. A better way to earn, a better way to build, a better way to learn, a better way to care."[56] Likewise, in his 1985 Annual Message, Governor Mario Cuomo explains how the state is continuously put to work to facilitate opportunity and assistance to improve the lives of New Yorkers:

> We make new efforts to enhance and improve our system, striving always to perfect it. New efforts to realize more fully the truth and potential of the simple aspirations we have for ourselves. Only the government we need, but all the government we need—a government that cherishes above all things common sense, competitiveness and compassion, a government that is both progressive and pragmatic, a government that helps people to go as far as they can on their own merits and then finds in the strength and the goodness of the successful the opportunity to help those who through no fault of their own were not able to help themselves.[57]

New York has created a fairly extensive apparatus that is oriented toward the public welfare rather than personal gain. As a result, the state has tended to provide public policies that are fairly generous by American standards. New York not only provides for the poor, it provides fairly generous public services for all New Yorkers. The state consistently outspends the national average on general expenditures, which include education, social services, and public safety spending. For example, in 2004, New York spent over $5.6 million per capita on general expenditures, a rate higher than the $4.1 million per capita national average, California's $4.8 million per capita, and Washington's $4.3 million per capita.[58] In terms of education spending per pupil, New York ranks third in the nation, well ahead of twenty-first-ranked Washington and fortieth-ranked California.[59] In terms of spending on health care assistance, New York ranks first in Medicaid expenditures per recipient as compared to the lagging forty-eighth-ranked California and fiftieth-ranked Washington.[60]

In terms of more conventional social welfare spending, New York ranks sixth in Temporary Aid to Need Families expenditures per recipient, compared to fourteenth-ranked California and twenty-eighth-ranked Washington.[61] We should also note here that Washington, in characteristic fashion, looks after its workers, laborers, and producers much more than does California and New York. Despite its relatively low state revenue per capita (Washington ranks thirtieth on general revenue per capita as compared to third-ranked New York and twelfth-ranked California), Washington outspends both states on its average weekly unemployment benefits.[62] In terms of public safety, New York spends more per capita than California and Washington on both police protection and corrections.[63] In terms of overall state spending, these figures suggest that New York not only generates more money than most other states, it also spends it at much higher rates on public services.

In the words of Governor Rockefeller, New Yorkers expect their "hard-earned tax dollars" to "produce a correspondingly high level of efficient and economical public services."[64] By mobilizing technical, social science, and professional knowledge to get results, New York has tended to follow more pragmatic forms of collective agency than purely ideological or strictly partisan politics. New York has tended to provide fairly generous public services not so much for a great love of the people but because it is more efficient to bring the poor along than let them drag on the economy or rot in the poorhouse. Embodying the "can-do" spirit of American politics, pragmatists want results.[65] In the hopeful words of Governor Rockefeller, pragmatists take action as if "there is nothing wrong with America that we don't have the human and natural resources to overcome."[66] To get results, pragmatists are more than willing to change courses of action, compromise, and change their own rules and principles to adapt to new situations. Again, Governor Cuomo expresses this practical approach to governance: "Indeed one of our greatest challenges is to be able to innovate, to anticipate, to provide new modes for making our principles work in a constantly changing society."[67]

To demonstrate the state's utility in solving pressing problems and doing so efficiently, pragmatic governance relies heavily on state elites, expert commissions, and other government insiders to get the job done. New York has created a governing machine, sorting and classifying risks, seeking to manage and control disorder. New York is big government. Today, New York has many more state and local employees per resident than both Washington and California. In 2005, for example, New York had 613 state and local government employees per 10,000 resident population, a figures above the 537 government employees per 10,000 resident population national average, Washington's 524 government employees per 10,000 resident population, and California's 490 government employees per 10,000 population.[68]

Pragmatic Action: Expert Commissions

Throughout the 1960s and well into the 1980s, New York relied heavily on expert commissions to sort through changing crime patterns and reassess whether the state should retain its indeterminate sentencing structure and rehabilitative approach to punishment or launch major sentencing reform. These commissions, unlike the hybrid state-citizen commissions discussed in the Washington case, tend to be made up entirely of professionals, law enforcement personnel, and various state representatives and often included the same people. Moreover, they do not proclaim to represent or include official "citizen representatives."

In 1961, for example, Governor Rockefeller appointed former Assemblyman Richard Bartlett to chair the New York Temporary Commission on Revision of the Penal Law and Criminal Code (commonly known as the Bartlett Commission), to update the state's penal code. By 1965, New York adopted the Bartlett Commission's recommendations to prioritize the crime control functions of imprisonment—that is, deterrence, rehabilitation, and incapacitation—rather than retribution.[69] Within a few years, Governor Rockefeller appointed the commissioners of both the Department of Corrections and the Division of Parole to head up the McGinnis-Oswald Committee, the Governor's Special Committee on Criminal Offenders, to figure out ways to implement rehabilitative programs in prison.[70] Other members included the commissioners of Social Services, Mental Hygiene, Narcotics Addiction Control Commission, Division of Youth, state administrator of the Judicial Conference, and several private attorneys.[71]

In 1968, in response to the federal Safe Streets Act, Governor Rockefeller created the New York State Crime Control Planning Board and charged it to come up with law enforcement policy and recommendations. The Crime Control Planning Board included chair Richard Bartlett, the New York County district attorney, the New York City police commissioner, the state attorney general, the state police superintendent, and the chair of the State Narcotics Addiction Control Commission.[72] In 1970, Governor Rockefeller created a fifteen-member special commission to reassess the state's penalties for marijuana.[73] After the bloody Attica Prison riot, the McKay Commission began to investigate the causes of the riots and make recommendations for major prison reform. In 1977, Governor Carey appointed Manhattan District Attorney Robert Morgenthau to chair the Executive Advisory Committee on Sentencing, the Morgenthau Committee. The Liman Commission and McQuillan Commissions followed to coordinate activities of the criminal justice system and to study sentencing patterns.

In 1983, Governor Cuomo and the New York state legislature created the Sentencing Guidelines Committee, the Bellacosa-Feinberg Committee, appointing six members each to evaluate the sentencing guidelines in New York. Chaired by law professor Joseph Bellacosa and replaced by Kenneth Feinberg, an attorney and former advisor to Senator Ted Kennedy, the commission included private attorney Arthur Liman, former president of the Legal Aid Society, chair of the Liman Commission and member of the McKay Commission; president of the State University of New York Vincent O'Leary; Ford Foundation and NAACP counsel Lynn Walker; Manhattan District Attorney Robert Morgenthau, member of the Liman Commission and chair of his own commission; and several other private attorneys and criminal justice officials.[74]

Pragmatism in Social Context: The Development of Managerial Penal Sanctioning

Like California and Washington, we again see that the period of the 1960s was not only a critical turning point in crime control policies and practices, it was a critical period in the ongoing processes of state governance. Like the populist revolt, the progressive reform era, and the New Deal response to the Great Depression, the 1960s was a period in which American states faced serious problems of governance. Youth and counterculture flourished, middle America joined the antiwar protest, urban riots intermixed violence and contentious racial politics, and the civil rights movement exposed the unfulfilled promises of American democracy—all of which exposed the contradictions of American democracy in the international context.

In the middle of this existential angst and political protest, crime bled across America. Crime rates doubled across the states between 1960 and 1970. In New York, violent crime more than doubled in the five short years between 1965 and 1970, increasing from 325 known violent offenses per 100,000 population to 685 known violent offenses per 100,000 population in 1970, figures well above the national average of 200 known violent offenses per 100,000 population in 1965 and 363 known violent offenses per 100,000 population in 1970.[75] New York's overall crime rate reached new heights as well, increasing from 3,065 index crimes per 100,000 population to over 4,900 index crimes per 100,000 population by 1970, a figure above the national average of just under 4,000 index crimes per 100,000 population.[76]

Crime had reached such dramatic proportions that the New York State Commission on Management and Productivity in the Public Sector, an influential crime control expert commission, expressed doubts about the public's confidence in criminal justice. The commission explained, "viewed from the victims' perspective, the promise of security becomes a cruel hoax."[77]

Welfarist Response to Crime Victims

To combat this growing sense of insecurity, state officials turned their attention to crime victims. They turned their attention to the consequences rather than the causes of crime: its costs, fear, and victims. In 1965, state officials began to manage and regulate the fear, insecurity, and anger of crime victims, defusing potential sources of vengeance through financial assistance. Governor Rockefeller explained the state's responsibility to victims: "Our citizens should not have to live in uncertainty and fear. They should be able to count in the security of their persons and property."[78] Adhering to New York's pragmatic agency, Rockefeller mobilized technical and expert knowledge to sort through victims' concerns. He appointed several state elites to head up a committee on crime victims. He asked the attorney general, the governor's counsel, and the presiding judge of the Court of Claims to come up with a proposal to provide some kind of financial assistance to crime victims and their families, particularly victims of violent crimes.[79] By the mid-1960s, another expert-led commissions, the New York Commission on the Revision of the Penal Law, had also been researching various ways to help crime victims.[80] By 1966, New York created the Crime Victims Board, a new state agency that would administer the crime victim compensation program.

Within a year, victim compensation increased five times, from awarding 43 victims $55,665 to awarding 220 victims a total of $386,585.[81] Within ten years, victim compensation reached over $4 million, awarding 1,764 victims a total of $4.3 million.[82] The Crime Victims Board provided (and continues to do so today) generous financial assistance to crime victims to pay for funeral costs, medical bills, counseling services, crime scene clean-ups, and other crime-related costs.[83] New York maintains one of the most generous compensation programs in the country. We should note that even though California was an innovator in victim compensation, the state maintains one of the stingiest victim compensation programs in the country—California caps awards at $6,000, whereas Washington caps at $20,000 and New York does not cap awards.[84]

As crime rates increased, state officials turned their attention rather quickly to victims. But they did so with financial aid rather than by increasing penal sanctions. I suggest that these early efforts to provide victims with a kind of criminal justice welfare may have averted victims' moral protests against an unresponsive state. The state's welfarist response may have defused victims' anger and resentment and circumvented a punitive response. However, we should also note that the state's centralization may have dampened the mass mobilization of victims, weakening or ignoring their demands for retribution in the late 1960s. By contrast, in California, crime victims' pain and suffering was amplified in the public sphere, legislated into the 1967 "great bodily harm" penalty. In California, the pain and suffering of victims helped justify and legitimate stiff penal sanctioning, a pattern that has been repeated in the 1980s with the Victims Bill of Rights and in the 1990s with three strikes initiative campaigns. By the mid-1960s, New York developed a relatively smart way to manage the unwieldy problem of criminal victimization, a problem that did not readily present a remedy. By relying more on a welfarist approach of compensation and public services, state officials proposed a technical rather than moral response.

Contagions and Public Health

From 1959 onward, Governor Rockefeller mobilized the political power of the executive branch to take on what he considered the biggest threat to public health and security: narcotics addiction and its associated crime. Although he was one the most influential and power politicians in New York, he did not necessarily act unilaterally, nor did he simply pursue partisan goals or private self-interest. Instead, he relied extensively on pragmatic collective agency. He formulated policy responses out his ongoing interaction with expert commissions, scientific inquiry, and key department officials, as evidenced by his own discourse on the subject and his gubernatorial papers, which are filled with state agency memos and reports, expert commissions, references to technical and scientific research, and public opinion polls.[85] New York's pragmatic tradition, with its reliance on collective inquiry and ongoing research, tended to support policy change and compromise. Embedded in this tradition, Rockefeller proposed and advocated nearly every kind of policy response to drugs that had been imagined and researched at the time. Next, I spend some time examining Rockefeller's discourse and policy developments on drugs because not only are a key component of New York's managerial approach to penal sanctioning, they represent the beginning of a shift away from penal-welfarist approaches to crime control.

In 1959, Rockefeller began to challenge the federal government to modernize its approach to drug traffic, calling for an all-out effort to stop the flow of drugs into the country, a move that could decrease the drug supply and therefore decrease drug addiction. Within a year, he advocated a public health approach to drug addiction, establishing state-run inpatient and outpatient facilities to treat addicts.[86] By 1962, he continued to press the federal government to develop more aggressive interdiction policies, a move that he hoped would slow the flow of drugs into the city and prevent addiction in the first place.[87] With pragmatism's emphasis on the application of scientific and expert knowledge, the same year, Rockefeller pressed the state to expand drug treatment facilities. In 1965, he reasserted his faith in scientific experimentation to solve social problems: "The nature of the affliction is such that the rate of cure is tragically low. To date there is frankly not sufficient knowledge of the causes of the disease, nor is there any known remedy. . . . To find the answer will take a massive effort in the laboratory, the hospital and the clinic."[88] From the early 1960s onward, he supported experimental research on drug addicts. By 1968, methadone maintenance became public policy in New York and New York City despite opposition from the federal government.[89] Medical researchers at Rockefeller University found a way to wean heroin addicts off the drug by injecting them with methadone shots.[90]

With this public health approach to drugs, Rockefeller frequently characterized drug addiction in epidemiological terms as a threatening disease, a threat "akin to cancer in spreading deadly disease among us" and "deserving all the brain power, manpower, and resources to overcome it."[91] In this context, narcotics addiction was a disease, and it was contagious, spreading indiscriminately across New York. In his Special Message to the State Legislature in 1966, he explained, "addiction spreads through a neighborhood like a virulent infection. Its unfortunate victims, prisoners of a relentless craving, lure the weak into the habit in order to help obtain drugs for themselves."[92] In this context, drug addiction was not the result of moral failing or even social deprivation, it was the result of a virus, a "virulent infection." Drug addicts were considered passive victims to a contagious disease. In his testimony before a joint hearing of the New York State Senate and Assembly Codes Committee, Rockefeller unequivocally made the link between drug addiction and disease. A few years later, when asked about the constitutionality of his proposal to have offenders physically examined for drugs addiction, he responded: "I would like to give you a precedent that was started under the days of Governor Dewey when tuberculosis was a contagious disease and our law says that you can isolate a contagious person, and I think these people are contagious people."[93]

By 1966, Rockefeller, key law enforcement officials, and various expert commissions became even more concerned with the "collateral effects" of drug addiction: crime. Drug addiction was perceived to be criminogenic—addiction caused crime. According to Rockefeller and expert officials, as more addicts turned to petty theft, random assaults, and prostitution to support their habits, crime increased across the state. In the mid-1960s, the New York State Commission of Investigation launched a major investigation into the drug-crime nexus and found similar results as the New York police commissioner. Both commissions concluded that narcotics addiction increased dramatically throughout the state and had increased crime. Myles Lane of the New York State Commission of Investigation explained: "From a social angle, narcotics is the most important problem in the United States ... the amount of crime generated by the need of addicts for money to feed the habit is appalling. It's a worse problem than alcohol."[94] In his 1966 Annual Message, Rockefeller incorporated the expert commission's research findings into his own analysis of drug addiction and crime. He explained how this link between addiction and crime spread across the state:

> Narcotics addicts are said to be responsible to one-half the crimes
> committed in New York City alone—and their evil contagion is
> spreading into the suburbs.
>   The problem of narcotics addiction is not confined to any class or
> area; it invades the split-level home as well as the cold-water tenement.[95]

In this context, crime itself was not caused by moral depravity or socioeconomic deprivation but was the result of drug addiction, itself the result of a disease ("an evil contagion"). Rockefeller explained: "With this infection comes crime—theft, burglary mugging, prostitution, assault and murder."[96] Drug addiction did not discriminate between ethnic groups or socioeconomic status—it claimed both city and suburban residents, rich and poor, white and black victims alike. To prevent its spread and to prevent drug-related crime, Rockefeller argued, the state had to find a way to prevent drug addiction. By doing so, he argued, the state would "strike a devastating blow at the roots of crime."

Rockefeller did not play up racial differences in drug use and drug crime but instead stressed collective vulnerability to an infectious disease. Nor did he focus on the blameworthiness or moral culpability of offenders and insist that they be held accountable. Although he argued that an inner-city problem, drug addiction, threatened to invade the whiter suburbs, he did not take that opportunity to condemn inner-city or black residents for the drug problem. He did not blame African Americans for drug addiction and drug crime. Instead, he blamed the disease. This particular drugs-as-disease characterization functioned to absorb potential urban and race conflicts. By characterizing drugs as a disease, Rockefeller, his administration, and those that followed diluted sources of intergroup conflict. We could easily imagine how drugs and drug crimes would play out differently in California, where social conflict is heightened rather than pacified. In New York, by posing drugs and associated crime as a public health problem, state officials necessitated a technical or managerial response. At the same time, we should note that this approach—the avoidance of contentious racial politics—probably prevented state officials from fully grasping the scale of urban plight and some of the underlying causes of drug addiction and drug crimes.

Quarantine and Containment: The Drug Laws

Now that Rockefeller and other state officials had created such apparently threatening and contagious public health problem, they had to find new ways to respond to drug addiction and associated crime. In a pragmatic mode of governance, state officials must get results, provide for the public, and demonstrate the state's utility to maintain legitimacy and public support. In the words of the governor: "They look to us to continue to meet urgent needs. And they expect the maintenance and improvement of essential State services on a prudent basis—and with emphasis on those services which will open up still further opportunities for their economic and social progress. They expect continued economy and efficiency in State government."[97] Turning to the drug problem in particular, Rockefeller pointed to public demand for some kind of state action: "Throughout the State, the people have made it clear to me that there was increasing concern about this cancerous growth in our society."[98] By commissioning a series of public opinion polls, Rockefeller was well aware that crime and narcotics were serious concerns to most New Yorkers throughout his administration. With this information, he pledged more state action. New York would respond to "eliminate this spreading disease."[99]

Based on the state's previous policy responses and additional scientific research, Rockefeller explained that there was "an emerging consensus" about the effectiveness of quarantine, the isolation of addicts from drugs.[100] To isolate addicts from drugs, New York would remove drug addicts and drug pushers from the public sphere. But they would do so in a highly differentiated way, separating addicts from dealers, one an illness, the other a crime. New York began to sort out more carefully addicts from dealers and proposed separate policy responses for each category. Rockefeller proposed stiffer penal sanctions for dealers and compulsory treatment for addicts. Emphasizing the need to quarantine threats, in his 1966 Annual Message, he argued: "We must remove narcotics pushers from the streets, the parks, and the schoolyards of our cities and suburbs."[101] He proposed an increased use of penal incapacitation to contain the risk associated with drug offenders.

Since then, New York has favored prison for drug dealers. To quarantine drug addicts, Rockefeller and the state legislature established the Narcotics Addiction Control Commission. Under the state's 1962 Metcalf-Volker Act, drug addicts arrested for lower level offenses could avoid prison terms by entering drug treatment facilities. Most chose prison instead of mandatory rehabilitation.[102] To ensure that drug addicts received some kind of treatment, Rockefeller introduced civil commitment. Operating under the Mental Hygiene Department, the Narcotics Addiction Control Commission forced treatment onto drug addicts.[103] Citing the U.S. Supreme Court and California's civil commitment program, Rockefeller justified civil commitment—the removal of risks from the public sphere—as a way to "prevent crime and to protect the people's health and welfare."[104] State officials began to managing the drug problem out of the public sphere in the name of public health, suppressing the individual freedom and autonomy of offenders in favor of the public health. Here, the use of state force is grounded in a different set of assumptions and practices than retribution and take on entirely different meanings. The objective and justification is to contain and regulate "contagions" rather than punish them.

By 1971, Rockefeller expanded his administration's antidrug approach, enlisting more expertise, more police, and more efficient court processing to manage the crime and narcotics problem. He expanded the funding and duties of the New York Crime Control Planning Board, expanded the police department and increased police training, asked for court reform recommendations from the Temporary Commission to Study the Courts, and proposed another drug commission, the Temporary Commission to Evaluate the Drug Laws. As justification for this expansion, he again pointed to the collateral negative effects of drugs:

> The tragedy of individual frustration and fear that rises out of the failure to stem the tide of crime in our communities creates an environment for the further spread of crime and general disrespect for our entire system of criminal justice.
>
> Because of their corrosive effect in the basic fabric of community life, the control of crime and narcotics abuse is an absolute necessity in solving the problems in our communities.[105]

In his 1971 Annual Message, he reaffirmed his resolve to quarantine threats to public health:

> Despite the massive effort—and despite a number of notable successes—we are regrettably still immersed in the tragedy of drugs and drug addiction.
>
> Nonetheless, if we are to survive as a society, we cannot permit ourselves to become subservient to the unreal world of drugs, we must, accordingly, be prepared to redouble our efforts to eradicate this dreaded cancer.[106]

By 1971, New York had quarantined nearly 20,000 addicts—about half of whom were in state-run facilities and the other half in private facilities.

After a decade long battle and a wide range of policy instruments, by 1973 and $1 billion later, Governor Rockefeller acknowledged that the state had failed to curb drug addiction and its associated crime. He explained: "Let's be frank...We have achieved very little permanent rehabilitation—have found no cure."[107] Like a contagious disease and threat to public health, once again he described how drug addiction and its collateral crime spread across New York, afflicting "every background and economic level." He continued: "Whole neighborhoods have been effectively destroyed by addicts as by an invading army."[108] Consequently, he told New Yorkers: "We face the risk of undermining our will as a people—and the ultimate destruction of our society as a whole."[109]

To Rockefeller, drug addiction posed a serious threat not only to public health but to the viability of society. Over the years, he had invested so much of the state's resources as well as his own political capital to curb drug addiction that he was not about to back away from this ever-expanding challenge. Rockefeller was determined to get results on drugs. Maximizing the flexibility of pragmatism, he pressed on. Shifting his attention toward the drug supply once again, he turned to law enforcement. Rockefeller wanted to unleash the full force of the state power against drug dealers, trying once again to stop the flow of drugs into the cities and suburbs and thereby decrease addiction and crime. Reversing much of his own longtime treatment-oriented approach to drug addiction, he introduced mandatory prison terms for drug felonies, sales and possession alike, as a deterrent and as punishment. He did so to signal to the public that he was committed to dealing with drug offenders, particularly drug dealers. After trying other methods and approaches to drug offenses, Rockefeller and the state legislature eventually resorted to harsh imprisonment in frustration rather than as a primary or automatic response to crime.

Pragmatism and Black Activism

Although Rockefeller certainly dominated the policy-making process and was particularly invested in the drug laws, he was not alone in his desire to mobilize the state's resources and technical expertise to intervene in a growing social problem. Despite opposition from the New York American Civil Liberties Union and various criminal justice officials who worried about an overburdened system, the state legislature passed the drug laws without too much dissension. Compromising with fellow state officials, Rockefeller toned down his stiffest proposals by restoring the possibility of parole and he agreed to the second felony laws, changes to the penal code that would increase sanctions for repeat felony offenders.[110] The Senate voted forty-one to fourteen and the Assembly voted eighty to sixty-five in favor of the drug laws.[111] But perhaps more important, Rockefeller found support for the laws in the communities most adversely affected by crime and the drug trade: black residents of Harlem. Many black residents of Harlem and the rest of New York City, church leaders, and the NAACP anticrime committee, for example, demanded more state protection against what they considered another threat to the viability of black neighborhoods, drugs and its associated crime.

Since the late 1960s, many black activists have pushed the state to take a tougher stand against lawlessness in their communities. African Americans wanted the state to fulfill its responsibility and provide protection. Black residents wanted to "escape the reign of criminal terror."[112] In the late 1960s, for example, the NAACP Citizens' Mobilization Against Crime advocated stronger law enforcement presence in black neighborhoods and lobbied Governor Rockefeller for stiffer penalties against violent offenders. In "Harlem Likened to the Wild West," the *New York Times* reported that African American activists sent Rockefeller and the state legislature telegrams supporting increased police presence and minimum prison terms, including five years for muggers, ten years for drug dealers, and thirty years for first-degree murderers.[113] Vincent Baker, chair of the NAACP anticrime committee, explained how black residents had started taking the law into their own hands to protect themselves against crime and violence. He explained his opposition to vigilantism and demands for state action: "We don't want gunslingers, paid or unpaid, in our community. We want law enforcement by and through the law. . . . Vigilantism is inherently undemocratic, antisocial and unsound . . . [it is brought about by] anarchy and complete helplessness against marauding hoodlums."[114] Well into the late 1960s, many black activists continued to patrol their own neighborhoods in an effort to root out drug dealers. For example, John Shabazz, leader of the Harlem-based Black Citizens Patrol, an organization made up of 155 reported members, explained that his voluntary association would try to root out drug dealers from the city's public schools: "We have the names and photographs of pushers . . . and we have people inside the schools to turn over the names to the proper authorities. If they [the police] don't deal with the problem, we will have to deal with it our own way."[115] By the early 1970s, African American community groups, social activists, church leaders, and ordinary residents wanted more state action; they wanted the state to intervene in the drug trade and its associated violence and crime. Many African Americans supported Rockefeller's drug laws. Consider, for example, Reverend Oberia Dempsey of Harlem, who argued: "Citizens have a right to be protected. We're being punished [by drug pushers] punishment is being meted against you, me, our children."[116] Dr. Benjamin Watkins, the honorary "mayor of Harlem," explained that stiff sanctions were necessary to "remove this contagion from the community."[117] Likewise, Jocelyn Cooper, a civil servant, stated: "I'm very much a liberal and a militant most of the time, but in terms of what he's [Rockefeller] advocating I'd like to see it happen."[118] Similarly, the *Amsterdam News*, the major black newspaper in the city, argued, "Aggressive state action against narcotics addiction is long overdue."[119] The *Amsterdam News* supported mandatory life sentences for the "non-addict drug pusher of hard drugs" because, as the editors explained, this kind of drug dealing "is an act of cold calculated, pre-meditated, indiscriminate murder of our community."[120] In Harlem, Reverend Earl B. Moore of the Baptist community and Dr. George Weldon McMurray of the AME Zionist Church supported Rockefeller's strong stance against drug pushers characterized as "merchants of death."[121] Similarly, the NAACP's Citizens Mobilization Against Crime supported tougher penalties, proposing "lengthening minimum prison terms for muggers, pushers, 1st degree murders."[122]

Mrs. Spring Anne Bell, a Bronx resident, explained her support: "What is being done to our youth who fall prey to some unscrupulous pusher is awful . . . our children are dying on rooftops, in dirty basements and hallways."[123] But she, like many other residents and the *Amsterdam News*, opposed any attempts to criminalize addicts or low-level addict-pushers. In this context, drug pushers were characterized as murderers to be punished and drug addicts were characterized as weak victims to be treated.

During a community meeting with state legislators at the West 125th Street YMCA, many African Americans expressed opposition to Rockefeller's mandatory prison term for all kinds of drug offenders, seeking to distinguish between hard-core dealers and addict-sellers.[124] At the same time, residents clearly wanted state protection and state intervention. Fred Samuel, leader of the Haryou-Act Community Corporation, explained how drugs and its associated crime was "a crisis that is holding us prisoners in our homes."[125]

Drug addiction, particularly heroin addiction, and associated crime were clearly concerns for black communities in New York. Embedded in New York's pragmatic political context, African Americans demanded the state take action and deal with this particular social problem. From the 1930s onward, African Americans, particularly the middle class, have been incorporated into New York politics.[126] Throughout the 1960s, New York pursued integrative civil rights policies, pursued pro–black community programs, and strengthened antidiscrimination laws in housing and employment.[127] These acts of political and economic incorporation may help explain not only black support for the drug laws but also the influence of African American activists on the passage of the drug laws. Within this context, African Americans made particular demands on the state, and they expected some level of response.

At the same, however, we should note that state officials did not alter their proposals to meet African Americans' opposition to mandatory penalties against drug addicts. The elite-oriented, highly insulated, pragmatic state may have used black support for its own advantage. Like its technical approach to crime victims, the pragmatic state sought to manage and appease potential sources of conflict, be seen to respond to demands, and avoid discontent. State officials tried to capture the social group most likely to be impacted by this particular use of state force without fully responding to their demands. By doing so, officials gained strategic support for their managerial response to perceived threats and contagions. The centralized or "top-down" pragmatic state is one that is primarily driven by elites and insiders. In this context, elites tend to use public support and cooperate with groups in civil society when it works to their advantage, but they are also less willing to cede decision-making ground to civil society. This is a state of elites and experts, not of the people. The centralized pragmatic state routinely blocks access to decision-making, a move that tends to stunt rather than expand full democratic participation. State officials shrewdly calculate the degree to which they must respond to democratic demands without ceding ground.

Ongoing Managerial Response

Over time, the drug laws transformed New York's prison population, increasing the proportion of drug offenders in prison.[128] From the mid-1980s and well into the 1990s, New York arrested more drug offenders, intensifying its response to an ongoing and all-out effort to manage and contain drug-related crimes.[129] Since then, some of these efforts have had a significant impact on African Americans. Since the mid-1980s, the proportion of African American men incarcerated for drug offenses has doubled, increasing from 14 percent in 1987 to 22 percent by 2001.[130] In the mid-1980s, in the broader context of deindustrialization, a growing black underclass, and decaying urban life, Governor Mario Cuomo redoubled New York's efforts to contain drug-related crime. I think that the focus on drug crimes worked to absorb and defuse sources of social and racial conflict. Focusing on drugs and its associated crime linked more to disease and contagions than to moral depravity necessitated a more technical and managerial response rather than a social response.

In 1985, Cuomo added over 200 narcotics police officers, called in technological and analytical support with the creation of LEAN, New York's Law

Enforcement Assistance Network, and created a special narcotics commission, a "working council of the State's frontline narcotics officials" to research and develop new approaches to drug traffic.[131] By 1989, working with the state legislature, Cuomo called the drug problem the "single most ominous phenomenon of our time" and the most "severe threat to our future."[132] Posing the problem in such ominous terms necessitated a proportional state response. Cuomo raised the stakes. To maintain legitimacy, officials had to make the state useful. New York went after drug offenders in a big way. In 1987, drug offenders made up 21 percent of New York prison population.[133] Within a few years, by 1990, drug offenders made up nearly 34 percent of the state's prison population; by 2000, drug offenders dropped slightly but still made up 30 percent of the overall prison population, up from 11 percent in 1975.[134] From the late 1980s onward, officials have made the state useful.

Differentiated Penal Sanctioning: Expert Commissions Sort Risk

At the same time that the drug laws filled New York's prisons, crime control experts and key lawmakers urged the state to develop a more differentiated response to crime. Many of the expert and legislative commissions, task forces, and committees urged the state to revise the penal code in ways that would better distinguish between hard-core violent and repeat felony offenders and low-level nonviolent offenders. Rather than lock up every convicted offender, for example, the New York Temporary Commission on Revision of the Penal Law and Criminal Code, the New York State Commission on Management and Productivity in the Public Sector, the Bellacosa-Feinberg Committee, the Black and Puerto Rican Legislative Caucus, and the Citizens Committee on Parole and Criminal Justice, all called for differentiated penal sanctions—sanctions that included prison sentences for the most violent offenders and alternatives to incarceration for low-level offenders.[135]

In the early 1960s, Governor Rockefeller had appointed former Assemblyman Richard Bartlett, a Republican, to chair the New York Temporary Commission on Revision of the Penal Law and Criminal Code. Charged with updating the state's penal code, the Bartlett Commission sought to link criminal sentencing primarily with crime control rather than retribution. To do so, the commission recommended increased rather than decreased judicial discretion; they also recommended the elimination of all mandatory sentences and began to push for the elimination of the death penalty.[136] The commission developed a more differentiated sentencing scheme, which would provide longer terms for more serious offenders and shorter terms for low-level offenders. According to the Bartlett Commission, discretionary penal sanctions would match "the possible *dangers* to society from the particular criminal conduct."[137] By 1965, the state legislature and Governor Rockefeller adopted many of the Bartlett Commission's recommendations. By 1967, the commission advocated the expansion of alternatives to incarceration for low-level offenders and supported mandatory prison terms for the most serious class A felonies.[138]

Adapting some of the strategic plans developed by its expert and legislative commissions on crime control, by 1973, the state legislature and Governor Rockefeller established differentiated penal sanctions for different kinds of offenses. Alongside the notorious drug laws, the legislature and the governor created the "alternative definite sentence" in 1973. By revising the state's penal code, Article 70 on Sentences of Imprisonment, New York created an institutionalized mechanism that would direct low-level felony offenders away from long-term prison sentences and away from custodial sanctions. The "alternative definite sentence" enabled judges to sentence low-level felony offenders and class D, E, and some C felony offenders to fixed short prison terms of less than one year rather than subject them to the uncertain and longer indeterminate sentence if they thought a prison sentence was necessary in the first place.[139] Under this provision, judges retained the discretion to sentence low-level offenders to noncustodial sanctions or short prison terms. Despite the introduction of mandatory prison terms for class A felony drug offenses in 1973, the New York penal code did not include mandatory prison terms for many other felony offenses, especially for low-level felony offenders. For over thirty years, the New York state legislature and Governors Rockefeller, Carey, Cuomo, and George Pataki have all left the alternative definite sentence in place, enabling judges to divert low-level offenders away from custodial sanctions.

By contrast, in California, low-level offenders are subject to mandatory prison terms vis à vis "three strikes" legislation, which mandates prison terms for repeat felony offenders, including nonviolent and low-level felonies (e.g., petty theft). As noted, California maintains much higher parole revocation rates than many other states, including New York and Washington, sending parolees to prison for technical violations rather than new crimes. In Washington both low-level and more serious felony offenders are considered for noncustodial sanctions.

Within a few years, still concerned about rising crime, the New York State Assembly commissioned the New York State Commission on Management and Productivity in the Public Sector to develop more effective anticrime legislation. The Commission on Management and Productivity hired James Q. Wilson, one of the leading crime control experts in the nation at the time, along with Mark Harrison Moore and Ralph Gants to research and analyze the state's current anticrime legislation and propose alternatives. To prepare their 1978 report, "A Proposal for Concentrating the Resources of New York's Criminal Justice System on the 'Hard Core' of the Crime Problem," Wilson, Moore, and Gants consulted with a wide range of crime control experts and state criminal justice officials in the Corrections and Probations Departments. Experts and officials included Henry Donnelly and Floss Frucher of the Department of Correctional Services; Les Cohen and Michael O'Connor of the Probation Department; Captain Daley and Lieutenant Newborn of the Youth Division of the New York City Police Department; Henry Dogin, William Bonacum, and Mo Silver of the Division of Criminal Justice Services; Judges David Ross and Richard Bartlett; Michael Smith, Sherri Farber, Lucy Friedman, and Bob Davis; and the Vera Institute, an independent criminal justice research center.[140]

Based on these consultations, their own research, and the work of Joan Petersilia, then a RAND criminal justice policy expert, Wilson and his colleagues recommended that New York devote more state resources and criminal justice attention to repeat and violent offenders rather other types of offenders. According to their "diagnosis" of the state's crime problem, violent crime, particularly "violent attacks by strangers," generated the most fear and insecurity among New Yorkers.[141] The researchers identified robbery as the key crime that New York should focus on because it was not only a violent attack but often led to an escalation of violence. According to their report, "one quarter of murders" in New York involved robberies.[142] To respond to this highly specified and somewhat limited notion of the state's crime problem, the researchers proposed a "triage" system and differentiated penal sanctions. First, to sort out the most serious and violent offenders from others, New York would have to improve its ability to identify the violent and chronic offender. It would then have to further differentiate the kinds of penal sanctions to better fit the type of crime. As Moore, Wilson, and Gants explain:

A crucial part of our criminal justice system must be a "triage" system: we must be able to discern when we are dealing with serious offenses and chronic offenders and when we are not. Moreover, for the different kinds of offenses and offenders, we may want different kinds of processing and different kinds of dispositions. Specifically, we many want to focus much of our attention and concern on the relatively small number of cases that involve serious, unprovoked attacks on strangers committed by people who are chronic offenders. Such cases should be processed quickly, and in cases where guilt is established beyond a reasonable doubt, the dispositions should be designed to incapacitate and deter within the bounds of just deserts. This does not preclude the pursuing of rehabilitation objectives within this framework. However, we are not optimistic that we can rehabilitate any large portion of the violent offender group by means that are consistent with our standards of justice and humanity.[143]

To increase the state's ability to classify and sort out targeted offenders, repeat violent offenders in particular, the researchers recommended the creation of triage systems. To get the system up and running, New York would have to improve the effectiveness and efficiency of certain information processing criminal justice programs, such as the Major Offense Bureau, the Career Criminal Programs, and the Early Case Assessment program. Once identified, repeat and violent offenders would be subject to increased criminal justice supervision and incapacitation. The researchers also proposed a wider range of penal sanctions that would further differentiate the degrees of criminal justice supervision. The state could then match "convicted offenders who are differentially wicked, uncontrollable and irretrievable" with an effective degree of supervision or security.[144]

Although the researchers did not reject rehabilitative or treatment approaches to punishment, they emphasized incapacitation and custody as a more effective use of limited state resources. They did not want to use incapacitation or custody as a crude or blunt instrument in which all kinds of offenses are simply warehoused in the same kind of facility. Instead, they proposed the creation differentiated levels of incapacitation and criminal justice supervision. Finally, they proposed increasing the criminal justice supervision of "at-risk" populations—that is, in the commission's words, youthful offenders who "pose continuing risks to the society."[145]

The same year, in 1978, New York apparently followed the advice of Commission on Management and its crime control experts as the state set out to implement their policy recommendations. The legislature and Governor

Carey passed the Violent Felony Offender law and a tough Juvenile Offender law. The Violent Felony Offender law created specific penal sanctions for violent felonies and established the "persistent violent felony offender," subjecting repeat violent felony offenders to mandatory minimum prison terms.[146] Seeking to match the penal sanction with the purported dangerousness of the offender, judges could sentence offenders with a wide range of options. For example, under this provision, judges could impose a three- to four-year sentence for lower level felonies or a ten- to twenty-five-year sentence for more serious felonies, rather than the conventional and undifferentiated one year to life imprisonment for a wide range of offenders. This legislation increased the likelihood that repeat violent offenders would serve relatively long prison terms. In addition, the Juvenile Offender law increased the likelihood that youthful offenders convicted of murder and other serious offenses would be incapacitated in state facilities, either the Division of Youth or in some cases in the adult prisons.[147]

While state officials took a rather aggressive approach to violent offenders and youthful violent offenders, newly identified as a high-risk group from the perspective of criminal justice, New York lawmakers also pursued diversion for lower level, especially nonviolent offenders. By 1979, New York institution-alized noncustodial sanctions for lower level offenders. The state established the New York City Intensive Supervision Program, which provided an alternative to incarceration for offenders who could have been sentenced to prison.[148] The state has maintained this program, among many others, for over twenty years.

By the early 1980s, Governor Cuomo and the state legislature continued the previous efforts to sort out violent offenders from nonviolent offenders. To isolate violent offenders from nonviolent offenders, Cuomo redistributed the state's police resources. In his 1983 Annual Message, he explained how the state sought to "make the most effective use of the police resources" and would therefore take redundant police officers out of low-crime areas and reassign them to "fight against serious, violent, and organized crime."[149] Embedded in the context of New York's pragmatic and technical approach to governance, Cuomo expanded the state's crime laboratory technology and resources. He explained his rationale: "Successful prosecution of dangerous criminals often depend upon the expert analysis of physical evidence by forensic scientists."[150]

While New York continued to pursue violent offenders, Cuomo picked up on early commissions' recommendations for diversion for low-level offenders. Cuomo explained his support and rationale for alternatives to incarceration:

Clearly, not everyone who breaks a law belongs in jail. At the same that we are establishing more specific sentencing procedures, we must also expand the use of alternatives to jail, especially for nonviolent crimes and first-time youthful offenders. Substantial fines, meaningful restitution and community service as a condition of probation must be utilized to a greater degree. The combined resources of the Divisions of Probation and Parole will be directed to finding and implementing alternatives to incarceration in appropriate case.[151]

To carry out these goals, Cuomo created the Division of Correctional Alternatives. From the early 1980s, the division increased community-based alternatives to incarceration in the middle of the state's prison boom. Collaborating with civil society organizations and community services providers, the Division of Correctional Alternatives established a wide range of locally run programs and relied on the New York City Legal Action Center for research and program development. Throughout the 1980s, New York established a number of new programs, including Project Greenhope in 1983, the Education and Assistance Staten Island Treatment Alternatives to Street Crime Program in 1985, the New York City Fortune Society in 1985, the King County Juvenile Offender Program in 1986, the Queens Treatment Alternatives to Street Crime in 1986, the Osborne Treatment Services El Rio in 1988, and the NYC Center for Alternative Sentencing and Employment Services in 1989.[152] These programs and many others are still operating today.

The Back End: Managerial Parole Practices

In 1985, the New York State Division of Parole adopted the state's managerial approach to crime control and penal sanctions. The division developed what they referred to as a "differentiated supervision" approach to parole supervision. The Division of Parole created a parole policy that would distinguish between different kinds of offenders and respond differently according to the degree of risk posed by each type. Rather than respond to parolees as individuals with individualized needs or as morally corrupt wrongdoers in need of moral guidance, the division responded to parolees as a type of risk or what Feeley and Simon refer to as an aggregate, as part of a population to be managed rather than reformed. The Division of Parole defined "risk" in terms of the probability that offenders will commit new crimes and end up back in prison. To manage this risk, the division decided to concentrate its resources and intensify its supervision of "high-risk" parolees. They targeted newly released inmates because this group as an aggregate is the most likely to commit new crimes. The division explains the "differentiated supervision" concept:

> The concept targets resources on parolees with the highest levels of
> need for surveillance and social services in an attempt to meet the
> agency's goals. Allocation of these resources is based on a model of
> risk management under which newly released parolees are placed on
> Intensive supervision which requires extensive contact standards.
> After 12 months, most parolees are moved to Regular supervision
> where their potential threat to the community and level of
> service needs have been reduced.[153]

By adopting a managerial approach to parole, the Division of Parole set specific goals for itself, namely, to keep new parolees out of prison to "enhance public safety and protection."[154] As Anthony Bottoms explains, a managerial approach to crime control often involves the specification of departmental goals and the development of key indicators that measure the department's efficiency and effectiveness.[155] The New York Division of Parole created an indicator of success that would provide tangible results and accountability. The rate of parolees' return to prison could provide concrete a measurement and visible statistics to assess the division's efficacy. Rather than measure their own success by the ex-offenders' integration back into society—a goal that could depend too much on the parolees' ability to find a job and stay employed—the division measured their own success by the number of parolees returned to prison. To a results-oriented agency, concepts such as rehabilitation or reintegration are too elusive and ill defined to measure in a concrete way, and these terms depend too much on the ex-offenders themselves.

By contrast, in Washington, the Department of Corrections creates a transition plan for soon to be released and newly released inmates, incorporating inmates' family, community volunteers (Neighborhood Readiness Team), service providers, and job training in a self-described effort to ease reentry and reintegration, decrease recidivism, and increase public safety.[156]

As part of New York's calculating machine of governance, the Division of Parole created an indicator that it could control to a certain extent. Consider, for example, that New York maintains relatively low rates of parolee returns to prison. In the 1999–2000 fiscal year, for example, New York returned

18 percent of parolees to prison.[157] In 2001–2002, the state returned 17 percent of parolees to prison, less than a third the rate of California, which returned nearly 65 percent to prison.[158] New York's low rate of parolee return indicates the division's apparent success in keeping parolees out of prison. More empirical research is needed to tease out the extent to which this success indicates that parolees themselves simply stay out of trouble and the extent to which it indicates that the Division of Parole itself is simply unwilling to send parole violators back to prison. We should note that New York's approach to parolees and possible parole violators is markedly different than that of California. As noted earlier, California locks up parole violators at extraordinary high rates. Unlike New York's calculated use of state repression, California uses parole violators, easy targets, to demonstrate its crime control prowess. New York, by contrast, actively seeks to keep parolees out of prison. With this strategy, the division itself not only appears successful but also prevents the unnecessary inflation of the prison population. The Division of Parole helps the state manage the overall scale of the prison population by keeping low-level parole violators out of prison.

At the same time, the Division of Parole actively seeks to manage and control the types of offenders it will release and take under its supervision in the first place. Working with the context of New York's selective incarceration regime, the Division of Parole tends to release nonviolent offenders at much higher rates than violent offenders. For example, in the 1999–2000 fiscal year, the most recent figures available, the division released 8,734 inmates from state prisons, the majority of which were nonviolent offenders. Of those released, 87 percent had not used a weapon during their crime, nor had they used force.[159] By contrast, 13 percent of those released had used a weapon and 12 percent had used forced during their crimes.[160] The Division of Parole was also much more likely to release first-time prison inmates rather than those who had served prior terms. For example, of those released, 58 percent had not served a prior term, whereas only 14 percent of those released had served two or more prison terms.[161] Like the criminal sentencing phase, the Division of Parole sorts high and low risks and responds with differentiated penal practices. In the context of parole, the state is more likely to release nonviolent offenders and prolong the incapacitation of violent offenders.

In recent years, under Governor Pataki, state officials have institutionalized this practice with the creation of the Presumptive Release Initiative. The Department of Corrections can now release nonviolent offenders on their own and bypass the parole board.[162] We should note here that offenders with no history of violence are the only ones eligible for the presumptive release program. With this new policy, the Department of Corrections has gained more systematic control over the size of the prison population. In other words, the department can manage the overall size of the prison population by regulating the release of an entire pool of offenders. It can decrease the prison population by releasing hundreds of inmates at a time. By the end of the 2004 fiscal year, the Department of Corrections released 1,000 inmates under this program alone.[163]

Along similar lines, in 2003, Governor Pataki established the Governor's Merit Time Credit for A-1 drug offenders. The Merit Time Credit program allows nonviolent drug offenders who are serving at least a fifteen-year sentence to substantially reduce their prison terms.[164] New York released fifty-seven drug offenders who on average had reduced their prison terms by thirty-seven months or just over three years.[165] With this policy initiative, Governor Pataki and the Department of Corrections have created a back-end corrective device for the stiff drug laws. By reducing the length of prison terms from inside the prison, the Department of Corrections has gained some leverage over the system's inputs, the size of prison admissions.

Recent Developments: Antidemocratic Tendencies and a Punitive Turn

Like California and Washington, New York's political and penal regimes are much more complicated and less uniform than the ideal types they approximate. All of the empirical cases have mixed elements and inherent tensions that have not been fully resolved. In New York, the state's pragmatism has been in tension with its antidemocratic tendencies ever since the early twentieth century. New York's political power is highly centralized and insulated from public participation. With political authority concentrated in the executive branch and low civic engagement, New York is to a certain degree under-democratized. The state is even under court order to improve voter participation. The state's pragmatic traditions have kept actors oriented toward the public welfare, trying to solve emergent social problems with expert knowledge and doing so with efficiency and rationality. However, elites have also been mired in their own internal power dynamics, cut off from public debate, and absorbed by cronyism and patronage politics. Under this kind of regime, public safety and security become key organizing features of governance.

Public safety is the most basic duty of state governance and a public good that even the most limited state must provide. According to Governor Pataki: the "government's most important responsibility [is] ensuring the safety and security of its people."[166] Describing New York's historic crime drop, he explained how the state had "saved" its people: "more than 86,000 families saved from being torn apart by a murder, rape or vicious assault."[167] As many commentators have noted, public safety and security also provide state actors with powerful cultural resources to pacify the public. In this context, penal policies are more likely to take a punitive and less managerial turn.

During Governor Pataki's administration (1994–2005), we can see elements of both kinds of political and penal regimes: pragmatic and managerial, antidemocratic and punitive.

In the aftermath of the World Trade Center bombing in 1993, the bloody Long Island Railroad (LIRR) shooting, and at the time what seemed like the state's persistent high crime rate (New York ranked second in the nation in 1992), state lawmaker George Pataki ran his gubernatorial campaign on public safety and security. Like many other politicians at the time, he exploited the volatile and emotional aspects of criminal victimization, tapping into an emerging moral calculus that demanded harsh penal sanctions to make up for victims' pain and suffering. In his televised campaign commercials, for example, he relied on the "tearful appeal" of the mother of one of the LIRR shooting victims to press his case for more punitive sanctions.[168] Likewise, during his quest to return the death penalty to New York, Governor Pataki again called on the parents of murdered children to testify in favor of more punitive crime policies. Devorah Halberstam, the mother of a teenage murder victim, linked her own suffering and pain with the need for justice: "I'm a mother who's suffering every day. I have children at home who are suffering all the time for the loss of their brother. No. 1, there has to be justice."[169] Pataki then connected the family members' needs as justification for the death penalty. He explained, "What demeans a society is when Devorah and David Halberstam can't get justice for their son who was killed by a terrorist because we don't have the death penalty in this state."[170] In this configuration, justice serves crime victims' needs. In 1995, Pataki pushed for and won legislation that reinstated in the death penalty in New York, which had been abolished for most crimes since 1965 under Governor Rockefeller. Although the return of the death penalty was perceived to be a major victory for Pataki and his punitive approach to crime control, the sanction did not last long, and none of the seven people sanctioned under the law have been executed. By 2004, New York's highest court proclaimed the penalty unconstitutional. By 2005, the New York State Assembly's Codes Committee defeated reinstatement, putting an end to the death penalty.

Despite Pataki's mobilization of the pain and suffering of crime victims and appeals to public insecurity, his administration should not be confused with a populist regime. Quite the contrary. Recall from the case of California that a populist regime depends on an open political system in which political power is decentralized and accessible to ordinary people. In New York, the executive branch monopolizes much of the political power and does so through its control of the budget, executive orders, appointments, agenda setting, and unlimited terms. This is not a case of politicians bending to or taking advantage of a clamoring punitive public. Pataki used the budget process to pass major crime control reform, using his leverage against the legislature, and bypassed public input. Unlike the regular legislative process, the budget process is not open to public debate or public input; there are no requirements for public hearings or testimony. The budget process is not subject to the same kind of public scrutiny as the legislative process. In 1996, Pataki used the budget process to press a harsher approach to crime control, increasing reliance on confinement by lengthening prison terms for first-time violent felons and eliminating their right to parole.[171]

Opposed to the reforms and the undemocratic process, State Assembly member Catherine Abate lamented: "Doesn't the public have the right to now what the impacts are? Where is the truth in budgeting?"[172] Similarly, in 1995, the New York Times criticized the state's closed budgetary-legislative process, a process that led to the increase in penal sanctions. Describing Governor Pataki and the legislature's agreement on sentencing reform as "secret deals hurriedly patched together to end the budget impasse," the editorial suggested the reform was undemocratic: "It is simply outrageous that the most significant change in the state's sentencing laws in two decades was fashioned without public scrutiny or debate under time pressures imposed by the need to agree on a budget."[173]

In addition to the insular and clubby budget process, Pataki issued a series of executive orders that increased reliance on confinement, and he did so without public debate. In 1995, he signed an executive order prohibiting sex offenders from certain probation programs, stating: "I will not gamble with the safety of the public. People who commit felony sex crimes must serve their time in prison."[174] In 1998, he signed "Jenna's law," ending parole for first-time violent offenders. He had already signed an executive order barring violent felons from work release,[175] curtailing one of the state's institutional mechanisms that regulate the size of the prison population. Further infringing on the rights and liberties of criminal offenders, Pataki introduced legislation mandating HIV testing for all crime suspects. By doing so, the state essentially depressed offenders' right to privacy, justifying this imposition in the name of crime victims, "so victims do not suffer needlessly."[176] In 2005, Pataki issued another executive order seeking to expand the collection of DNA to a wide range of offenders, including those on probation, parole, temporary release, and those who plea bargained.[177] The expansion of the DNA database greatly increased the state's capacity to regulate the population in the name of public safety and security.

Through a set of questionable democratic practices, the Pataki administration introduced a rougher and more punitive approach to crime control.

Steely Pragmatism and the Longevity of New York's Managerial Penal Regime

At the same time, Pataki's administration maintained aspects of both pragmatic governance and a managerial approach to crime control. By 2000, New York's prison population actually began to decline, one of the few states to experience such a dramatic downward turn. Continuing the state's long-term trend toward bifurcated penal sanctions (that is, longer prison terms for violent offenders and shorter terms, early release, or diversion for nonviolent offenders), Pataki called his contribution to this trend "right-sizing," "common sense," and "smart criminal justice policies." According to the New York State Department of Corrections Prison Commissioner Glenn S. Goord, Pataki's right-sizing policy increased the early release of nonviolent offenders from prison, releasing over 50,000 of them since 1995.[178] As already noted, Governor Pataki also introduced Merit Time for nonviolent drug offenders, increasing their early release from prison. With a declining prison population, the Department of Corrections recently proposed a major takedown plan to consolidate inmates in prison facilities both by vacating double bunks and closing a few facilities.[179]

Perhaps what is most remarkable about the mixed legacy of the Pataki administration was his effort to reform the Rockefeller drug laws. From the beginning of his term, he sought to weaken the harshest aspects of the laws, reducing the severe sanctions and channeling nonviolent offenders away from prison. In the mid-1990s, his reform efforts were characterized

by commentators as "decidedly out of line with the current Republican thinking in the rest of the country. While New Yorkers appear to like the idea of
emptying prisons of nonthreatening criminals, and perhaps slowing the costly
business of prison construction, the newly triumphant conservatives elsewhere
are moving in the other direction."[180] In 2004, after a protracted struggle
between the governor and state legislature, Pataki signed a major reform bill,
restructuring the drug laws for the first time since they were passed in 1973.
The drug reform effectively reduced penal sanctions for almost all drug
offenses. It replaced the indeterminate sentences of fifteen to twenty-five
years to life for the most serious offense, with less severe determinate sentences of eight to twenty years; increased the possession weights; allowed for
resentencing to lesser sanctions; and increased drug offenders' eligibility for
merit time and early release.[181] In a discourse that contrasts sharply with his
appeals to the death penalty and his law and order rhetoric, Pataki acknowledged the humanity and suffering of criminal offenders sanctioned under the
drug laws. In signing the legislation, he stated: "Hundreds of nonviolent
offenders serving unduly long sentences will have an opportunity to be imme-
diately reunited with their families"; this new law "provides opportunities for
relief for all nonviolent offenders sentenced under the previous law"; and "I am
proud that together, we've enacted meaningful reform that is both just and
balanced."[182] Here the governor connects justice with offenders' liberty, relief,
and release from prison. At the same time, this shift away from reliance on
imprisonment for drug offenders will keep prison costs down, a central tenet
of the state's managerial approach to crime control. At present, state officials
are again considering a major reform to the Rockefeller drug laws to decrease
their severity.

Until his resignation in 2008, Governor Eliot Spitzer seemed to be
continuing the state's pragmatic tradition and managerial approach to crime.
Campaigning as a reform candidate, Spitzer filled his public speeches with
appeals to pragmatism and desire to overcome some of the internal power
struggles endemic to the state run by elites. In his Inaugural Address, for
example, he explained: "We chose pragmatism and ethics over partisan politics
and disfunction [sic], and we demanded an end to gridlock."[183] He continued to
map out his rationality of governance, quoted here at some length:

> We must embrace a progressive vision of government once more—a
> vision that upholds the values of individuality and community; of
> entrepreneurship and opportunity; of responsibility and fairness. No

one any longer believes in government as a heavy hand that can cure
all our ills, but rather we see it as a lean and responsive force that can
make possible the pursuit of prosperity and opportunity for all—by
softening life's blows, leveling its playing field and making possible
the pursuit of happiness that is our god given right. . . . We will
succeed not because we point fingers or refuse to budge, but because
we compromise enough to find principled consensus, and because
we listen enough to find wise solutions.[184]

Here Spitzer revisits many of the themes central to New York governance that
were especially visible during the Rockefeller administration, already discussed
at some length. Spitzer calls for a government that is "lean and responsive"—
one that must take action to maintain its legitimacy. A pragmatic state demon-
strates its worthiness of public support through its utility, its ability to respond
to and solve emergent social problems, soften life's blows, and level its playing
field. He also emphasizes the government's responsibility to compromise and
find solutions to complex problems through consensus rather than asserting
ideological or partisan positions. Of course, Spitzer's invocation of pragmatism
may just be political rhetoric without material substance. We should always
note that discourse, the expression of meaning, is a central cultural resource
out of which actors make sense of their world and orient their actions. Within
three months of taking office, Spitzer issued Executive Order no. 10 to establish a state Commission on Sentencing Reform. The commission is expected
to review the state's sentencing structure, propose proportionate sanctions, and
find cost-effective ways to manage the criminal justice system, "to make the
most of efficient use of the correctional system and community resources."[185]
In other words, the commission is charged with finding and imposing a
certain degree of rationality on the state's criminal justice system. In the
pragmatic tradition of the state, the commission itself is made up of state elites
and professional experts, including but not limited to the commissioner of
the Department of Correctional Services, the chair of the Board of Parole, the
commissioner of the Division of Criminal Justice Services, the chair of
the Crime Victims Board, state legislators, and a judge. Unlike the case of
Washington's Sentencing Guidelines Commission, New York's Commission
on Sentencing Reform has no citizen representatives. Although more research
is needed to assess the former Spitzer administration, particularly its relationship with the state legislature and its approach to crime control, at this point
in time, we can clearly see the resiliency of pragmatism.

Conclusion

Together, for over thirty years, the New York state legislature; Governors Rocke-feller, Carey, Cuomo, and Pataki; the Department of Corrections; the Division of Parole; and a slew of crime control experts have developed a managerial res-ponse to crime and penal sanctioning. State officials have created a system to identify, classify, and sort perceived risks to public security and allocated re-sources accordingly: prison for violent and drug offenders, diversion for others. By rationalizing crime, defusing its emotional tenor in favor of a more epi-demiological view, state officials portrayed crime as a contagion that could be contained. As such, crime and its control demanded a technical rather than moral response, favoring a differentiated rather than indiscriminate use of state force (imprisonment). The view of drugs and its associated crimes may have also defused sources of urban and racial conflict because it recast social conflict in a more palatable way, universalizing drugs as a public health problem rather than the moral failings of particular individuals.

Governed by pragmatism, state officials economized penal sanctioning, strategically deploying force against calculated risks, justified in the name of public health. And they did so without much protest. New York's highly centralized governing apparatus concentrates political power among elites and depresses citizen participation; as a consequence, state officials have tended to prioritize public security, quarantining contagions at the expense of individual freedom and autonomy. The state's antidemocratic tendencies make it vulnerable to periods of increased punitiveness and increased reliance on confinement and other forms of state coercion, creating a restrictive form of citizenship in the name of the public good.

6

Democratic Governance, Social Trust, and Penal Order

The Democratic Process Shapes Penal Regime Variation

In the late 1960s and early 1970s, Americans changed the way they punish criminal offenders. By doing so, they changed the basic governing relationship between the state and citizens, creating new conditions of citizenship and new conditions of inclusion and exclusion. Since the mid-1970s, American penal policies have effectively excluded thousands of offenders from full economic, social, and political participation in the United States, often with dire consequences for the individuals, their families, and communities.[1] African Americans along with other socially and economically marginalized groups such as the poor and undereducated have been especially hard hit by these policies. Policy makers and the public are just beginning to feel the blowback of mass imprisonment as the problems of prisoner reentry and strained state budgets have forced many state governments and penal reformers to rethink the character and effectiveness of their crime control policies. This book has been motivated by a desire to understand this major transformation in American penal policy.

Perhaps more important, this book has been motivated by a desire to understand and explain a relatively understudied facet of U.S. penal policy: subnational variation, the chronic long-term differences we see across the states. American penal sanctioning is much more varied, complex, fragmented and localized than discussions of the national trend allow. American states punish differently from one another and do so in ways that have not been fully documented or fully explained. As many commentators have noted, in the face of high crime, social upheaval, and lost confidence in government, many states tried to revive their flagging political authority and re-create social solidarity through repressive means. Yet what is less clear is why and how many American states did *not* do so. Some even began a long-term push toward de-escalation and reintegration, policies and practices that are still viable today. By paying attention to these differences, particularly countertrends, this book may provide some lessons for contemporary policy makers and penal reformers seeking to challenge mass imprisonment. By paying attention to these differences, this book opens up a new and potentially useful way to think about and explain American punishment.

To explain American penal regime variation, this study examined the political process and collective action, surprisingly understudied factors in the literature. I argued that the way Americans engage in the democratic process significantly shapes the way they punish offenders. The way ordinary people get involved in politics—the way they make demands and how and why they provide emotional and cultural support to state action—all of these factors influence and shape the nature and character of penal sanctioning against others. By focusing on the democratic process, this book highlights how people self-govern and how they mobilize collectively do so. It looks at how ordinary people engage in public life and how this participation can expand and deepen social ties and norms of reciprocity, factors that can moderate or exacerbate the repressive powers of the state. At the same time, the democratic process shows, sometimes very clearly, how certain social groups come to dominate other groups, integrating and excluding others through public policies. Penal sanctioning provides a dramatic staging for this collective process of social inclusion and exclusion.

This study also examined how the organization of the state itself, the underlying structures of power and authority, shapes the nature and meaning of political conflict in a particular place. Here each state's configurations of power and public access (e.g., initiative process, town hall meetings, expert commissions) created certain unavoidable and legitimate channels of action while blocking others. In addition, each state's initial policy response to rising crime and other perceived problems of order in the late 1960s and early 1970s created resilient path dependencies, policy legacies that continue to shape the substance and trajectory of each state's crime control measures today. Past decisions created unavoidable policy paths.

Taken together, collective agency and political structures provide the under-lying texture of politics. They shape broader debates about the nature of state responsibility and debates about the provision of public goods versus the pursuit of private self-interest. They enable and constrain the possibilities of action. They give meaning to the ways political actors understand and take action against major policy issues, such as internal order and security, public safety, and crime control. Even in a postmodern society infused by global trends, democratic traditions are still closely linked to place and locality, inscribing their differences onto contemporary politics. These varying democratic processes shape the na-ture of political conflict differently place to place with varying effects on subna-tional penal regimes. Table 6.1 illustrates the key analytical features of the democratic process as conceptualized here. Different kinds of collective agency combined with varying patterns of decentralization create specific patterns of democratic governance: deliberative democracy; polarized populism; elite prag-matism; and corporatism (not discussed in the case studies).

Penal sanctioning is fundamentally linked to the ways states exercise power and maintain legitimacy.[2] Penal sanctioning provides the means and symbolic resources to resolve and also perpetuate conflict over social ordering. As a form of social classification, it is also tied to the ways democratic states establish conditions of citizenship and collective identity in complex political communities. Penal sanctioning is shaped by political struggles over the con-ditions of citizenship, the legitimacy and authority of the state, and the nature of social relations in civil society, particularly the level of social trust and reciprocity across diverse social groups. Understanding the democratic process is essential to our understanding of penal sanctioning because they tend to be mutually constitutive.

TABLE 6.1. Democratic Governance by Decentralization and Civic Engagement

Civic Engagement	Decentralization	
	High	Low
High	Deliberative democracy	Corporatism*
Low	Polarized populism	Elite pragmatism

* This type is a theoretical construct that was not examined in the case studies. Minnesota represents this type with a high degree of civic engagement, high social trust, and relatively high degree of centralization.

Findings from the Case Studies

To explain penal regime variation, the initial change in penal sanctioning in the late 1960s and early 1970s, and the chronic long-term differences across the American states, I investigated and systematically compared three case studies spatially and temporally, using many of the analytical strategies available to comparative and historical research. California, Washington, and New York were selected because the democratic process works differently in these places but in ways that is representative of broader American traditions rooted in populism, deliberation, and pragmatism. The small number of cases allowed for a close reading of the policy-making process in three different places over a relatively long period of time, highlighting the long-term and ongoing causal processes of democratic governance on crime control, and highlighting the patterns of similarity and difference across the cases. The small number of cases increased the familiarity with the detail and nuance of each case study, enabling me to go back and forth between theory and data. This interactive process forced to me to rethink some of my initial observations about the primary role of state elites and devote considerable more attention to collective agency, specifically civic engagement and social capital. The limitations of this approach and its applicability are discussed shortly.

The findings suggest that the character and degree of democratization significantly shaped the character and intensity of penal sanctioning but in unexpected and counterintuitive ways. High levels of civic engagement and social trust can constrain the intensity of penal sanctioning, enabling inclusionary but normalizing conditions of citizenship. Underdemocratized polities with lower levels of social capital can amplify state coercion, creating restrictive and exclusionary conditions of citizenship, often in the name of the public good. The character of collective agency played a significant role in shaping the public debate and policy development. It was also one of the key differences between California and Washington, two open polities with direct citizen participation and histories of leniency toward criminal offenders. But California's weakened ties between civil society and the state, its depressed and acrimonious civic engagement, helped foster the state's more retributive approach to crime control, undoing much of the state's progressive past.

CALIFORNIA: POLARIZED POPULISM AND RETRIBUTION. Specifically, in California, neopopulist politics dominate the character of political debate and shape the development of public policies. Here we see a technically open polity with highly decentralized political power and a tradition of successful popular movements. Yet this kind of democratic process has been shaped by and constitutive of a high degree of social polarization and contentious politics. In this kind of uncompromising, winner-take-all environment, political actors tend to downplay mutual obligation and social trust. In this case, neopopulism supported a discourse on crime control and criminality that viewed crime as a result of moral depravity, individual failing, and social indecency. Criminals were perceived to be free loaders, getting something for nothing, moral failures, and linked to popular anxiety about declining moral cohesion and increasing diversity.[3] In response, citizens supported and often demanded that state officials pursue a more retributive penal regime. In this zero-sum political environment, the crime victims' movement was also quite successful. By dramatizing the pain and suffering of victims (and by extension the general public), activists helped change the moral calculus of justice, using victimization as justification for increased sanctions. Over time, neopopulism has encouraged and may have come to depend on the repressive powers of the state to resolve social conflict as it has created more exclusionary conditions of citizenship.

WASHINGTON: DELIBERATIVE DEMOCRACY, PARSIMONY, AND DE-ESCALATION. By contrast, in the state of Washington, more deliberative politics shaped the character and trajectory of public debate and public policy. Here decentralized political power has been complemented by intensive civic engagement, creating a highly democratized polity that prioritizes compromise and self-governance. In this environment, political actors tended to emphasize mutual obligation, norms of reciprocity, and public welfare. This deliberative democracy tended to support a crime control discourse based on the social causes of crime and the result of routine activities in affluent societies. Criminals were considered part of the political community, they were just failed members who needed another chance and whose liberty actually mattered in the calculus of justice. First-time offenders were given special consideration and accommodation. State officials, special interest groups, citizens, and social movement groups to some degree were all reluctant to impose the repressive powers of the state on others, extending a sense of social solidarity to criminal offenders. In this parsimonious penal regime, officials and activists sought to limit the intensity of penal sanctioning, using the least repressive options whenever possible. At times, state officials even pursued de-escalation, imposing institutional constraints on the state's capacity to punish.

However, Washington's apparent leniency toward offenders has been counterbalanced by an insidious form of state power: disciplinary power. While Washington has consistently diverted offenders away from prison, it has pushed them toward noncustodial sanctions based on communal labor. The state's legacy of cooperatives and self-governance provided the cultural and institutional support necessary to pursue intensive work release programs, work camps, and community service. In this penal regime, the discipline of labor has been imposed in part through civil society as volunteer groups and other community service organizations take on the role of correctionalism, resocializing offenders for reentry and reintegration. Together, Washington's deliberative democracy restrains state coercion, enabling more inclusionary but normalizing conditions of citizenship.

NEW YORK: ELITE PRAGMATISM AND MANAGERIALISM. In New York, the democratic process has been informed by a mix of pragmatism and elitism, a tension between providing for the public good and private self-interest. In this insular and underdemocratized polity, political power is highly centralized and to a certain degree blocked from public access and participation. Here a concentrated group of state officials—particularly the governor, technocrats, and other policy experts—dominate the business of governing, discouraging public input. When pragmatism dominates, we see generous public welfare, the provision of public goods, but when the state's more elitist tendencies emerge, we see a government mired in private power struggles with little regard to public welfare. In this bureaucratized policy environment, New York has been spared the brunt of popular anticrime movements with their demands for harsh justice, as evidenced in California. By contrast, New York state officials developed a more managerial approach to crime control, defusing some of the more emotional and moral undertones of penal policy. However, at the same time, state officials have not pursued parsimonious penal policies (as the Rockefeller drug laws surely attest), nor have they have they protected individual liberty and autonomy from the encroachment of state power.

Instead, state officials mobilized penal sanctioning against specific kinds of offenders in the name of the public good. Here the discourse on crime was dominated by epidemiological terms, especially in the critical period of the late 1960s and early 1970s. Crime was perceived to be a major threat to public health, a contagion to be quarantined. It is interesting to note that criminals were not necessarily vilified but perceived more as a health risk to the larger

TABLE 6.2. Case Study by Democratic Process and Penal Regime

Case	Democratic Process	Penal Regime
California	Polarized populism	Retributive
Washington	Deliberative democracy	De-escalation
New York	Elite pragmatism	Managerial

community. State officials developed a triage approach to penal sanctioning, sorting and classifying the most serious perceived risks and allocating precious state resources accordingly. New York's managerial regime sought to regulate and minimize collective risk rather than expose, reform, or punish the supposed moral depravity of individual criminal offenders. It tried to accomplish these tasks in the most cost-efficient way possible. For over thirty years, New York sorted violent and drug offenders into prison and diverted most others away. This managerial approach supported differentiated and moderate imprisonment rates, a targeted use of state power, referred to by state officials as "smart" criminal justice policies. This apparently reasonable and pragmatic approach to crime with its strategic use of state power nevertheless tended to suppress individual autonomy and liberty in favor of the perceived public good, creating restrictive conditions of citizenship. Table 6.2 illustrates the case studies by varying democratic processes and their associated penal regimes: polarized populism and retribution; deliberative democracy and de-escalation; pragmatism and managerialism.

Discussion and Implications

What can readers take away from this study? How does it advance, challenge, or complement sociological and criminological thinking about punishment in America? How is it relevant to policy makers or penal reformers? Where do we go from here?

I want to draw attention to several key points raised by this study, clarify its relationship to existing accounts, introduce a few policy notes, and discuss its applicability to other states and policy areas. The discussion is organized around the following claims and concerns:

1. Civic engagement as a definitive factor in penal sanctioning;
2. Social trust underpins the process of inclusion and exclusion;

3. Importance of place, locality, and context in a globalizing social world;
4. Role of black incorporation in mitigating state coercion;
5. Resiliency of institutions and path dependencies in shaping public policies;
6. Public policy implications: legitimacy gaps; and
7. Applicability.

Civic Engagement and Social Trust

First, the democratic process is vital to understanding American punishment. Civic engagement—how ordinary people get involved in politics—is perhaps the definitive factor in determining the degree to which states infringe on the rights and freedoms of others.

Most recent scholarship on crime and punishment has tended to view the public as an undifferentiated mass and uniform source of vengeance, unnecessarily reducing the complexities of public opinion and public participation. This book challenges conventional arguments about the inherent link between punitiveness and democratization. James Whitman, for example, argues that democratization—public participation in politics—partially accounts for the relative harshness in American penal sanctioning, especially compared to European counterparts, such as France and Germany. Likewise, Joachim Savelsberg argues that the openness of the American political system, the public's participation in policy making, helps account for high rates of imprisonment in the United States. Others such as Katherine Beckett, for example, argue that electoral politics, especially the politicization of crime in electoral politics, partially explains increased punitiveness in crime control as politicians ratchet up penalties to both meet and shape public demand and public voting. My work suggests that these findings may only be true in specific contexts under specific historical conditions rather than generalized American patterns.

Moreover, the findings point to the opposite pattern: democratization can constrain rather than expand the repressive powers of the states. Depressed democratization can intensify state coercion rather than restrain it. Here I take cues from Robert Putnam by connecting civic engagement with social trust. Intensive and deliberative civic engagement can reflect but also facilitate social trust. Social trust indicates a social group's ability and capacity to recognize and acknowledge others and treat them with mutual respect, even those who are different. Social trust indicates group members' sense of mutual obligation toward others and their norms of reciprocity. Higher levels of social trust can facilitate processes of social inclusion, making polity members less willing to inflict state coercion against others. Here we see an inclusive political community that even incorporates criminal offenders into group membership. By contrast, social polarization and lower levels of social trust can foster processes of social exclusion, enabling majoritarian social groups to dominate others, making them more likely to call on state coercion to settle problems of order and group conflict.

The findings also show that the democratic process is not a single unitary or coherent development. Democratization not only varies across the American states, it is dependent on certain institutional configurations and practices of social mobilization. This book suggests that prior discussions about democracy and punishment have been partial and underdeveloped.

Consider, for example, in the political contexts in which voter participation and other complex forms of civic engagement were relatively weak, penal regimes tended to be more coercive (e.g., California and New York). By contrast, in Washington where voter participation and complex forms of civic engagement were relatively high, the penal regime tended to be less repressive. Specifically, in Washington, a highly democratized polity that prioritized deliberation, discussion, compromise, and mutual obligation supported the principle of parsimony. Public dialogue, debate, negotiation, and engagement with different points of view provided essential support for less coercive public policies. In California, an open polity with surprisingly low rates of civic engagement, contentious collective agency, and social polarization tended to support retributive and more punitive penal sanctioning. In New York, the elitist and pragmatic tendencies tended to depress democratization yet support more strategic forms of coercion, repressive for certain risks, benign for others.

We should note here that state centralization or bureaucratization is often put forward as a more favorable approach to crime control as state elites and experts can control policy formation, downplaying or ignoring the public's emotional attachments and irrational impulses, leading to more rational, technical responses. State centralization in New York certainly supported a managerial penal regime, but it also intensified state repression against certain classified risk categories (entire social groups) and depressed individual liberty. Moreover, this regime was produced, for the most part, through an antidemocratic process, raising questions about its long-term legitimacy and the authority of the state.

Importance of Place

The case studies have emphasized the importance of place, locality, and context. Even in an era of globalization and associated social change, social actors continue to understand their world with the raw materials available to them in a particular place. People take action with the cultural resources available to them in their immediate environment. This account lends further empirical weight to Stuart Scheingold's early work on local politics and crime control, and it lends support to the innovative work of Evi Girling, Ian Loader, and Richard Sparks on the localized experience of crime and globalization.

In the case studies, we can see how the historical development of the democratic process varied state by state, creating different kinds of democratic traditions across the US which continue to inform contemporary politics. The case studies also show how place, locality, and context significantly shaped the discourse on crime control and penal sanctioning and did so differently in different places. The meaning of crime, justice, and the role of penal sanctioning took on radically different meanings with radically different effects from place to place. In California, moral indecency and individual responsibility dominated the discourse on crime, in Washington it was failed socialization, and in New York it was threats to public health. These varied conceptualizations of the crime problem supported different but associated kinds of penal sanctioning so that in California we see the coupling of moral outrage and retribution, in Washington public empathy and parsimony, and in New York concerns about collective risk and managerialism.

By focusing on subnational variation, this book reminds readers that broad social transformation is made up and made meaningful by particular experiences of change, experiences that are grounded in specific places and localities. If we are to make sense of general trends in American punishment, we need to investigate the particular and the local. This book focused on the subnational level, but more could be done to examine how municipal or county-level politics influence and shape crime control policy. Lisa Miller's new book, *The Perils of Federalism*, nicely illustrates how the policy debate on crime control loses its texture, nuance, and complexity moving from city politics to the state legislature to the federal government.

Racial Politics: Black Incorporation

What about race? If not for the legacy of racism, the backlash against civil rights, and persistent racial inequalities, how else can we account for American punitiveness? This book modifies this account on two levels. First, as noted, punitiveness has not been a uniform, totalizing, or necessary response to crime across the states. Second, the case studies have shown that black political *incorporation* in addition to black exclusion played a key role in the development of American penal regimes in the late 1960s and early 1970s, the period under investigation. The case studies have shown that racial politics played out in much more complicated ways than the arguments about racial social control allow.

Black Americans were not passive victims but active participants in the transformation of American social order. Consider that the political incorporation of African Americans most likely changed the way state officials understood and responded to crime. Black incorporation not only indicates a more inclusive notion of citizenship, it gives political actors opportunities to develop social trust and norms of reciprocity across social groups, an imperative in complex political communities such as the United States, which depend on compromise and negotiation. Black political incorporation may have mitigated against state coercion.

In Washington, state officials and black civic associations made extensive efforts to incorporate African Americans into the political process and economic mainstream, moves that may have increased a sense of mutual obligation across social groups, depressing crude forms of social control. By contrast, in California, the political exclusion of African Americans, dramatically illustrated by the history of the initiative process and its legislation of racial intolerance, may have decreased the opportunities to develop social trust and mutual obligation across social groups, and subsequently supported retributive penal sanctions, especially as they were perceived to be used against racial and ethnic minorities. In New York, the political incorporation of African Americans provided key public support to the Rockefeller drug laws and over time may have tempered the indiscriminate use of imprisonment. However, at the same time, state elites may have co-opted black public support to help justify and legitimate a much tougher approach to drug crimes that over time significantly impacted black communities across New York. Black incorporation and political participation have made them both accomplices and victims of penal reform. Of course, we should note the African American "community" is quite diverse and fragmented and middle-class blacks who are more active in politics may not in fact speak for the interests of poor blacks. What this study indicates, however, is the need for more careful analysis of black participation in the development of crime control policies rather than reliance on demographics.

Institutional Constraints and Path Dependencies

This study shows how contemporary American penal regimes were shaped by the legacies of past practices and institutions. For example, the case studies illustrated how specific power arrangements shaped each state's initial response to rising crime. These initial responses then created path dependencies for subsequent responses to crime and other perceived problems of order. What this means is that contemporary penal regimes were shaped in part by events, actions, and policies that took place much earlier. Contemporary penal trends cannot be explained fully by recent or proximate causes (e.g., arrest, sentencing). Instead, we need to take a long-term view of policy formation. By developing this theme, this book lends further empirical support to the growing field of historical and political institutionalism. By doing so, my work expands the scope of this field and contributes to a much-needed historical sociology of crime policy.

The case studies suggest that the specific structure of the democratic process both constrained and enabled certain forms of civic engagement and collective agency with varying effects on the development of American penal regimes. In other words, we cannot separate the effects of human agency from the political contexts in which people are operating. The findings suggest that certain kinds of institutional configurations are more likely to encourage public participation while others are more likely to depress it.

For example, New York's highly centralized political power reduces the opportunities as well as the political will to participate in politics. Here state elites dominate policy making without the necessary checks on power, sometimes providing for the public welfare and at other times pursuing private self-interest. In California, the state's decentralized political power should theoretically encourage public participation. However, the state's initiative process, its direct democracy measures, tends to depress civic engagement. The initiative process tends to bring about highly contentious and polarizing collective action, forcing out those who do not necessarily take a strong or oppositional stand. It forces out middle-of-the-road voters whose views may not be represented by the dichotomous language of zero-sum political debates. What's more, the initiative not only undermines compromise, it weakens social trust. In California the initiative process institutionalized racial intolerance, further weakening social bonds and mutual recognition across diverse social groups. By contrast, Washington's use of public forums and hybrid state-citizen commissions allowed for more deliberative political discussion, discussion based more on a mutual respect for others than on winner-take-all politics. These institutions allowed for the expression of different opinions, encouraged governmental accountability and citizen input, and to a certain extent promoted compromise and social trust. The findings suggest that certain kinds of institutional configurations were more likely to deepen demands for retribution as well as provide their legal and political expression, while others were more likely to bring about more conciliatory measures.

These findings not only lend further empirical weight to the emerging literature on the structuring effects of political institutionalism on penal regimes (namely, the work of David Downes, Joachim Savelsberg, Marie Gottschalk, John Sutton, James Willis, Tim Newburn, and Trevor Jones, among others), they also raise difficult questions about social change and penal reform. Political institutions and their subsequent path dependencies cannot be easily overcome or willed away. Political institutions that depress public participation or facilitate harsh penal sanctioning cannot be easily changed without determined and sustained collective action, collective action that is itself shaped by the same institutions.

Public Policy Implications

This study has some important and potentially unpopular policy implications. First, I think the public needs to be more not less involved in crime control policy. Second, I think it is a mistake for penal policy makers to retreat behind bureaucratic insulation or expert commissions.

The public is not stupid, cultural dupes, nor a uniform source of vengeance and irrationality. That relationship is dependent on specific historical conditions and political configurations, none of which are universal across the American states. Given the opportunity for deliberative discussion, ordinary people can support more rational and pragmatic responses to crime. Given the opportunity to interact with one another, debate a range of policy proposals, learn from experts, and hold state lawmakers and policy makers accountable, citizens can make informed decisions about crime control policy. Deliberative forums can promote compromise. Consider, for example, that Jason Barabas has shown how deliberative forums can alter a person's deeply held views even on such sensitive policy issues as Social Security.[4] David Green found that citizens' participation led to more "liberalizing" views on crime and punishment and decreased their demands for vengeance and custodial sanctions.[5] Likewise, Gerry Johnstone has argued that public participation can expose more people to the negative effects of penal sanctioning and expand their views of the public interest.[6]

Moreover, public support is necessary for state legitimacy. Public support is especially critical in policy areas fraught with emotional and moral dilemmas. Crime and punishment raise unresolved moral questions about pain, suffering, the value of human life, the limits of freedom, justice, and the principles of safety and security in highly complex democracies that value personal liberty. How these problems are temporarily resolved depends on the nature and character of collective agency. This means that attempts to block public access to crime control policy can backfire, creating legitimacy problems for the state. Purely technocratic responses to crime, generated by bureaucratic insulation, may provoke more populist and punitive responses. The public may feel that their concerns, insecurities, and anxieties about their own safety and security are either taken for granted or deemed irrelevant by policy makers. When people feel excluded, they may withdraw their trust and confidence in government, intensifying their moral outrage and redirecting it against more vulnerable and less integrated social groups. This is what happened in California. By contrast, in Washington, state officials consistently incorporated citizen input into policy making. Washington created its Sentencing Commission through a high-profile and highly public process and included citizen representatives on the commission itself.

Applicability and New Lines of Research

The findings of this study are limited. It would be useful to be clear about their generalizability. The small number of cases raises doubts about whether we can extend the findings to other times and places. It is entirely possible the findings may only account for the penal regime variation in California, Washington, and New York and may not explain the full range of penal sanctioning in the United States. There is good reason, however, to think that the findings may be applicable to other cases. First, these three cases are certainly not the same thing as three observations. Comparing the policy-making process spatially and temporally in cases that represent common patterns rather than extreme cases substantially increases the number of observations and improves analytical leverage. Because the findings are grounded in empirical detail, prior research, and comparative methodology, the core theoretical framework developed here may provide some insight into other contexts within the United States and beyond. To be sure, more research is necessary to assess these claims, but the point here is to highlight *implications* for future thinking about penal sanctioning.

THE OTHER AMERICAN STATES AND DEDEMOCRATIZATION. The selected cases represent major democratic traditions in the United States: populism, pragmatism, and deliberative democracy. The arguments developed here have relevance for other American states steeped in those traditions. Texas and many other western states grew up with populist politics and retributive penal policies; Pennsylvania and Illinois may provide further examples of pragmatic politics and its associated managerial penal regime; whereas Maine and Vermont may provide examples of deliberative democracy with its associated less coercive penal sanctioning. Minnesota may represent the corporatist type (illustrated in Table 6.1) with a high degree of civic engagement, high social trust, and relatively high degree of centralization and associated low imprisonment rates. States that fall along the top tier in Table 6.1 with higher rates of civic engagement tend to have less coercive penal regimes; state that fall along the bottom dimensions with lower rates of civic engagement, more social polarization, or more elite dominated politics tend to have more coercive penal regimes.

To get a preliminary look at how this study might help explain differences across the fifty states, we can graph the relationship between the democratic process and penal regimes. Figure 6.1 maps the relationship between social capital (as a composite measure of social trust and civic engagement taken from Putnam) and imprisonment rates across the nation. Of course, this is only a crude illustration and reduction of a much more complicated process, but the figure provides a visual reference point to an intriguing finding. In states with a high degree of social capital, like Vermont and Minnesota, we tend to see lower rates of imprisonment. In states with low degrees of social capital, like Alabama, Texas, and Louisiana, we tend to see higher imprisonment rates. More research is needed to assess the degree to which this is a significant relationship across the states given varying degrees of crime, economic inequality, and ethnic diversity. I suspect that this relationship will be important because social trust underpins more general social processes of inclusion and exclusion.

From this configuration, I suggest a further argument about the general upward trend in American punishment. Despite the important differences we continue to see across the states, the United States as a whole has increased its reliance on imprisonment. If we extend the findings from the case studies,

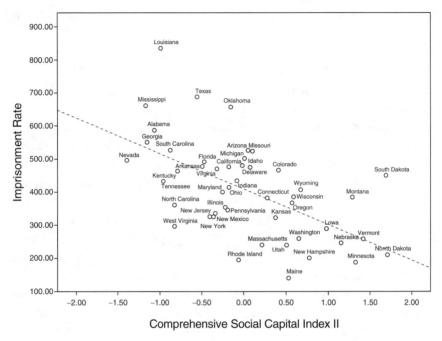

FIGURE 6.1. Social capital and imprisonment rates in American states.

it may be dedemocratization, the retrenchment of American democracy, that partially accounts for high rates of imprisonment in the United States. Americans by and large have retreated into the private sphere, becoming detached from a sense of mutual obligation and civic responsibility, instead experiencing social isolation and social polarization. They have weakened the emotional and political support necessary to sustain inclusive public policies, policies that are responsive to public welfare and not just private interest. Concomitantly, they have failed to restrain the repressive powers of the state, especially as they have been directed at the most vulnerable social groups—the poor and racial and ethnic minorities. Of course, more research is needed to confirm this claim. It is nevertheless a provocative claim worth exploring in further detail.

What about the South? Some readers may argue that the South has high imprisonment rates because southern states continue to maintain racial hierarchies and rely on the criminal law to repress African Americans. The racial dynamics in the cases were much more complicated and perhaps more insidious than a strict racial social control perspective allows. This book does not dispute the importance of race, but it tries to connect racial dynamics to the democratic process. To fully account for penal regime variation in the South, this study suggests that we trace out the effects of black incorporation and black exclusion. In the aftermath of the civil rights movement, some southern states did incorporate African Americans politically and economically, whereas others continued to resist with force. Where we see higher rates of civic engagement, white and black, we might see greater social trust across diverse social groups, increasing norms of mutual obligation and reciprocity, forces that undermine punitiveness and may support more lenient penal regimes. Southern states as a whole tend to have lower rates of civic engagement and social capital, but where we see variation, we may see variation in imprisonment rates. On a related point, we would want to further investigate the extent to which racial diversity can generate or limit social trust, especially across social groups.

This study also suggests that the structure of political power plays an important role in shaping penal outcomes. It suggests that we take a look at how modes of governance facilitate the provision of public welfare or private self-interest. In the southern states, I expect that some are more or less centralized and more or less open to public participation. Unlike the western states, the southern states, except Florida, do not allow for the initiative or direct democracy measures. But neither are the southern states especially centralized like their northeastern counterparts. At the same time, many southern states have historical roots in more feudal-like political orders in which a group of power elites (landowners, planters) dominate governing, using public office for private gains rather than the general welfare. In these types of underdemocratized polities, state officials are more likely to reaffirm their political authority and legitimacy through the criminal law and penal sanctioning. Here penal sanctioning is visible, forceful, and a brutal reminder of unequal power relations. It is also one of the few policy mechanisms available to states that fail to invest in public goods and public welfare. According to this perspective, it is not all that surprising that many of these underdemocratized southern states have relatively high imprisonment rates.

BEYOND THE BORDER: PENAL SANCTIONING IN EUROPE. Most American criminological research has been focused on the United States. However, since the terrorist attacks of September 11, 2001, many researchers have been forced to take a look at crime control, policing, and other security concerns beyond the U.S. border. Those tragic and bloody events may spark some much-needed comparative criminology, opening up the field to global trends, international justice, and nation-specific particularities of criminal justice. This book may provide some groundwork for future comparative research, despite its focus on American states.

European governance is being transformed in real time. Governments there are facing increased immigration and ethnic diversity, rising crime, economic restructuring, and changing political borders. These post-cold war developments have raised questions about the nature and character of national sovereignty and citizenship. They have raised questions about group member-ship and social classification, pushing nation-states into a rapid process of social incorporation and exclusion. An understanding of the criminal law and penal sanctioning will be key to explaining the remaking of European nation-states.

Take the case of Sweden, for example. This is a country with one of the highest levels of social trust, intensive civic engagement, a corporatist or power-sharing political structure. This is also a country with a historically lenient approach to crime and punishment. Yet it also has a long history of social engineers, a moralizing civil society, and strict prohibitions against alcohol. Sweden now has one of the largest foreign-born populations in Europe. Swedish criminologists have tied the country's zero-tolerance approach to drugs to fear of outsiders, especially those coming from former Soviet satellites and the Balkans.[7] Given the country's historically generous social welfare state and inclusive notions of citizenship, it is an interesting and pressing empirical question as to how or to what degree Swedes will mobilize the criminal law and penal sanctioning to resolve new questions of social order.

Sweden is not alone in this dilemma. France and Germany, among many others, have experienced rapidly changing social orders, particularly the conflu-ence of crime and immigration. France recently watched its suburbs burned by second- and third-generation North African immigrants frustrated by their social exclusion and conflicts over policing. France provides an interesting counter-point to Sweden because it has a highly centralized government but weak civil society, weak ties between civil society and the state, and relatively low social trust. So far, France has responded to these changing social conditions with much more stringent police regulation and state coercion. Germany may pro-vide another contrasting case; it has a decentralized government, much more local input, and mid-level social trust, but it has created exclusionary conditions of citizenship, especially for its Turkish "guest workers" and other immigrant groups. Its period of imprisonment liberalization may be under threat.

Given these historical conditions, some democracies more than others will come to rely on the criminal law and penal sanctioning to reestablish social order, redefining group membership and collective identity through coercive means. These responses most likely will be filtered and made meaningful through culturally distinct legal traditions, political institutions, and forms of collective agency as well as by global trends. By focusing on the diversity of democratic processes across Europe, researchers may be better able to explain cross-national penal regime variation.[8] By focusing on the nature of collective agency and the intensity of social trust, researchers may gain some insight into the way criminal law and penal sanctioning bring societies together and tear them apart. A comparative focus on other Western democracies may also illustrate that there is nothing inevitable about democratization and punitiveness.

The Future of American Penal Sanctioning?

This book has pointed to the long-term institutional and cultural differences in American democracy as the explanation for the long-term differences in American penal sanctioning. This kind of argument raises some troubling questions about the nature and possibility of change. If current patterns of punishment are inextricably tied to past policies, how can we change them? Can California become more like Washington or New York? Or vice versa? Can the United States as a whole reverse its prison boom? The response is both yes and no.

From a pessimistic view, penal reformers, social activists, and state officials cannot just shake off past policies, cultural legacies, or entrenched political structures because these are overriding causal forces that continue to shape penal sanctioning today. It is difficult to undo enduring political traditions and years of harsh punishment. Even under the best conditions, reformers cannot focus exclusively on revising the criminal law, lessening or abolishing penal sanctions, because they also need to consider broader social support. In policy areas such as crime and punishment—areas that generate moral and emotional struggles about life and death, justice, and group membership—public engagement and public support are necessary to develop and sustain legitimate public policies. Prison populations are dependent on both immediate events like legislative reform and long-term processes like cultural values and democratic institutions. Both aspects are hard to change but necessary for meaningful reform. To reverse the U.S. case, we would need to see serious legislative activity coupled with significant increases in social trust across diverse social groups and sustained efforts at social integration, including efforts to reincorporate the most marginalized people, like ex-offenders, the poor, the undereducated, and racial and ethnic minorities.

On the more optimistic side, reformers can take advantage of this particular political moment, which offers a rare opportunity for change. State governments are indeed faced with tough budget choices, and many have been forced to rethink their approaches to crime control. Many state officials are coming to realize that imprisonment has tended to generate more social problems than its resolves, creating a revolving door of social exclusion that brings with it tremendous economic and social costs. Plus, crime rates are down. Reformers can try to leverage the institutional and cultural tools available at this moment and in particular places to bring about change. By being cognizant of how institutional environments frame policy debates and policy problems, reformers can better develop proposals that resonate rather than repel state officials and the public. Taking examples from the case studies, in New York reforms that highlight crime and punishment as a public health issue with pragmatic solutions may be more effective than mobilizing moral outrage. In California, reformers could channel populist fervor against the prison itself as a failed institution and graphic reminder of the excesses of state power. In Washington, reforms that come from below may be more effective than reforms from above. In other words, reformers can use the institutional environment to change existing policies. Moreover, the history of American social movements tells us that sustained collective action that is strategic and morally pressing has successfully brought about radical social change in American public life, as it could be with American penal sanctioning.

Notes

CHAPTER 1

1. Bureau of Justice Statistics, "Prisoners in 2007," available at http://www.ojp.usdoj.gov/bjs/pub/pdf/p07.pdf (March 12, 2009); Bureau of Justice Statistics, "Jail Statistics," available at http://www.ojp.usdoj.gov/bjs/jails.htm (June 23, 2008); Bureau of Justice Statistics, *Sourcebook of Criminal Justice Statistics—1976* (Washington, D.C.: U.S. Government Printing Office, 1977); The Sentencing Project, "Incarceration," available at http://www.sentencing-project.org/IssueAreaHome.aspx?IssueID=2 (June 23, 2008).

2. Marc Mauer, "Comparative International Rates of Incarceration: An Examination of Causes and Trends" (Sentencing Project, 2003), 2.

3. On the devastating effects of mass imprisonment on economic and social life, see Bruce Western, *Punishment and Inequality* (New York: Russell Sage, 2006); on the difficulties of prisoner reentry into mainstream society, see Joan Petersilia, *When Prisoners Come Home: Parole and Prisoner Reentry* (New York: Oxford University Press, 2003); on the negative effects of mass imprisonment on particular social groups and neighborhoods, see Todd Clear, *Imprisoning Communities: How Mass Incarceration Makes Disadvantaged Neighborhoods Worse* (New York: Oxford University Press, 2007).

4. Bureau of Justice Statistics, "Prisoners in 2007," 8.

5. For a vivid look at Angola prison, see the documentary film by Jonathan Stack and Liz Garbus, *The Farm: Life inside Angola Prison* (New York: A&E Home Video, 1998).

6. On the emotional toll capital punishment has on corrections staff, see Bob Herbert, "In America; Inside the Death House," *New York Times*, October 9, 2000.

7. Oregon Department of Corrections, "What Is Community Corrections," available at http://www.oregon.gov/DOC/TRANS/CC/whatiscc.shtml (June 12, 2008).

8. Judith A. Greene, *Smart on Crime: Positive Trends in State-Level Sentencing and Corrections Policy* (Washington, D.C.: Families against Mandatory Minimums, 2003), 12.

9. Greene, *Smart on Crime*.

10. Greene, *Smart on Crime*.

11. For important exceptions, see recent work on subnational imprisonment variation: David F. Greenberg and Valerie West, "State Prison Populations and Their Growth, 1971–1991," *Criminology* 39.3 (August 2001): 615–653; Katherine Beckett and Bruce Western, "Governing Social Marginality: Welfare, Incarceration, and the Transformation of State Policy," *Punishment & Society* 3.1 (January 2001): 43–59; on spending, see David Jacobs and Ronald Helms, "Collective Outbursts, Politics, and Punitive Outbursts: Toward a Political Sociology of Spending on Social Control," *Social Forces* 77.4 (June 1999): 1497–1523.

12. See David Garland, "Limits of the Sovereign State," *British Journal of Criminology* 36.4 (1996): 445–471.

13. In 2007, the most current Bureau of Justice Statistics figures available, California imprisoned 471 inmates per 100,000 population, Washington imprisoned 273 inmates per 100,000 population, New York imprisoned 322 inmates per 100,000 population, and the U.S. states overall averaged 447 inmates per 100,000 population. Bureau of Justice Statistics, "Prisoners in 2007," 18.

14. Political institutional theory has been particularly influential. See Theda Skocpol, *Protecting Soldiers and Mothers: The Political Origins of Social Policy in the United States* (Cambridge: Cambridge University Press, 1992); Edwin Amenta, *Bold Relief: Institutional Politics and the Origins of Modern American Social Policy* (Princeton, N.J.: Princeton University Press, 1998); for review see Edwin Amenta, "State-Centered and Political Institutional Theory: Retrospect and Prospect," in *Handbook of Political Sociology: States, Civil Societies and Globalization*, eds. Thomas Janoski, Robert Alford, Alexander Hicks, and Mildred Schwartz (Cambridge: Cambridge University Press, 2005), 96–114. On the character of democratic politics, see Benjamin Barber, *Strong Democracy: Participatory Politics for a New Age* (Berkeley: University of California Press, 1984); Robert Putnam, *Making Democracy Work: Civic Traditions in Modern Italy* (Princeton, N.J.: Princeton University Press, 1993).

15. Political scientists have studied how American federalism allows for political variation on the state level, which subsequently influences subnational policy development. See, for example, Daniel Elazar, *American Federalism: A View from the States* (New York: Thomas Y. Crowell, 1966); Virginia Gray and Russell L. Hanson, eds., *Politics in the American States: A Comparative Analysis* (Washington, D.C.: Congressional Quarterly Press, 2004); Thomas Dye, *Politics in States and American*

Communities (Englewood Cliffs, N.J.: Prentice Hall, 1988). This study takes cues from this work but is ultimately tied to sociological theories of action.

16. On the localized experience of crime and globalization, see Evi Girling, Ian Loader, and Richard Sparks, *Crime and Social Change in Middle England: Questions of Order in an English Town* (London: Routledge, 2000). On the importance of local politics of crime control, see the classic Stuart Scheingold, *The Politics of Street Crime: Criminal Process and Cultural Obsession* (Philadelphia: Temple University Press, 1991); Lisa L. Miller, *The Perils of Federalism: Race, Poverty and the Politics of Crime Control* (New York: Oxford University Press, 2008).

17. David Downes, *Contrasts in Tolerance: Post-War Penal Policy in the Netherlands and England and Wales* (Oxford: Clarendon Press, 1988).

18. U.S. Census Bureau, "Participation in Elections for President and US Representatives: 1932–2006, Table 406," available at http://www.census.gov/compendia/statab/tables/08s0406.pdf (January 30, 2008); Theda Skocpol, *Diminished Democracy: From Membership to Management in American Civic Life* (Norman: University of Oklahoma Press, 2003); Robert Putnam, *Bowling Alone: The Collapse and Revival of American Community* (New York: Simon & Schuster, 2000).

19. Michel Foucault vividly describes this process in *Discipline and Punish* as he traces the transformation of political power through changing penal practices. He explains how the prison represented a different kind of political power than the terrorizing and brutal power displayed by the public executions so central to monarchical rule. The prison, through its strict routine, intensive surveillance, and insidious use of social scientific knowledge, exercised a form of power designed to control and transform criminal offenders rather than maim or kill them. By doing so, it helped create a specific kind of modern political subject, disciplined, self-censoring, industrious, and conditioned for self-rule. For Foucault, this development was no less repressive than monarchical rule because it simply replaced one strategy of power for another, replacing blood and death with conformity and normalization. But it was also productive in the sense that the prison helped establish a particular type of political subjectivity resonant with the new political order based on freedom. Michel Foucault, *Discipline and Punish: The Birth of the Prison* (New York: Pantheon, 1977); Thomas Dumm, *Democracy and Punishment: Disciplinary Origins of the United States* (Madison: University of Wisconsin Press, 1987); Marie Gottschalk, *The Prison and the Gallows: The Politics of Mass Incarceration in America* (Cambridge: Cambridge University Press, 2006); Jonathan Simon, *Governing through Crime: How the War on Crime Transformed American Democracy and Created a Culture of Fear* (New York: Oxford University Press, 2007).

20. On the role of emotions, political community, and state sanctions, see Ian Loader and Neil Walker, *Civilizing Security* (Cambridge: Cambridge University Press, 2007); Ian Loader, "Policing, Recognition and Belonging," *Annals of the American Academy of Political and Social Science* 605.1 (May 2006): 202–221; and Ian Loader, "Playing with Fire?: Democracy and the Emotions of Crime and Punishment,"

in *Emotions, Crime and Justice*, eds. S. Karstedt, Ian Loader, and Heather Strang (Oxford, UK: Hart, forthcoming).

21. On cumulative causality, see Paul Pierson, "Big, Slow-Moving, and Invisible: Macrosocial Processes in the Study of Comparative Politics," in *Comparative Historical Analysis in the Social Sciences*, eds. James Mahoney and Dietrich Rueschemeyer (Cambridge: Cambridge University Press, 2003), 177–207.

22. On path dependencies, see Paul Pierson, *Dismantling the Welfare State? Reagan, Thatcher, and the Politics of Retrenchment* (New York: Cambridge University Press, 1994). On the problem of change and continuity in political institutionalism, see Elisabeth Clemens and James Cook, "Politics and Institutionalism: Explaining Durability and Change," *Annual Review of Sociology* 25 (1999): 441–466.

23. For a helpful discussion on a genealogical approach to historical material, see David Garland, *The Culture of Control: Crime and Social Order in Contemporary Society* (Chicago: University of Chicago Press, 2001), 2.

24. According to the Bureau of Justice Statistics (BJS), forty-two people were executed in 2006. This figure contrasts sharply with the 2.2 million people imprisoned in state or federal prisons or local jails. See BJS, "Capital Punishment Statistics: Summary Findings," available at http://www.ojp.usdoj.gov/bjs/cp.htm (January 21, 2008); BJS, "Prison Statistics: Summary Findings," available at http://www.ojp.usdoj.gov/bjs/prisons.htm (January 21, 2008).

25. On the dehumanizing aspects of confinement, particularly the nearly total loss of individual autonomy, see Gresham Sykes, *Society of Captives: A Study of Maximum Security Prison* (Princeton, N.J.: Princeton University Press, 1958). On the psychological and debilitating effects of long-term isolation, see Craig Haney, "Psychological Impact of Incarceration: Implications for Postprison Adjustment," in *Prisoners Once Removed: The Impact of Incarceration and Reentry on Children, Families, and Communities*, eds. Jeremy Travis and Michelle Waul (Washington, D.C.: Urban Institute Press, 2003), 33–66.

26. BJS, "Prisoners in 2007," available at http://www.ojp.usdoj.gov/bjs/pub/pdf/p05.pdf (January 30, 2008), 18.

27. BJS, "Prisoners in 2007," 18.

28. BJS, "Prisoners in 2007," 18.

29. BJS, "Prisoners in 2007," 18.

30. BJS, "Prisoners in 2007," 18.

31. The total crime rate in Washington has fluctuated between 6,100–6,500 since the mid-1970s, compared to 5,200 of the national average, New York's 4,500–5,600 and California's 7,200–5,800. Although Washington's violent crime rate has been relatively low, under 500, and under the national average since the 1960s, the violent crime rate there as well as in New York and California increased substantially between 1965 and 1975, a critical period under investigation. See Federal Bureau of Investigation (FBI), *Uniform Crime Report 1965* (Washington, D.C.: Government Printing Office); FBI, "Uniform Crime Report 2006," available at http://www.fbi.gov/ucr/hc2006/index.html

(February 1, 2008); BJS, *Sourcebook of Criminal Justice Statistics—1976*; BJS, *Sourcebook of Criminal Justice Statistics—1986* (Washington, D.C.: U.S. Government Printing Office, 1987).

32. See discussion in Katherine Beckett, *Making Crime Pay: Law and Order in Contemporary American Politics* (New York: Oxford University Press, 1997).

33. Consider, for example, that the rate for murder and non-negligent man-slaughter increased from 5.1 in 1965 to 9.6 by 1975. See "Estimated number and rate (per 100,000 inhabitants) of offenses known to the police. By offense, United States, 1960–2006, Table 3.106.2006," available at http://www.albany.edu/sourcebook/pdf/t31062006.pdf (January 30, 2008).

34. See Scheingold, *Politics of Street Crime*; Theodore Sasson, *Crime Talk: How Citizens Construct a Social Problem* (New York: Aldine de Gruyter, 1995).

35. See review on racial threat hypothesis, in Greenberg and West, "State Prison Populations."

36. In 1960, New York's black population was 8.4 percent compared to 5.6 percent in California or 1.7 percent in Washington State. By 1975, New York's black population reached nearly 12 percent, compared to 7 percent in California and 2 percent in Washington. In 2006, New York's black population measured over 17 percent, com-pared to less than 7 percent in California or about 3.5 percent in Washington. See U.S. Census Bureau, "The 1966 Statistical Abstract," available at http://www2.census.gov/prod2/statcomp/documents/1966-01.pdf (February 1, 2008); U.S. Census Bureau, "The 1978 Statistical Abstract," available at http://www2.census.gov/prod2/statcomp/documents/1978-01.pdf (February 1, 2008); U.S. Census Bureau, "The 2007 Statistical Abstract," available at http://www.census.gov/compendia/statab/index.html (February 1, 2008).

37. Duane Lockard, *Toward Equal Opportunity: A Study of State and Local Antidis-crimination Laws* (New York: Macmillan, 1968).

38. Lockard, *Toward Equal Opportunity*; John H. Mollenkopf, "New York: The Great Anomaly," in *Racial Politics in the American Cities*, eds. Rufus P. Browning, Dale Rogers Marshall, and David H. Taub (New York: Longman Press, 1990).

39. Jeffrey S. Adler, "Introduction," in *African American Mayors: Race, Politics and the American City*, eds. David R. Colburn and Jeffrey S. Adler (Urbana: University of Illinois Press, 2001).

40. Raymond Wolfinger and Fred Greenstein, "Repeal of Fair Housing in California: An Analysis of Referendum Voting," *American Political Science Review* 62.3 (September 1968): 753–769.

41. On the populist movement, see Lawrence Goodwyn, *The Populist Moment: A Short History of Agrarian Revolt in America* (Oxford: Oxford University Press, 1978); on populism and the progressive movement in California and Washington, see Elisa-beth Clemens, *The People's Lobby: Organizational Innovation and the Rise of Interest Group Politics in the United States, 1890–1925* (Chicago: University of Chicago Press, 1997).

42. New York has relatively low voter participation. In 2006, for example, 37.6 percent of the voting age population voted, compared to 43.6 percent of the national average. See U.S. Census Bureau, "Persons Reported Registered and Voted by State: 2006, Table 405," available at http://www.census.gov/compendia/statab/tables/08s0405.pdf (January 30, 2008).

43. Thad Beyle has compiled a very useful index of governors' institutional powers. He measures the degree to which governors control budgets, legislation, appointments, political parties; the strength of veto power; and the length of tenure, including the presence or absence of term limits. New York scores well above the national average on Beyle's index. See Thad Beyle, "The Governors," in *Politics in the American States: A Comparative Analysis*, 8th ed., eds. Virginia Gray and Russell Hanson (Washington, D.C.: Congressional Quarterly Press, 2004), 212–213.

44. For important exceptions and insightful analyses of political processes and punishment, see Gottschalk, *The Prison and the Gallows*; Joachim J. Savelsberg, "Knowledge, Domination, and Criminal Punishment," *American Journal of Sociology* 99.4 (Jan. 1994): 911–943; James J. Willis, "Transportation versus Imprisonment in Eighteenth- and Nineteenth-Century Britain: Penal Power, Liberty, and the State," *Law & Society Review* 39.1 (2005): 171–210; James Q. Whitman, *Harsh Justice: Criminal Punishment and the Widening Divide between America and Europe* (Oxford: Oxford University Press, 2003); Miller, *The Perils of Federalism*.

45. On the "harshness" of American punishment and a useful conceptualization, see Whitman, *Harsh Justice*, chapter 2.

46. Garland, *Culture of Control*; Simon, *Governing through Crime*; Beckett, *Making Crime Pay*; Loïc Wacquant, "Deadly Symbiosis: When Ghetto and Prison Meet and Mesh," *Punishment & Society* 3.1 (2001): 95–134.

47. Jean Cohen, "Civil Society and Globalization: Rethinking the Categories," in *State and Civil Society in Northern Europe: The Swedish Model Reconsidered*, ed. Lars Trägårdh (New York: Berghahn, 2007), 2.

48. Cohen, "Civil Society and Globalization," 2.

CHAPTER 2

1. On the localized experience of crime and globalization, see Girling, Loader, and Sparks, *Crime and Social Change*; on the role of local politics in crime control, see Scheingold, *The Politics of Street Crime*.

2. John Hagan argues that the criminal justice system should be understood as a "loosely coupled" organization rather than as a coherent entity because the various actors and agencies do not always act in unison nor simply reflect structural imperatives. See John Hagan, John Hewitt, and Duane Alwin, "Ceremonial Justice: Crime and Punishment in a Loosely Coupled System," *Social Forces* 58.2 (Dec. 1979): 506–527.

3. Anthony Giddens, "Problems of Action and Structure," in *The Giddens Reader*, ed. Phillip Cassells (Stanford, Calif.: Stanford University Press, 1993).

4. On the "state" as a set of institutions, see Max Weber, *Politics as Vocation* (Philadelphia: Fortress Press, 1965 [1919]).

5. See Dumm, *Democracy and Punishment;* Simon, *Governing through Crime.*

6. For an useful discussion on how imprisonment works as a classification scheme, see John Sutton, "Imprisonment and Social Classification in Five Common Law Countries," *American Journal of Sociology* 106.2 (Sept. 2000): 350–386.

7. On felon disenfranchisement, see Jeff Manza and Chris Uggen, *Locked Out: Felon Disenfranchisement and American Democracy* (New York: Oxford University Press, 2006).

8. Stuart Scheingold, "New Political Criminology: Power, Authority, and the Post-Liberal State," *Law & Social Inquiry* 23.4 (Fall 1998): 857–895; John Pratt, "Emotive and Ostentatious Punishment: Its Decline and Resurgence on Modern Society," *Punishment & Society* 2.4 (Oct. 2000): 417–439.

9. Franklin Zimring and Gordon Hawkins, *The Scale of Imprisonment* (Chicago: University of Chicago Press, 1991); Michael Tonry, *Malign Neglect: Race, Crime and Punishment in America* (New York: Oxford University Press, 1995); Bruce Western and Katherine Beckett, "How Unregulated Is the US Labor Market? The Penal System as a Labor Market Institution," *American Journal of Sociology* 104 (1999): 1135–1172.

10. For important exceptions, see Gottschalk, *The Prison and the Gallows;* James Morone, *Hellfire Nation: The Politics of Sin in America History* (New Haven, Conn.: Yale University Press, 2003).

11. Darryl Brown, "Democracy and Decriminalization," *Texas Law Review* 86.2 (2007): 223–275.

12. For an analysis of how "institutional homes," administrative jurisdiction and policy priorities, shape the development of public policy, see Chris Bonastia, *Knocking on the Door: The Federal Government's Attempt to De-Segregate the Suburbs* (Princeton, N.J.: Princeton University Press, 2008).

13. On the role of the state in facilitating and hampering the rise of a global economy, see Nitsan Chorev, *Remaking US Trade Policy: From Protectionism to Globalization* (Ithaca, N.Y.: Cornell University Press, 2007).

14. For a discussion of ideal types as useful methodological tools, see Max Weber, *Economy and Society*, eds. Guenther Roth and Claus Wittich (Berkeley: University of California Press, 1978), 4–5.

15. Barber, *Strong Democracy;* Putnam, *Making Democracy Work.*

16. Edwin Amenta and Michael P. Young, "Democratic States and Social Movements: Theoretical Arguments and Hypotheses," *Social Problems* 46.2 (May 1999): 153–168.

17. In twenty-four American states, nonelected, ordinary people can create legally binding legislation through the initiative process, a process by which citizens collect qualifying signatures to place new statutes or constitutional amendments on electoral

ballots and then vote on them; the proposed measures become law if they gain a specified proportion of electoral support. For more on the initiative process, see Larry Sabato, Howard Ernst, and Bruce A. Larson, eds., *Dangerous Democracy? The Battle over Ballot Initiatives in America* (Lanham, N.J.: Rowman & Littlefield, 2001).

18. James Madison, "Federalist No. 47," in *The Federalist: A Commentary on the Constitution of the United States*, Alexander Hamilton, John Jay, and James Madison (New York: Modern Library, 2001), 308.

19. Evan Schofer and Marion Fourcade-Gourinchas, "The Structural Contexts of Civic Engagement: Voluntary Association Membership in Comparative Perspective," *American Sociological Review* 66.6 (Dec. 2001): 806–828.

20. Skocpol, *Protecting Soldiers and Mothers*.

21. Edwin Amenta, Kathleen Dunleavy, and Mary Bernstein, "Stolen Thunder? Huey Long's Share Our Wealth, Political Mediation, and the Second New Deal," *American Sociological Review* 59.5 (Oct. 1994): 678–702.

22. Putnam, *Making Democracy Work*.

23. Charles Tilly, "Parliamentarization of Popular Contention in Great Britain, 1758–1834," *Theory & Society* 26.2/3 (April 1997): 245–273.

24. Hugh Heclo and Henrik Madsen, *Policy and Politics in Sweden: Principled Pragmatism* (Philadelphia: Temple University Press, 1987); Thomas Anton, "Policy-Making and Political Culture in Sweden," *Scandinavian Political Studies* 4 (1969): 88–102.

25. Göran Rosenberg, "The Crisis of Consensus in Post-War Sweden," in *Crisis and Culture: The Case of Germany and Sweden*, eds. Lars. Trägårdh and Nina Witoszek (New York: Berghahn Books, 2002).

26. Gunnar Broberg and Mattias Tyden, "Eugenics in Sweden: Efficient Care," in *Eugenics and the Welfare State*, eds. Gunnar Broberg and Nils Roll-Hansen (East Lansing: Michigan State University Press, 1996).

27. Piero Colla, "Race, Nation, and Folk: On the Repressed Memory of World War II in Sweden and Its Hidden Categories," in *Crisis and Culture: The Case of Germany and Sweden*, eds. Lars Trägårdh and Nina Witoszek (New York: Berghahn Books, 2002).

28. Official classification of ethnic differences and immigrants in Sweden falls into two categories: citizenship and country of birth. For more on ethnicity and crime in Sweden, see Peter Martens, "Immigrants, Crime and Criminal Justice in Sweden," *Ethnicity, Crime and Immigration: Comparative and Cross-National Perspectives*, ed. Michael Tonry (Chicago: University of Chicago Press, 1997).

29. Putnam and his colleagues later developed an index of social capital in *Bowling Alone*. This index measures how often people volunteered, worked on a community project, attended a town or school meeting, served on a local committee, how often people socialized with community members, rates of civic associations, voting participation, and levels of social trust. For more on the development of the social capital concept, see Pierre Bourdieu, "The Forms of Capital," in *Handbook of Theory and Research for the Sociology of Education*, ed. J. G. Richardson (New York: Greenwood Press,

1986), 241–258; James Coleman, "Social Capital in the Creation of Human Capital," *American Journal of Sociology* 94 (1988): S95–S120. For a critical review of the term, see Alejandro Portes, "Social Capital: Its Origins and Applications in Modern Sociology," *Annual Review of Sociology* 24 (1998): 1–24.

30. John Braithwaite and Philip Pettit, *Not Just Deserts: A Republican Theory of Criminal Justice* (Oxford: Oxford University Press, 1990).

31. On the violence inherent in criminal case processing and punishment, see Robert Cover, "Violence and the Word," *Yale Law Journal* 95 (July 1986); on the dehumanizing aspects of confinement, see Sykes, *Society of Captives*; on the psychologically debilitating effects of imprisonment, particularly long-term isolation, see Haney, "Psychological Impact."

32. Hagan et al., "Ceremonial Justice."

33. For an insightful discussion of the relationship between penal sanctioning and political authority, see David Garland, *Punishment and Modern Society: A Study in Social Theory* (Chicago: University of Chicago Press, 1990), 47–81. Also see David Garland, *Punishment and Welfare: A History of Penal Strategies* (Aldershot, U.K.: Gower, 1985).

34. S. Karthick Ramakrishnan and Mark Baldassare, *The Ties That Bind: Changing Demographics and Civic Engagement in California* (San Francisco: Public Policy Institute of California, 2004), 48.

35. Bruce Cain and Kenneth Miller, "The Populist Legacy: Initiatives and Undermining of Representative Government," in *Dangerous Democracy? The Battle over Ballot Initiatives in America*, eds. Larry Sabato, Howard R. Ernst, and Bruce Larson (Lanham, Md.: Rowman & Littlefield, 2001).

36. John Allswang, *The Initiative and Referendum in California, 1898–1998* (Stanford, Calif.: Stanford University Press, 2001).

37. Clemens, *The People's Lobby*.

38. Jürgen Habermas, *The Theory of Communicative Action* (Boston: Beacon Press, 1981).

39. Lars Trägårdh, "Democratic Governance and the Creation of Social Capital in Sweden: The Discreet Charm of Governmental Commissions," in *State and Civil Society in Northern Europe: The Swedish Model Reconsidered*, ed. Lars Trägårdh (Oxford: Berghahn Books, 2007), 255–270.

CHAPTER 3

1. On rehabilitation in the California Department of Corrections, especially its parole practices, see Jonathan Simon, *Poor Discipline: Parole and the Social Control of the Underclass* (Chicago: University of Chicago Press, 1993). On correctionalism more generally, see Garland, *Culture of Control*, chapter 2.

2. Jerry Gillam, "3 Reagan Anti-Crime Bills Approved by Assembly Unit," *Los Angeles Times*, April 19, 1967, 3. Also see Richard Berk, Harold Brackman, and Selma

Lesser, *A Measure of Justice: An Empirical Study of Changes in the California Penal Code, 1955–1971* (New York: Academic Press, 1977); Lou Cannon, *Governor Reagan: His Rise to Power* (New York: Public Affairs, 2003).

3. California Department of Corrections, *Historical Trends, 1982–2002* (Sacramento, CA: Youth and Adult Correctional Agency Data Analysis Unit, 2003); U.S. Census Bureau, "California: Quick Facts," available at http://quickfacts.census.gov/qfd/states/06000.html (February 13, 2008).

4. BJS, "Prisoners in 2005," 4.

5. Ramakrishnan and Baldassare, "Ties that Bind," 48; California Field Poll, "Release #1547, 1990," California Field Research Corporation, San Francisco. Available at the Institute of Governmental Studies Library, University of California, Berkeley.

6. In the policy areas of crime and punishment, I have not found supporting evidence concerning the use of more conciliatory mechanisms of conflict resolution, such as town hall meetings in California from the mid-1960s onward.

7. Cain and Miller, "The Populist Legacy."

8. Allswang, *The Initiative and Referendum in California.*

9. Clemens, *The People's Lobby*; Robert McMath, *American Populism: A Social History 1877–1898* (New York: Hill & Wang, 1993).

10. McMath, *American Populism*; Goodwyn, *Populist Moment.*

11. Norris, quoted in Joan Didion, *Where I Was From* (New York: Alfred Knopf, 2003), 44.

12. McMath, *American Populism*; Cain and Miller, "The Populist Legacy."

13. McMath, *American Populism.*

14. Goodwyn, *Populist Moment.*

15. Cain and Miller, "The Populist Legacy"; McMath, *American Populism.*

16. Allswang, *The Initiative and Referendum in California*; Neal R. Peirce and Jerry Hagstrom, *The Book of America: Inside the 50 States Today* (New York: Norton, 1983).

17. Kevin Starr, *Inventing the Dream: California through the Progressive Era* (New York: Oxford University Press, 1985).

18. Clemens, *The People's Lobby.*

19. Cain and Miller, "The Populist Legacy."

20. V. O. Key and Winston Crouch, *The Initiative and Referendum in California* (Berkeley: University of California Press, 1939).

21. Allswang, *The Initiative and Referendum in California*; Cain and Miller, "The Populist Legacy."

22. Allswang, *The Initiative and Referendum in California*; Key and Crouch, *The Initiative and Referendum in California.*

23. Allswang, *The Initiative and Referendum in California*; Key and Crouch, *The Initiative and Referendum in California.*

24. Allswang, *The Initiative and Referendum in California*; Starr, *Inventing the Dream*; Clemens, *The People's Lobby.*

25. Allswang, *The Initiative and Referendum in California*; Starr, *Inventing the Dream*.

26. Johnson, quoted in Allswang, *The Initiative and Referendum in California*, 15; also see Amenta, *Bold Relief*.

27. Starr, *Inventing the Dream*.

28. Johnson, quoted in Key and Crouch, *The Initiative and Referendum in California*, 439.

29. *Los Angeles Express*, September 9, 1911, quoted in Key and Crouch, *The Initiative and Referendum in California*, 440.

30. Allswang, *The Initiative and Referendum in California*.

31. Starr, *Inventing the Dream*; Allswang, *The Initiative and Referendum in California*.

32. Allswang, *The Initiative and Referendum in California*.

33. *California Weekly*, quoted in Starr, *Inventing the Dream*, 260.

34. See discussion in Elisabeth Gerber, Arthur Lupia, Mathew D. McCubbins, and D. Roderick Kiewiet, *Stealing the Initiative: How State Government Responds to Direct Democracy* (Upper Saddle River, N.J.: Prentice Hall, 2001).

35. Key and Crouch, *The Initiative and Referendum in California*.

36. Key and Crouch, *The Initiative and Referendum in California*.

37. Key and Crouch, *The Initiative and Referendum in California*; Allswang, *The Initiative and Referendum in California*.

38. David Mayhew, *Placing Parties in American Politics* (Princeton, N.J.: Princeton University Press, 1986).

39. Amenta, *Bold Relief*; Mayhew, *Placing Parties*.

40. Clemens, *The People's Lobby*; Cain and Miller, "The Populist Legacy."

41. Cain and Miller, "The Populist Legacy."

42. Clemens, *The People's Lobby*, 254.

43. Amenta, *Bold Relief*.

44. Amenta, *Bold Relief*.

45. Amenta, *Bold Relief*.

46. Lisa McGirr, *Suburban Warriors: The Origins of the New American Right* (Princeton, N.J.: Princeton University Press, 2001). For a fascinating documentary on the cultural impact of the military build-up in San Diego, see Garrett Scott, *Cul de Sac: A Suburban War Story* (First Run/Icarus Films, 2002). These conditions may have been counterbalanced by strong collectivist traditions and strong labor movements, which were underdeveloped in California but central to other war industry boomtowns, such as Seattle, Washington.

47. McGirr, *Suburban Warriors*; Chip Berlet and Matthew Lyons, *Right-Wing Populism in America: Too Close for Comfort* (New York: Guilford Press, 2000); Rebecca Klatch, *Women of the New Right* (Philadelphia: Temple University Press, 1987); Sara Diamond, *Roads to Dominion: Right-Wing Movements and Political Power in the United States* (New York: Guilford Press, 1995).

48. Quoted in McGirr, *Suburban Warriors*, 162–163.

49. Allswang, *The Initiative and Referendum in California*.

50. Allswang, *The Initiative and Referendum in California*.

51. Matthew Dallek, *The Right Moment: Ronald Reagan's First Victory and the Decisive Turning Point in American Politics* (New York: Free Press, 2000).

52. Dallek, *The Right Moment*.

53. Campaign material, quoted in Dallek, *The Right Moment*, 60.

54. Cannon, *Governor Reagan*; Dallek, *The Right Moment*.

55. Peirce and Hagstrom, *The Book of America*.

56. Reagan, quoted in Kiron Skinner, Annelise Anderson, and Martin Anderson, eds., *Reagan, in His Own Hand* (New York: Touchstone Books, 2002), 444–445.

57. Ronald Reagan, "Address before the Merchants and Manufacturers Association, Los Angeles," and "Speech at the Republican State Convention, Anaheim," in *The Creative Society: Some Comments on Problems Facing America* (New York: Devin-Adair, 1967), 16.

58. Cannon, *Governor Reagan*.

59. FBI, *Uniform Crime Report 1965*; FBI, *Uniform Crime Report 2006*; BJS, *Sourcebook of Criminal Justice Statistics—1976*; BJS, *Sourcebook of Criminal Justice Statistics—1986*.

60. California Department of Justice, *Crime in California* (Sacramento: California Department of Justice, 2002).

61. Cannon, *Governor Reagan*.

62. Dallek, *The Right Moment*.

63. Schrade, quoted in *New York Times*, January 5, 1965, 68.

64. California Field Poll, "Release #558, May 11, 1967," and "Release #554, April 5, 1967," Field Institute, San Francisco. Available at the Institute of Governmental Studies Library, University of California, Berkeley; also see Dallek, *The Right Moment*.

65. Dallek, *The Right Moment*.

66. Gladwin Hill, "Isolation of Poorer Negroes Called Key to Los Angeles Riots," *New York Times*, August 29, 1965, 54; Peter Bart, "Officials Divided in Placing Blame," *New York Times*, August 15, 1965, 81; Dallek, *The Right Moment*.

67. Hill, "Isolation of Poorer Negroes"; Bart, "Officials Divided."

68. Hawkins, quoted in Peter Bart, "Negro Gains Vex Coast Mexicans," *New York Times*, October 17, 1965, 82.

69. Quoted in Bart, "Negro Gains."

70. Bart, "Negro Gains."

71. Hill, "Isolation of Poorer Negroes."

72. Dallek, *The Right Moment*.

73. California Field Poll, "Release #558, February 6, 1968," Field Institute, San Francisco. Available at the Institute of Governmental Studies Library, University of California, Berkeley.

74. Ronald Reagan, "The Morality Gap at Berkeley, Speech at Cow Palace, May 12, 1966," in *The Creative Society*, 125.

75. Reagan, "The Morality Gap," 126.

76. Reagan, "The Morality Gap," 126.

77. Daniel Evans, "Statewide Television Address on Citizen Unrest, June 4, 1970," Office of the Governor, Daniel Evans Gubernatorial Papers, Washington State Library and Archive, Olympia.

78. Evans, "Citizen Unrest, June 4, 1970."

79. California Field Poll, "Release #558."

80. Ronald Reagan, "Joint Conference of California School Boards Association and California Association of School Administrators, December 8, 1968," California Council on Criminal Justice, Governor Speeches, 1968, F3869:106 (Sacramento, CA), 1–2.

81. Reagan, "Joint Conference, December 8, 1968," 2.

82. Reagan, quoted in *New York Times*, August 1, 1968, 20.

83. Lindsay, quoted in *New York Times*, August 1, 1968, 20.

84. Reagan, in Berk et al., *A Measure of Justice*, 58.

85. Reagan, "Joint Conference, December 8, 1968," 3.

86. Reagan, in Berk et al., *A Measure of Justice*, 58.

87. Reagan, "Joint Conference, December 8, 1968," 3.

88. Cannon, quoted in Berk et al., *A Measure of Justice*, 61; Lou Cannon, *Ronnie and Jesse: A Political Odyssey* (Garden City, N.Y.: Doubleday, 1969).

89. Ronald Reagan, "Speech to Members of the Legislature of California, April 10, 1969," California Council on Criminal Justice, Governor Speeches on Crime Control, F3869:106 (Sacramento, CA), 2.

90. Berk et al., *A Measure of Justice*.

91. For a discussion of California's determinate sentencing reform, see April Kestell Cassou and Brian Taugher, "Determinate Sentencing in California: The New Numbers Game," *Pacific Law Journal* 9 (1978): 1–106; Sheldon Messinger and Philip E. Johnson, "California's Determinate Sentencing Statute: History and Issues," in *Determinate Sentencing: Reform or Regression* (Washington, D.C.: U.S. Government Printing Office, 1977); David Greenberg and Drew Humphries, "The Cooptation of Fixed Sentencing Reform," *Crime and Delinquency* 26 (1980): 205–225.

92. Cassou and Taugher, "Determinate Sentencing."

93. California Council on Criminal Justice, "Memo to Staff, May 19, 1971," California Council on Criminal Justice, Governor Speeches on Crime Control, F3869:106 (Sacramento, CA).

94. California Department of Corrections, "Time Served on Prison Sentence," Policy and Evaluation Division, Offender Information Services Branch, Estimates and Statistical Analysis Section, Data Analysis Unit (Sacramento, CA, 2004); Franklin Zimring and Gordon Hawkins, *Prison: Population and Criminal Justice Policy in California* (Berkeley: Institute of Governmental Studies Press, 1992).

95. California State Constitution, Article 1, Declaration of Rights, Section 28, available at http://www.leginfo.ca.gov/const-toc.html (September 29, 2005).

96. Editorial, *Los Angeles Herald Examiner*, November 17, 1981, available at the Paul Gann Archive, Box 1395 Folder 1 (Sacramento: California State Library, California History Section).

97. Treena Davis, Letter to Paul Gann, 1981, available at the Paul Gann Archive, Proposition 8: Analyses and Correspondence, Box 1393, Folder 6 (Sacramento: California State Library, California History Section).

98. G. Mielke, Letter to Paul Gann, September 14, 1981, available at the Paul Gann Archive, Proposition 8: Analyses and Correspondence, Box 1393, Folder 6 (Sacramento: California State Library, California History Section).

99. For an alternative account based on state elites, see Candace McCoy, *Politics and Plea Bargaining: Victims' Rights in California* (Philadelphia: University of Pennsylvania Press, 1993). McCoy argues that Proposition 8 was the handiwork of George Nicholson and John Doolittle, conservative Republican lawmakers who used the initiative process to limit the discretion of the California judiciary. While my account does not dispute state elite involvement in the campaign, Proposition 8 was nevertheless a voters' initiative that resonated on some level with the voting public to become law.

100. Edmund G. Brown, "Report to the Legislature, January 7, 1976," Governor's Office, Sacramento, California.

101. Darryl Gates, quoted in "Burglary Victim Dies from Beating," *Los Angeles Herald Examiner*, December 30, 1980, available at the Paul Gann Archive, Box 1395, Folder 2 (Sacramento: California State Library, California History Section).

102. California Field Poll, "Release #1128, August 25, 1981," Field Institute, San Francisco, available at the Institute of Governmental Studies Library, University of California, Berkeley.

103. Mike Curb, "Citizen's Committee to Stop Crime," Citizen's Committee to Stop Crime, Sacramento.

104. Curb, "Citizen's Committee," emphasis in original.

105. Editorial, *San Francisco Chronicle*, May 23, 1982, available at the Paul Gann Archive, Newsclippings, Box 1395, Folder 9 (Sacramento: California State Library, California History Section).

106. Carol Hallett, Letter to Paul Gann, June 17, 1981, Paul Gann Archive, Endorsements: Proposition 8, Box 1394, Folder 1 (Sacramento: California State Library, California History Section).

107. Robert Agnew, Letter to Paul Gann, June 2, 1981, Paul Gann Archive, Proposition 8: Analyses and Correspondence, Box 1392, Folder 5 (Sacramento: California State Library, California History Section).

108. Doris Walker, Letter to Paul Gann, August 17, 1981, Paul Gann Archive, Proposition 8: Analyses and Correspondence, Box 1393, Folder 6 (Sacramento: California State Library, California History Section).

109. California Secretary of State, "A History of California Initiatives," available at http://www.ss.ca.gov/elections/init_history.pdf (July 20, 2006).

110. California Field Poll, "Release #1163, April 22, 1982," and "Release #1164, April 20, 1982," Field Institute, San Francisco, available at the Institute of Governmental Studies Library, University of California, Berkeley.

111. California Field Poll, "Release #1164, April 20, 1982."

112. California Field Poll, "Release #1163, April 22, 1982," 30.

113. Mark Baldassare, *PPIC Statewide Survey: Special Survey on Californians and the Initiative Process* (San Francisco: Public Policy Institute of California, October, 2005): vi–6.

114. Mike Curb, George Deukmejian, and Paul Gann, "Arguments in Favor of Proposition 8, 1981," California Ballot Measures Database, Hastings Library, available at http://traynor.uchastings.edu/cgi-bin/starfinder/729.caproptext (July 28, 2006), capitals in original.

115. Richard Gilbert et al., "Arguments Opposed to Proposition 8, 1981," California Ballot Measures Database, Hastings Library, available at http://traynor.uchastings.edu/cgi-bin/starfinder/729.caproptext (July 28, 2006), capitals in original.

116. Baldassare, *PPIC Statewide Survey*, vii.

117. Paul Gann Archive, Newsclippings, Box 1395, Folder 9 (Sacramento: California State Library, California History Section).

118. Paul Gann, television interview, Channel 24, Los Angeles, September 16, 1981, Paul Gann Archive (Sacramento: California State Library, California History Section).

119. Mrs. Robert Mays, Letter to Paul Gann, 1981, Paul Gann Archive, Proposition 8: Analyses and Correspondence, Box 1393, Folder 6 (Sacramento: California State Library, California History Section).

120. Anne R. Brockman, Letter to Paul Gann, 1981, Paul Gann Archive, Proposition 8: Analyses and Correspondence, Box 1393, Folder 6 (Sacramento: California State Library, California History Section).

121. Mickey Wakefield, Letter to Paul Gann, December 15, 1981, Paul Gann Archive, Proposition 8: Analyses and Correspondence, Box 1393, Folder 6 (Sacramento: California State Library, California History Section).

122. C. T. Wise, Letter to California Assemblywoman Carol Hallett, July 8, 1981, Paul Gann Archive, Proposition 8: Analyses and Correspondence, Box 1393, Folder 5 (Sacramento: California State Library, California History Section).

123. Milton Collins, Letter to Paul Gann, August 2, 1981, Paul Gann Archive, Proposition 8: Analyses and Correspondence, Box 1393, Folder 6 (Sacramento: California State Library, California History Section).

124. Collins, Letter to Gann, August 2, 1981.

125. McCoy, *Politics of Plea-Bargaining*, 181.

126. Wakefield, Letter to Gann, December 15, 1981.

127. Collins, August 2, 1981.

128. California Secretary of State, "History of Initiatives."

129. Tom Tyler and Robert J. Boeckmann, "Three Strikes and You Are Out, but Why? The Psychology of Public Support for Punishing Rule Breakers," *Law & Society Review* 31.2 (1997): 237–266.

130. Beckett, *Making Crime Pay.*

131. Gann, television interview, Channel 24, Los Angeles, September 16, 1981.

132. California Secretary of State, "History of Initiatives," 8.

133. "Proposition 184: Increased Sentences, Repeat Offenders," California Ballot Measures Database, Hastings Library, available at http://traynor.uchastings.edu/cgi-bin/starfinder/6757/calprop.txt (December 19, 2006).

134. James Austin, John Clark, Patricia Hardyman, and D. Alan Henry, "The Impact of 'Three Strikes and You' re Out,'" *Punishment and Society* 1.2 (1999): 131–162.

135. Governor Arnold Schwarzenegger, "Swearing-In Remarks, November 13, 2003," Sacramento, CA, available at http://gov.ca.gov/index.php?/print-version/speech/3086/ (August 21, 2007).

136. Governor Arnold Schwarzenegger, "Swearing-In Remarks"; capitals in original.

137. Public Policy Institute of California, "PPIC Statewide Survey: Californians and Their Government," Public Policy Institute of California and James Irvine Foundation, San Francisco, May 2007, 22.

138. Office of the Governor of California, Fact Sheet, 2007, available at http://gov.ca.gov/index.php?/fact-sheet/6116 (August 17, 2007).

139. Office of the Governor of California, Fact Sheet, 2007.

140. For further discussion of this optimistic view of California's prison reform, particularly of Petersilia's involvement in state government, see Jonathan Simon's blog for *Governing through Crime,* "The Professor and the Governor," posted May 11, 2007, available at http://governingthroughcrime.blogspot.com/2007_05_01_archive.html (August 21, 2007).

141. Office of the Governor, "Comprehensive Prison Reform, Fact Sheet: More Rehabilitation, Fewer Victims," available at http://gov.ca.gov/index.php?/fact-sheet/6089 (March 21, 2008).

142. Jennifer Warren, "Prison Plan Ignores Major Issues," *Los Angeles Times,* April 27, 2007, B1.

143. Office of the Governor of California, "Fact Sheet: Governor Signs Prison Agreement," available at http://gov.ca.gov/index.php?/fact-sheet/6116 (August 17, 2007).

144. Austin et al., "Impact of Three Strikes."

145. California Attorney General, "Proposition 66: Official Title and Summary with Analysis by the Legislative Analyst," Sacramento, CA, 2004, 44–45.

146. Robert Salladay and Megan Garvey, "California Elections," *Los Angeles Times,* November 1, 2004, B1.

147. Red Hodges, Rev. Rick Schlosser, and Ronald Hampton, "Argument in Favor of Proposition 66, 2004," in "Proposition 66: Official Title and Summary," emphasis in original.

148. Families to Amend California's Three Strikes (FACTS), "150 Stories of Inmates," available at http://facts1.live.radicaldesigns.org/article.php?list+type&type+20 (August 16, 2007).

149. American Civil Liberties Union of Southern California, "Three Strikes Reform: Time for the Ballot, 2004," available at http://aclu-sc.org/News/OpenForum/100443/10445 (August 16, 2007).

150. California Field Poll, "Release #2141, October 13, 2004," Field Institute, San Francisco, 2, available at the Institute of Governmental Studies Library, University of California, Berkeley.

151. California Secretary of State, available at http://www.sosca.gov/elections/sov/2004_general (August 16, 2007).

152. Cam Sanchez, Jon Coupal, and Sheila Anderson, "Rebuttal to Argument in Favor of Proposition 66," in "Proposition 66: Official Title and Summary," 46.

153. Arnold Schwarzenegger, Bill Lockyer, and Harriet Salarno, "Arguments against Proposition 66," in "Limitations on 'Three Strikes' Laws, Sex Crimes, Punishment Initiative Statute," Attorney General of California (Sacramento, 004), 47.

154. Schwarzenegger et al., "Arguments against Proposition 66," 47.

155. Schwarzenegger et al., "Arguments against Proposition 66," 47.

156. Mike Reynolds, "Three Strikes and You' re Out: Stop Repeat Offenders: An Official Online Resource," available at http://www.threestrikes.org/index.html (August 16, 2007).

CHAPTER 4

1. Samuel Walker, *Taming the System: The Control of Discretion in Criminal Justice, 1950–1990* (New York: Oxford University Press, 1993).

2. Walker, *Taming the System.*

3. Christopher Bayley, "Good Intentions Gone Awry—Proposals for Fundamental Change in Criminal Sentencing," *Washington Law Review* 51 (1976): 529–564; Barbara McEleney, *Correctional Reform in New York: The Rockefeller Years and Beyond* (Lanham, Md.: University Press of America, 1985); American Friends Service Committee Working Party, *Struggle for Justice: A Report on Crime and Punishment in America* (New York: Hill and Wang, 1971).

4. Daniel Evans, "State of the State, 1974," Office of the Governor, 2S-4-42, Washington State Library and Archive, Olympia.

5. Evans, "State of the State, 1974."

6. Daniel Evans, "The Evans Administration: A Record of Continuing Achievement 1972–1973," Office of the Governor, Daniel Evans Gubernatorial Papers, 2S-I-44, Washington State Library and Archive, Olympia.

7. Evans, "Evans Administration, 1972–1973"; Washington State Department of Corrections, "Community Corrections," available at http://www.doc.wa.gov/aboutdoc/communitycorrections.asp (February 22, 2008).

8. Norval Morris, *The Future of Imprisonment* (Chicago: University of Chicago Press, 1974), 59.

9. William Henry, Law and Justice Planning Division, "Testimony to the House Institutions Committee, July 28, 1978," Office of the Governor, Dixie Lee Ray Gubernatorial Papers: Governor's Council on Crime and Justice, 2T4012, Washington State Library and Archive, Olympia, 9–10.

10. For an insightful and useful discussion of punishment as degradation, see Whitman, *Harsh Justice*, 19–37.

11. Revised Code of Washington State, "Sentencing Reform Act of 1981, 9.94A.010," available at http://apps.leg.wa.gov/RCW/default.aspx? (February 22, 2008).

12. On the diversion of low-level offenders away from prison and subsequent drop in imprisonment rates, see David Boerner and Roxanne Lieb, "Sentencing Reform in the Other Washington," in *Crime and Justice: A Review of the Research*, ed. Michael Tonry (Chicago: University of Chicago Press, 2001), 71–135.

13. BJS, "Prisoners in 2007," 18.

14. BJS, "Prisoners in 2007," 18; Sentencing Project, "Comparative International Incarceration Rates: An Examination of Causes and Trends," Report to U.S. Commission on Civil Rights, June 20, 2003.

15. BJS, *Probation and Parole in the United States, 2002* (Washington, D.C.: U.S. Department of Justice, 2003), 2. Also see Washington State Department of Corrections, "Community Corrections Population Characteristics," available at http://www.doc.wa.gov/general/communitypopcharacteristics.htm (December 10, 2003).

16. Daniel Evans, "State of the State Address, January 11, 1967," Office of the Governor, Daniel Evans Gubernatorial Papers, 2S-4-42, Washington State Library and Archive, Olympia.

17. Daniel Evans, "State of the State Address, January 10, 1972," Office of the Governor, Daniel Evans Gubernatorial Papers 2S-4-42, Washington State Library and Archive, Olympia.

18. Daniel Evans, "Speech to the National Council on Crime and Delinquency, September 24, 1968," Office of the Governor, Evans Gubernatorial Papers, 2S-4-38, Washington State Library and Archive, Olympia.

19. See for example, Evans, "Speech September 24, 1968"; Evans, "State of the State, January 12, 1971," Office of the Governor, Daniel Evans Gubernatorial Papers 2S-4-42, Washington State Library and Archive, Olympia.

20. U.S. Census Bureau, "Persons Reported Registered and Voted by State: 2000, No. 420," Statistical Abstract of the United States, available at http://www.census.gov/statab; Gray and Hanson, *Politics in the American States*, table 3.4. Washington ranks tenth in the nation in terms of social capital, scoring 0.65, according to Putnam's social capital index, *Bowling Alone*.

21. Putnam, *Bowling Alone*.

22. On the violence inherent in criminal case processing and punishment, see Cover, "Violence and the Word"; on the dehumanizing aspects of confinement, see Sykes, *Society of Captives*; on the psychologically debilitating effects of imprisonment, particularly long-term isolation, see Haney, "Psychological Impact."

23. Western, *Punishment and Inequality in America*; Manza and Uggen, *Locked Out*.

24. Petersilia, *When Prisoners Come Home*.

25. On progressive populism, see Clemens, *People's Lobby*.

26. Clemens, *People's Lobby*; Goodwyn, *Populist Moment*; Christopher Lasch, *The True and Only Heaven: Progress and Its Critics* (New York: Norton, 1991), 337.

27. Goodwyn, *Populist Moment*; Berlet and Lyons, *Right Wing Populism in America*.

28. Rogers, quoted in Carroll H. Wooddy, "Populism in Washington: A Study of the Legislature of 1897," *Washington Historical Quarterly* (1930): 108.

29. Clemens, *People's Lobby*; Goodwyn, *Populist Moment*; Lasch, *True and Only Heaven*.

30. Wooddy, "Populism in Washington," 103.

31. Clemens, *People's Lobby*.

32. Washington State Constitution, Amendment 7, Article 2, Section 1 "Legislative Powers, Where Vested," 1911, available at http://www.leg.wa.gov/LawsAndAgencyRules/constitution.htm (February 22, 2008).

33. Clemens, *People's Lobby*, 260; Berlet and Lyons, *Right Wing Populism*.

34. Clemens, *People's Lobby*.

35. Clemens, *People's Lobby*, 271.

36. Lasch, *True and Only Heaven*; Didion, *Where I Was From*.

37. Lasch, *True and Only Heaven*, 93.

38. Evans, "State of the State, 1974" and "Budget Message," Office of the Governor, 2S-4-42 and 2S-4-37, Washington State Library and Archive, Olympia.

39. Schofer and Fourcade-Gourinchas, "The Structural Contexts of Civic Engagement."

40. Peirce and Hagstrom, *Book of America*.

41. Margaret Ada Miller, *The Left's Turn: Labor Welfare Politics and Social Movements in Washington State, 1937–1973* (Ph.D. diss., University of Washington, 2000).

42. Amenta, *Bold Relief*.

43. Miller, *Left's Turn*; Amenta, *Bold Relief*.

44. Amenta, *Bold Relief*, 167.

45. Amenta, *Bold Relief*; Beckett and Western, "Governing Social Marginality."

46. Amenta, *Bold Relief*.

47. Peirce and Hagstrom, *Book of America*.

48. The Index of Governors' Institutional Powers is a useful indicator of the degree of centralization because it measures the degree to which governors control budgets, legislation, appointments, political parties, the strength of veto power, and the length of tenure, including the presence or absence of term limits. The stronger the governors' powers, the more centralized political authority, and vice versa. Both decentralized California and Washington (3.2) score below the national average (3.5) in terms of governors' powers and well below more centralized states like New York or Illinois (4.1); see Beyle, "The Governors," 212–213.

49. California and Washington use the initiative process differently. Californians have tried to use and have passed many more voter initiatives than Washington. Between 1914 and 2002, Californians voted on 290 initiatives and approved 99. For details, see California Secretary of State, "A History of California Initiatives." By contrast, between 1914 and 2005, Washingtonians voted on 125 ballots and approved 63. For details, see Washington State Secretary of State, "Elections: Index to Initiatives and Referendum History and Statistics, 1914–2005," available at http://www.secstate.wa.gov/elections/initiatives/statistics.aspx (July 20, 2006). Washington has a higher approval rate on fewer ballots, suggesting that they are possibly better understood, are better discussed, and represent compromises.

50. "Give us a piece of your mind, March 22–27, 2004," town hall meeting with state lawmakers Debbie Regala, Jeannie Darneille, Dennis Flannigan, available at http://access.wa.gov.

51. "8th District lawmakers schedule town hall meeting, February 9, 2004," town hall meeting with state lawmakers Pat Hale, Kennewick, Hankins, Delvin, available at http://access.wa.gov.

52. "Save the Date, March 22, 2004," town hall meeting with state representatives Sharon Tomiko Santos and Eric Pettigrew, available at http://access.wa.gov.

53. On deliberation and pluralist politics, see Amy Gutman and Dennis Thompson, *Why Deliberative Democracy?* (Princeton, N.J.: Princeton University Press, 2004).

54. David Green, "Public Opinion versus Public Judgment about Crime: Correction the 'Comedy of Errors,'" *British Journal of Criminology* 46 (January 2006): 131–154.

55. Gerry Johnstone, "Penal Policy Making: Elitist, Populist or Participatory," *Punishment & Society* 2.2 (2000): 161–180.

56. Stephen Knack, "Social Capital and the Quality of Government: Evidence from the US States," *American Journal of Political Science* 46.4 (October 2002): 772–785.

57. Daniel Evans, "The Courts: Key to Civilizing an Urban Society, November 11, 1966," Speech to Citizens' Conference on Washington's Courts, Office of the Governor, Daniel Evans Gubernatorial Paper, 2S-4-38, Washington State Library and Archive, Olympia. Also see Daniel Evans, "Proposal for a Combined Structure for Administering the Juvenile Delinquency Prevention and Omnibus Crime Control and Safe Streets

Act, 1968," Office of the Governor, Daniel Evans Gubernatorial Papers, 2S-2-432, Washington State Library and Archive, Olympia.

58. Quintard Taylor, *The Forging of a Black Community: Seattle's Central District from 1870 through the Civil Rights Era* (Seattle: University of Washington Press, 1994); U.S. Census Bureau, cited in Taylor, *Forging Black Community*, 192.

59. Taylor, *Black Community*.

60. In 1960, Washington's violent crime rate hovered around 57 reported incidents per 100,000 population. Five years later, in 1965, that rate nearly doubled, reaching 103 reported incidents per 100,000 population. By 1970, the rate doubled again, reaching 221 reported incidents per 100,000 population. For details, see Federal Bureau of Investigation (FBI), *Uniform Crime Report 1965*; FBI, "Uniform Crime Report 2006"; BJS, *Sourcebook of Criminal Justice Statistics—1976*; BJS, *Sourcebook of Criminal Justice Statistics—1986*.

61. For details, see FBI, *Uniform Crime Report 1965*; FBI, "Uniform Crime Report 2006"; BJS, *Sourcebook of Criminal Justice Statistics—1976*; BJS, *Sourcebook of Criminal Justice Statistics—1986*.

62. For details, see FBI, *Uniform Crime Report 1965*; FBI, "Uniform Crime Report 2006"; BJS, *Sourcebook of Criminal Justice Statistics—1976*; BJS, *Sourcebook of Criminal Justice Statistics—1986*.

63. Washington State Law and Justice Planning Division, "Comprehensive Plan for Law Enforcement, 1970," Office of the Governor, Planning and Community Affairs. Washington State Library and Archive, Olympia.

64. J. Edgar Hoover, quoted in the Republican Party Policy Committee, "Richard Nixon Campaign Key Issues 1968," Office of the Governor, Daniel Evans Gubernatorial Paper, 2S-1-21, Washington State Library and Archive, Olympia; emphasis in original.

65. Richard Nixon, quoted in Beckett, *Making Crime Pay*, 38.

66. Ronald Reagan, quoted in "GOP Testimony on Violence," *New York Times*, August 1, 1968, 20.

67. Washington State Citizens Council on Crime and Delinquency, "Council Minutes, February 22, 1966," Office of the Governor, Daniel Evans Gubernatorial Papers, Washington State Library and Archive, Olympia.

68. Washington State Law and Justice Planning Division, "Comprehensive Plan for Law Enforcement, 1970."

69. For a discussion on the "new criminologies of everyday life," see Garland, *Culture of Control*, 127–131. For more on situational crime prevention, see Ronald Clarke, ed., *Situational Crime Prevention: Successful Case Studies* (Guilderland, N.Y.: Harrow and Heston, 1997).

70. Taylor, *Black Community*.

71. Taylor, *Black Community*.

72. Kramer, quoted in Washington State Commission on the Causes and Prevention of Civil Unrest, "Report on Race and Violence in Washington, 1969,"

Office of the Governor, Daniel Evans Gubernatorial Papers, Washington State Library and Archive, Olympia.

73. Kramer, quoted in "Report on Race."

74. "The Evans Administration: A Record of Continuing Achievement 1972–1973."

75. Richard Kitto, "Editor's Note, Symposium: Law and the Correctional Process in Washington," *Washington Law Review* 51 (1976): 491–528.

76. Law and Justice Planning Division, "Comprehensive Plan," 324.

77. Henry, "Testimony to House Institutions Committee, July 28, 1978."

78. Henry, "Testimony to House Institutions Committee, July 28, 1978," 9–10.

79. Washington State Citizens Council on Crime and Delinquency, "Council Minutes, February 1966."

80. Law and Justice Planning Office, "Comprehensive Plan, 1970," 338.

81. Sentencing Reform Act, Washington Laws Ch. 9.94A, Sec.725, Revised Code of Washington (1981), available at http://apps.leg.wa.gov/RCW/default.aspx?cite (February 25, 2008).

82. Washington State Department of Corrections, "Offender Crews," available ay http://www.doc.wa.gov/aboutdoc/offendercrews.asp (February 25, 2008).

83. Sentencing Reform Act. Also see Boerner and Lieb, "Sentencing Reform."

84. Sentencing Reform Act.

85. David Boerner, *Sentencing in Washington: A Legal Analysis of the Sentencing Reform Act of 1981* (Seattle, Wash.: Butterworth, 1985).

86. Boerner and Lieb, "Sentencing Reform," 95.

87. On deliberation and mutual respect, see Gutman and Thompson, *Why Deliberative Democracy?*

88. Washington Association of Prosecuting Attorneys, "Justice in Sentencing, 1981," House of Representatives, Committee on Institutions, Washington State Archive and Library, Olympia.

89. Washington Association of Prosecuting Attorneys, "Justice in Sentencing."

90. Bayley, "Good Intentions Gone Awry," 551.

91. Washington State House of Representatives Institutions Committee Task Force on Sentencing 1979–1980, Washington State Archive and Library, Olympia.

92. Jean T. Hueston, quoted in "Sentencing Guidelines Public Hearings and Written Testimony," Washington State Sentencing Guidelines Commission, 1981–1983, Office of the Governor: John Spellman's Gubernatorial Papers, 2U-08-045, Washington State Library and Archive, Olympia.

93. Tina Peterson, quoted in "Sentencing Guidelines Public Hearings and Written Testimony."

94. Maria Lindsey, quoted in "Sentencing Guidelines Public Hearings and Written Testimony."

95. Jonathan Nelson, quoted in "Sentencing Guidelines Public Hearings and Written Testimony."

96. "Sentencing Guidelines Public Hearings and Written Testimony."

97. See discussion in Boerner and Lieb, "Sentencing Reform."

98. See Putnam, *Making Democracy Work.*

99. *Seattle Post-Intelligencer,* January 29, 1990, B1.

100. The CPA defined "sexual predators" as a certain class of repeat violent sex offenders who are diagnosed with "mental abnormalities or personality disorders" and who are likely to recidivate unless confined. See Community Protection Act, Washington Laws Ch. 3, Sec 1002, Revised Code of Washington 71.09 (1990).

101. Norm Maleng, "Governor's Task Force on Community Protection Report, November 28, 1989," Governor's Task Force on Community Protection, Booth Gardner Gubernatorial Papers, Washington State Library and Archive, Olympia.

102. Washington State Department of Social and Health Services, "Statistics on the Number of Persons Civilly Committed to the Special Commitment Center Program," available at http://www1.dshs.wa.gov/hrsa/scc/Stats.htm (September 23, 2006); Washington State Institute for Public Policy, "Sex Offender Sentencing in Washington State: How Sex Offenders Differ from Other Felony Offenders," Washington State Institute for Public Policy, Olympia, September 2, 2005; Washington State Institute for Public Policy, "Sex Offender Sentencing in Washington State: Initial Sentencing Decision," Washington State Institute for Public Policy, Olympia, September 16, 2005.

103. Washington State Institute of Public Policy, "Sex Offender Sentencing."

104. Community Protection Act.

105. Washington State Department of Social and Health Services, "Statistics on the Number of Persons Civilly Committed to the Special Commitment Center Program."

106. Washington State Office of Crime Victim Advocacy, available at http://www.cted.wa.gov/portal/alias_lang_en/tabID_244 (September 23, 2006).

107. Lisa Miller, "Looking for Postmodernism in All the Wrong Places: Implementing a New Penology," *British Journal of Criminology* 41.1 (Winter 2001): 168–184.

108. Washington State Senate Law and Justice Committee, "Public Hearings on Community Protection, January 9–12, 1990," audiotapes, Washington State Library and Archive, Olympia.

109. Robert Cover, quoted in David Boerner, "Confronting Violence: In the Act and in the Word," *University of Puget Sound Law Review* 15 (1992): 576.

110. Boerner, "Confronting Violence," 576.

111. Quoted in Boerner, "Confronting Violence," 539.

112. Maleng, "Governor's Task Force."

113. Maleng, "Governor's Task Force."

114. Washington State Senate Law and Justice Committee, "Public Hearings on Community Protection, January 9–12, 1990."

115. Washington State Senate Law and Justice Committee, "Public Hearings on Community Protection, January 9–12, 1990."

116. Washington State Senate Law and Justice Committee, "Public Hearings on Community Protection, January 9–12, 1990."

117. Quoted in Stuart Scheingold, Toska Olson, and Jana Pershing, "Sexual Violence, Victim Advocacy, and Republican Criminology: Washington State's Community Protection Act," *Law & Society Review* 28.4 (1992): 740.

118. Washington State Senate Law and Justice Committee, "Public Hearings on Community Protection, January 9–12, 1990."

119. Quoted in Boerner, "Confronting Violence," 531.

120. Quoted in Boerner, "Confronting Violence," 536.

121. Elaine Scarry, *The Body in Pain: The Making and Unmaking of the World* (New York: Oxford University Press, 1987).

122. Washington State Senate Law and Justice Committee, "Public Hearings on Community Protection, January 9–12, 1990."

123. Quoted in Boerner, "Confronting Violence," 536; emphasis in original.

124. Washington State Senate Law and Justice Committee, "Public Hearings on Community Protection, January 9–12, 1990."

125. Helen Harlow, quoted in *Seattle Post-Intelligencer*, October 30, 1990, A1.

126. *Seattle Post-Intelligencer*, January 29, 1990, B1.

127. Booth Gardner, "State of the State Address, 1990," Office of the Governor, Booth Gardner's Gubernatorial Papers: Speeches, 8 93-A-24, Washington State Library and Archive, Olympia.

128. Gardner, "State of the State, 1990."

129. Maleng, "Governor's Task Force."

130. Maleng, "Governor's Task Force."

131. The Hard Time reform was originally introduced as a legislative bill but failed in both houses. It eventually passed as an initiative to the legislature. In Washington, citizens can write their own legislation, gather enough qualifying signatures, and put the proposal either before the public or state legislature for a vote.

132. The Three Strikes (I 593) Initiative to the People, Hard Time for Armed Crime (I 159) Initiative to the Legislature, juvenile justice reform (3 SHB 3900), and methamphetamine manufacture (HB 2628) increased Washington State's prison population. See Washington State Sentencing Guidelines Commission, "The Sentencing Reform Act at Century's End: An Assessment of Adult Felony Sentencing Practices in the State of Washington," Report to the Governor and the Legislature, January 2000.

133. Norm Maleng, quoted in Dave LaCourse, "Hard Time for Armed Crime: Policy Brief, 1997," Washington Policy Center, available at http://www.washingtonpolicy.org/CriminalJustice/PNHardTimeforArmed Crime97–04.html (August 26, 2007).

134. Austin, Clark, Hardyman, and Henry, "The Impact of 'Three Strikes and You're Out.'" Also see William Claiborne, "California Only State Applying 'Three Strikes' Law Extensively," *Washington Post*, September 1996, A3.

135. Chase Riveland, quoted in Claiborne, "California Only State Applying 'Three Strikes' Law Extensively."

136. For testimony in favor, see "Senate Bill Report: SI 159, 1995," Washington State Senate Committee on Ways and Means, 1995, 3.

137. LaCourse, "Hard Time for Armed Crime: Policy Brief, 1997."

138. For testimony against, see "Senate Bill Report: SI 159, 1995," 1–3.

139. "Senate Bill Report: SI 159, 1995," 1–3.

140. In Washington, voters voted on a death penalty and three strikes initiative. See Death Penalty Initiative 316 (1975) and the Sentencing of Criminals Initiative 589 (1993), Washington State Secretary of State, "Elections: Index to Initiatives and Referendum History and Statistics, 1914–2005."

141. California Secretary of State, "A History of California Initiatives." available at

142. Mike Lowry, "State of the State Address, January 9, 1996," available at http://www.digitalarchives.wa.gov/GovernorLowry/sos1.htm (August 26, 2007).

143. ESSB 6094, Section 708, Chapter 488, Laws of 2005. See Steve Aos, Marna Miller, and Elizabeth Drake, *Evidence-Based Public Policy Options to Reduce Future Prison Construction, Criminal Justice Costs, and Crime Rates* (Olympia: Washington State Institute for Public Policy, 2006), 2.

144. See SSHB 2338.

145. Between 1997 and 2000, Washington increased spending on prevention by 36 percent and increased spending on treatment by 27 percent. See Gary Locke, "Major Accomplishments: Public Safety," available at http://www.digitalarchives.wa.gov/governorlocke/accomplish/safety.htm (August 26, 2007).

146. See Washington State Sentencing Guidelines Commission, "The Sentencing Reform Act at Century's End."

147. See Locke, "Major Accomplishments: Public Safety."

148. Foucault, *Discipline and Punish*, 104.

CHAPTER 5

1. McKinney's Consolidated Laws of New York, 1973 Session Laws of New York.

2. McKinney's Consolidated Laws of New York, 1973 Session Laws of New York, 405.

3. McKinney's Consolidated Laws of New York, 1973 Session Laws of New York.

4. Nelson A. Rockefeller, "Annual Message to the Legislature, January 3, 1973," Public Papers of Nelson A. Rockefeller, Governor of the State of New York, Albany; Nelson A. Rockefeller, "Annual Message to the Legislature, January 6, 1971," Public Papers of Nelson A. Rockefeller, Governor of the State of New York, Albany, 53.

5. McKinney's Consolidated Laws of New York, 1973 Session Laws of New York; McKinney's Consolidated Laws of New York, 2004.

6. McKinney's Consolidated Laws of New York, 1973 Session Laws of New York; McKinney's Consolidated Laws of New York, 2004.

7. McKinney's Consolidated Laws of New York, 1978 Session Laws of New York; New York Consolidated Laws Article 70.

8. New York State Commission on Management and Productivity in the Public Sector, *Violent Attacks and Chronic Offenders: A Proposal for Concentrating the Resources of New York's Criminal Justice System on the "Hard Core" of the Crime Problem* (Albany: New York, 1978), 48.

9. New York State Commission on Management and Productivity in the Public Sector, *Violent Attacks*, 48.

10. New York State Commission on Management and Productivity in the Public Sector, *Violent Attacks*, 48.

11. Chauncey G. Parker, "Testimony of Chauncey G. Parker, New York State Director of Criminal Justice, February 2, 2004," Joint Legislative Fiscal Committees on the State 2004–05 Budget, Albany, New York.

12. On risk management, see Malcolm Feeley and Jonathan Simon, "The New Penology: Notes on the Emerging Strategy of Corrections and Its Implications," *Criminology* 30.4 (1992): 449–474; Anthony Bottoms, "The Philosophy and Politics of Punishment and Sentencing," in *The Politics of Sentencing Reform*, Chris Morgan Clarkson and Rod Morgan, eds. (Oxford: Clarendon Press, 1995), 17–49.

13. New York State Department of Correctional Services, "Inmates under Custody: By Crime, 1975–1979; 1980–1989; 1987–1992; 1991–2000," Albany, New York. Until relatively recently, the national average for violent offenders in prison was under 50 percent, with property offenders and drug offenders making up about 20 percent each (BJS 2007). We should note here that although the New York State Department of Correctional Services classifies burglary as a violent felony offense, for comparative purposes, I have calculated burglary under property offenses to make more meaningful comparisons across cases and across offense type with data from the California Department of Corrections, Washington Department of Corrections, and the BJS.

14. BJS, "Prisoners in 2007," 18; BJS, *Sourcebook of Criminal Justice Statistics—1976*; BJS, *Sourcebook of Criminal Justice Statistics—1986*.

15. New York has relatively low voter participation. In 2006, for example, 37.6 percent of the voting age population voted as compared to 43.6 percent of the national average. See U.S. Census Bureau, "Persons Reported Registered and Voted by State: 2006, Table 405." On rates of civic engagement and social capital, see Putnam, *Bowling Alone*. On the federal court order, see Edward Schneier and John Murtaugh, *New York Politics: A Tale of Two States* (Armonk, N.Y.: M.E. Sharpe, 2001).

16. Schneier and Murtaugh, *New York Politics*.

17. Schneier and Murtaugh, *New York Politics*.

18. Stephen Skowronek, *Building a New American State: The Expansion of National Administrative Capacities, 1877–1920* (Cambridge: Cambridge University Press, 1982); Mayhew, *Placing Parties*.

19. Peirce and Hagstrom, *Book of America*.

20. Edwin Burrows and Mike Wallace, *Gotham: A History of New City to 1898* (Oxford: Oxford University Press, 1999).

21. Burrows and Wallace, *Gotham*.

22. Sarah Liebschutz with Robert Bailey, Jeffrey Stonecash, Jane Shapiro Zacek, and Joseph Zimmerman, *New York Politics and Government: Competition and Compassion* (Lincoln: University of Nebraska Press, 1998).

23. Liebschultz et al., *New York Politics*.

24. McMath, *American Populism*; Burrows and Wallace, *Gotham*.

25. Ann Shola Orloff, "The Political Origins of America's Belated Welfare State," in *The Politics of Social Policy in the United States*, eds. Margaret Weir, Ann Shola Orloff, and Theda Skocpol (Princeton, N.J.: Princeton University Press, 1988).

26. Elizabeth Clapp, *Mothers of All Children: Women Reformers and the Rise of the Juvenile Courts in Progressive Era America* (University Park: Pennsylvania State University Press, 1998).

27. Clapp, *Mothers*; Clemens, *People's Lobby*; Stephen J. McGovern, *The Politics of Downtown Development: Dynamic Political Cultures in San Francisco and Washington D.C.* (Lexington: University Press of Kentucky, 1998).

28. Clapp, *Mothers*; David Rothman, *Conscience and Convenience: The Asylum and its Alternatives in Progressive America* (Glenview, Ill.: Scott, Foresman, 1980); Michael Katz, *In the Shadow of the Poorhouse: A Social History of Welfare in America* (New York: Basic Books, 1986).

29. Mayhew, *Placing Parties*.

30. Peirce and Hagstrom, *Book of America*.

31. Peirce and Hagstrom, *Book of America*; Orloff, "Political Origins."

32. McGovern, *Politics of Downtown*.

33. Katz, *Shadow of the Poorhouse*.

34. Bureau of Analysis and Investigation, cited in Katz, *Shadow of the Poorhouse*, 191.

35. Katz, *Shadow of the Poorhouse*.

36. Katz, *Shadow of the Poorhouse*.

37. On social pollution, see Mary Douglas, *Purity and Danger: An Analysis of the Concept of Pollution and Taboo* (London: Routledge, 1966).

38. Amenta, *Bold Relief*.

39. Amenta, *Bold Relief*.

40. Amenta, *Bold Relief*.

41. Herbert Jacob and Kenneth Vines, eds., *Politics in the American States: A Comparative Analysis* (Boston: Little, Brown, 1965), 390.

42. Jacob and Vines, *Politics in the American States*, 388.

43. Virginia Gray, Herbert Jacob, and Kenneth Vines, eds., *Politics in the American States: A Comparative Analysis* (Boston: Little, Brown, 1999), 4.

44. Thad Beyle has compiled a very useful index of governors' institutional powers. He measures the degree to which governors control budgets, legislation, appointments, political parties, the strength of veto power and the length of tenure, including the presence or absence of term limits; New York scores a 4.1 out of 5 to the

nation's average 3.5, California's 3.4, Washington's 3.2, and Alabama's low 2.7. See Beyle, "Governors," 212–13.

45. Beyle, "Governors."

46. Beyle, "Governors."

47. Beyle, "Governors."

48. Although Rockefeller resigned before the end of his fourth term, under his fifteen-year tenure, New York improved its roadways, created the Metropolitan Transportation Authority to administer mass transit; initiated the construction of the Twin Towers, home to New York's financial center; and established the State University of New York, subsidizing higher education for thousands of residents. See Peirce and Hagstrom, *Book of America*.

49. In the highly contentious 2000 presidential election that was later disputed in the Supreme Court, 51 percent of New York's voting age population turned out to vote, a figure lower than the 55 percent of the national average and 59 percent in Washington. See U.S. Census Bureau, "Statistical Abstract of the United States: Persons Reported Registered and Voted by State: 2000, Table 402"; Virginia Gray, Herbert Jacob, and Robert Albritton, *Politics in the American States* (Glenview, Ill.: Scott, Foresman, 1990).

50. Gray, Hanson, and Jacob, *Politics in the American States*, 100.

51. By 2002, New York ranked thirty-ninth in voter turnout, California ranked forty-fifth, and Washington ranked thirteenth. See figures in Gray and Hansen, *Politics in the American States*, 93.

52. In 1988, New York City created the Voter Assistance Commission to increase "participation in the democratic process." One mayoral appointee, Robert J. McFeeley of Staten Island, appears to be the only "citizen" representative, as he holds no title. Consider the other members and their various titles and professions. The mayor appointed Dr. Jeffrey Kraus, professor of Political Science, Wagner College, to chair the commission. The New York City Council appointed six members, including Jane Kalmus, executive director, National Non Partisan Voter Registration Campaign; Elizabeth Sunshine, executive director, New York State Institute on Disability; Morshed Alam, Department of Environmental Protection; and Glen D. Magpantay, staff attorney, Asian American Legal Defense and Education Fund. The commission also includes seven ex officio members: Carol Robles-Roman, deputy mayor for Legal Affairs; John Ravitz, executive director, NYC Board of Elections; Mark Page, director, Office of Management and Budget; Frederick A. O. Schwarz, NYC Campaign Finance Board; Betsy Gotbaum, public advocate; Michael A. Cardoza, Corporation Council, NYC Law Department; and Joel I. Klein, chancellor, NYC Department of Education (Voter Assistance Commission 2004). See Voter Assistance Commission, "About Commissioners," available at http://www.nyc.gov/html/vac/html/aboutcommissioners.html.

53. New York scores a relatively low 0.36, ranking thirty-fourth in the nation, just below twenty-eighth-ranked California at 0.18, and far below social capital-rich states like Minnesota (1.32), Vermont (1.42), and Washington (0.65). For details, see Putnam, *Bowling Alone*.

54. Putnam, *Bowling Alone*.

55. Putnam, *Bowling Alone*.

56. Hugh Carey, "Annual Message, January 4, 1978," in Public Papers of Hugh Carey, Governor of the State of New York, Albany.

57. Mario Cuomo, "Message to the Legislature, November 10, 1985," in Public Papers of Mario Cuomo, Governor of the State of New York, Albany.

58. U.S. Census Bureau, "Statistical Abstract of the United States: State Governments—Expenditures and Debt by State 2004, Table 440," available at http://www.census.gov/compendia/statab/tables/08s0440.pdf (March 10, 2008).

59. Gray, Hanson, and Jacob, *Politics in American States*, 4.

60. Gray, Hanson, and Jacob, *Politics in American States*, 333.

61. Gray, Hanson, and Jacob, *Politics in American States*, 333.

62. U.S. Census Bureau, "Statistical Abstract of the United States: State Unemployment Insurance by State and Other Area: 2002, No. 555," available at http://www.census.gov/statab/www.

63. U.S. Census Bureau, "Statistical Abstract of the United States: State and Local Government—Expenditures and Debt by State 2000, No. 447," available at http://www.census.gov/statab/www.

64. Nelson A. Rockefeller, "Annual Message to the Legislature, January 3, 1973," 10.

65. Gerald Benjamin and T. Normal Hurd, eds., *Rockefeller in Retrospect: The Governor's New York Legacy* (Albany, N.Y.: Nelson A. Rockefeller Institute of Government, 1984).

66. Nelson A. Rockefeller, "Annual Message to the Legislature, January 6, 1971."

67. Cuomo, "Message to the Legislature, November 10, 1985," 7.

68. U.S. Census Bureau, "Statistical Abstract of the United States: State and Local Government Employment and Average Monthly Earnings by State 1995 and 2004, Table 452," available at http://www.census.gov/compendia/statab/tables/08s0452.pdf (March 10, 2008).

69. Pamala Griset, *Determinate Sentencing: The Promise and the Reality of Retributive Justice* (Albany: State University of New York Press, 1991).

70. McEleney, *Correctional Reform*.

71. McEleney, *Correctional Reform*.

72. "Governor Creates State Crime Panel," *New York Times*, December 20, 1968, 31.

73. Richard Reeves, "Governor Will Seek Panel on Narcotics," *New York Times*, January 30, 1970, 1.

74. Griset, *Determinate Sentencing*.

75. FBI, *Uniform Crime Report 1965*; FBI, "Uniform Crime Report 2006"; BJS, *Sourcebook of Criminal Justice Statistics—1976*; BJS, *Sourcebook of Criminal Justice Statistics—1986*.

76. FBI, *Uniform Crime Report 1965*; FBI, "Uniform Crime Report 2006"; BJS, *Sourcebook of Criminal Justice Statistics—1976*; BJS, *Sourcebook of Criminal Justice Statistics—1986*.

77. New York State Commission on Management and Productivity in the Public Sector, *Violent Attacks*, 4.

78. Nelson A. Rockefeller, "Annual Message to the Legislature, January 5, 1966," in Public Papers of Nelson A. Rockefeller, Governor of the State of New York, Albany.

79. "Rockefeller Seeks State Fund to Aid Victims of Crime," *New York Times*, October 24, 1965: 1.

80. "Rockefeller Seeks State Fund to Aid Victims of Crime," 1.

81. *New York Statistical Yearbook 1979*, Table L-9 (Albany: New York State Division of the Budget).

82. *New York Statistical Yearbook 1979*, Table L-9.

83. New York State Crime Victims Board, "Victim Support Services," available at http://www.cvb.state.ny.us/services.

84. Nancy E. Marion, *Criminal Justice in America: The Politics Behind the System* (Durham, N.C.: Carolina Academic Press, 2002), 117.

85. Nelson A. Rockefeller Gubernatorial Papers, Rockefeller Archive Family Archives, Rockefeller Archive Center, Sleepy Hollow, New York.

86. Griset, *Determinate Sentencing*.

87. Rockefeller argued that the state's efforts to address drug addiction and treatment need to work in conjunction with increased federal law enforcement against drug trafficking. See Nelson A. Rockefeller, "Special Message to the Legislature, March 23, 1962," NAR Gubernatorial: Press Office, Folder 1907, Box 91, Series 25, Rockefeller Family Archive, Rockefeller Archive Center, Sleepy Hollow, New York.

88. John Silbey, "Governor Spurs Help for Addicts," *New York Times*, January 3, 1965, 1; John Silbey, "State to Allow Addicts Dosage," *New York Times*, July 21, 1965, 39.

89. Tom Buckley, "City and State to Join Disputed Narcotics Program," *New York Times*, December 9, 1968, 1.

90. Buckley, "Narcotics Program."

91. Rockefeller, quoted in James Underwood and William Daniels, *Governor Rockefeller in New York: The Apex of Pragmatic Liberalism in the United States* (Westport, Conn.: Greenwood Press, 1982), 140.

92. Rockefeller, quoted in McEleney, *Correctional Reform*, 48.

93. Nelson A. Rockefeller, cited in John Silbey, "Rockefeller Seeks New Addict Law," *New York Times*, January 30, 1966, 64.

94. Lane, cited in Charles Grutzner, "Rise in Addiction Studied by State," *New York Times*, February 19, 1965, 38.

95. Rockefeller, "Annual Message to the Legislature, January 5, 1966," 12.

96. Rockefeller, quoted in McEleney, *Correctional Reform*, 48.

97. Rockefeller, "Annual Message, 1966," 10.

98. Rockefeller, "Annual Message, 1966."

99. Rockefeller, "Annual Message, 1966."

100. Rockefeller, in John Silbey, "Rockefeller Seeks New Addict Law," *New York Times*, January 30, 1966, 64.

101. Rockefeller, in Silbey, "Rockefeller Seeks New Addict Law," 64.

102. Rockefeller, in Silbey, "Rockefeller Seeks New Addict Law," 64.

103. McEleney, *Correctional Reform*; also see Alan Chartock, "Narcotics Addiction: The Politics of Frustration," in *Governing New York State: The Rockefeller Years*, eds. Robert Connery and Gerald Benjamin (New York: Academy of Political Science, 1974).

104. Rockefeller, "Annual Message, 1966," 13.

105. Rockefeller, "Annual Message, 1971," 47.

106. Rockefeller, "Annual Message, 1971," 53.

107. Rockefeller, "Annual Message, 1973," 21.

108. Rockefeller, "Annual Message, 1973," 21.

109. Rockefeller, "Annual Message, 1973," 22.

110. Griset, *Determinate Sentencing*.

111. Chartock, "Narcotics Addiction."

112. "Addicts' Victims Turned Vigilante," *New York Times*, January 8, 1969: 1.

113. "Harlem Likened to Wild West," *New York Times*, January 8, 1969: 48.

114. "Harlem Likened to wild West," 48.

115. "Addicts' Victims Turn Vigilante," 1.

116. Nelson A. Rockefeller, "News Conference with Governor Nelson A. Rockefeller, January 22, 1973," NAR Gubernatorial: Press Office, Folder 1837, Box 89, Series 8, Record Group 15, Rockefeller Family Archive, Rockefeller Archive Center, Sleepy Hollow, New York.

117. Quoted in Gerald Fraser, "Harlem Response Mixed," *New York Times*, January 5, 1973: 65.

118. Quoted in Fraser, "Harlem Response Mixed," 65.

119. "Governor Rockefeller proposes new laws that impose mandatory life sentences for hard core drug pushers and on addicts who commit serious crimes while under the influence...What are your views?" *Amsterdam News*, January 13, 1973.

120. "Rockefeller and narcotics," *Amsterdam News*, January 13, 1973.

121. Rockefeller, "News Conference."

122. "Governor Rockefeller proposes."

123. "Governor Rockefeller proposes."

124. Robert Thomas, "New Drug Laws Scored in Harlem," *New York Times*, February 3, 1973: 30.

125. Thomas, "New Drug Laws Scored in Harlem," 30.

126. Roger Biles, "Mayor David Dinkins and the Politics of Race in New York City," in *African American Mayors: Race, Politics and the American City*, eds. David Colburn and Jeffrey Adler (Urbana: University of Illinois Press, 2001).

127. Mollenkopf, "New York: The Great Anomaly"; Lockard, *Toward Equal Opportunity*.

128. New York State Department of Correctional Services, "Men and Women Undercustody: 1987–2001," Division of Program Planning Research and Evaluation, Albany, 2002, 81.

129. New York State Department of Correctional Services, "Men and Women Undercustody," 81.

130. New York State Department of Correctional Services, "Men and Women Undercustody," 81.

131. Cuomo, "Message to the Legislature, November 10, 1985," 46.

132. Cuomo, in Phillip Gutis, "Praise and Skepticism Greet Drug Plan," *New York Times*, January 5, 1989, B4.

133. New York State Department of Correctional Services, "Inmates under Custody."

134. New York State Department of Correctional Services, "Inmates under Custody."

135. Griset, *Determinate Sentencing*.

136. John Silbey, "Overhaul Urged for Penal Code," *New York Times*, March 17, 1964.

137. Bartlett Commission, in Griset, *Determinate Sentencing*, 16.

138. Griset, *Determinate Sentencing*.

139. McKinney's Consolidated Laws of New York, 2004 Session Laws of New York.

140. New York State Commission on Management and Productivity in the Public Sector, *Violent Attacks*, 3.

141. New York State Commission on Management and Productivity in the Public Sector, *Violent Attacks*, 48.

142. New York State Commission on Management and Productivity in the Public Sector, *Violent Attacks*, 48.

143. New York State Commission on Management and Productivity in the Public Sector, *Violent Attacks*, 6.

144. New York State Commission on Management and Productivity in the Public Sector, *Violent Attacks*, 30.

145. New York State Commission on Management and Productivity in the Public Sector, *Violent Attacks*, 41.

146. McKinney's Consolidated Laws of New York, 1978 Session Laws of New York.

147. Griset, *Determinate Sentencing*.

148. New York State Probation and Correction Alternatives, "Programs and ATI Programs," available at http://dpca.state.ny.us.

149. Mario Cuomo, "Annual Message to the Legislature, January 5, 1983," in Public Papers of Mario Cuomo, Governor of the State of New York, Albany, 40.

150. Cuomo, "Annual Message, January 5, 1983," 40.

151. Cuomo, "Annual Message, January 5, 1983," 39.

152. New York State Probation and Correctional Alternatives, "Programs and ATI Programs."

153. New York State Division of Parole, "Board of Parole 1997–2000," available at http://criminaljustice.state.ny.us/crimenet/ojsa/cja99/parole.pdf.

154. New York State Division of Parole, "Board of Parole 1997–2000."

155. Bottoms, "The Philosophy and Politics of Punishment and Sentencing," 25; Feeley and Simon, "The New Penology."

156. Washington State Department of Corrections, "The DOC Re-entry Initiative: Smart on Crime," available at http://www.doc.wa.gov/docs/reentrywhitepaper.pdf (March 10, 2008).

157. New York State Division of Parole, "The Board of Parole, 1999–2002, Table 4," available at http://criminaljustice.state.ny.us/crimnet/ojsa/cja_00_01/parole.pdf (March 10, 2008). For recent initiatives to keep parolees out of local jails, see New York State Division of Parole, "Reducing the Number of Parole Violators in Local Correctional Facilities in New York State," available at http://parole.state.ny.us/PROGRAMpublications.asp (March 10, 2008).

158. New York State Division of Parole, "The Board of Parole, 1999–2002, Table 4." Compare California Department of Corrections, "Rate of Felon Parolees Returned to California Prisons," Data Analysis Unit, Sacramento, 2004, Table 1.

159. New York State Division of Parole, "The Board of Parole, 1999–2002, Table 2."

160. New York State Division of Parole, "The Board of Parole, 1999–2002, Table 2."

161. New York State Division of Parole, "The Board of Parole, 199–2002, Table 2."

162. Parker, "Testimony."

163. Parker, "Testimony."

164. Parker, "Testimony."

165. Parker, "Testimony."

166. George Pataki, quoted in "Pataki Signs Rocky Drug Reform into Law," in New York State Department of Correctional Services, *DOCS TODAY*, 13 (2002): 2.

167. New York State Department of Correctional Services, "Pataki Signs Rocky Drug Reform into Law," 2.

168. Todd Purdum, "The 1994 Campaign: The Ad Campaigns; Race for Governor: Cuomo Rebuts Pataki on Crime," *New York Times*, October 28, 1994, B4.

169. Devorah Halbersam, quoted in James Dao, "Death Penalty in New York Reinstated after 18 Years; Pataki Sees Justice Served," *New York Times*, March 8, 1995, A1.

170. George Pataki, quoted in Dao, "Death Penalty in New York Reinstated," A1.

171. Joyce Purnick, "Metro Matters; A Quiet Plan to Transform Criminal Law," *New York Times*, March 4, 1996, B1.

172. Catherine Abate, quoted in Purnick, "Metro Matters," B1.

173. Editorial, "Sentencing Reform, in Secret," *New York Times*, June 3, 1995, A18.

174. George Pataki, quoted in James Dao, "Pataki Bars Sexual Offenders from New Probation Program for Nonviolent Felons," *New York Times*, May 1, 1995, B4.

175. New York State 2005–06 Executive Budget, "Public Safety and Security, 2005–2006," available at http://www.budget.state.ny.us/archive/fy0506archive/fy0506littlebook/pubSafe.html (September 2, 2007).

176. George Pataki, quoted in Clifford Levy, "Legislation Would Allow Judges to Order HIV Tests for Suspects," *New York Times*, January 12, 1996, B1.

177. New York State 2005–06 Executive Budget, "Public Safety and Security"; Editorial, "A Step Too Far on DNA Profiles," *New York Times*, December 18, 2005, 14.

178. New York State Department of Correctional Services, "Press Release, January 23, 2004," available at http://www/docs.state.ny.us/PressRel/DOCSinitiatives.html (August 31, 2007).

179. New York State Department of Correctional Services, "Press Release, January 23, 2004."

180. Joseph Treaster, "Ideas & Trends: It's Pataki, Sounding Like Cuomo; Drug Wars Cont.: The Liberals' Unlikely Ally," *New York Times*, February 5, 1995, 4.3.

181. New York State Department of Correctional Services, "Pataki Signs Rocky Drug Reform into Law," 4–5.

182. New York State Department of Correctional Services, "Pataki Signs Rocky Drug Reform into Law," 4.

183. Eliot Spitzer, "Inaugural Address, January 1, 2007," available at http://www.ny.gov/governor/keydocs/0101071_speech_print.html (August 31, 2007).

184. Spitzer, "Inaugural Address, January 1, 2007."

185. Eliot Spitzer, "Executive Order No. 10: Establishing the New York State Commission on Sentencing Reform, March 5, 2007," available at http://www.ny.gov/governor/executive_orders/exeorders/10_print.html (August 31, 2007).

CHAPTER 6

1. On the devastating effects of mass imprisonment on economic and social life, see Western, *Punishment and Inequality*; on the effects of imprisonment on political participation, namely, felon disenfranchisement, see Manza and Uggen, *Locked Out*; on the difficulties of prisoner reentry into mainstream society, see Petersilia, *When Prisoners Come Home*; also see Clear, *Imprisoning Communities*.

2. Foucault, *Discipline and Punish*; Simon, *Governing through Crime*; Garland, *Punishment and Modern Society* and *Culture of Control*.

3. Tyler and Boeckmann, "Three Strikes and You Are Out, but Why?"

4. Jason Barabas, "How Deliberation Affects Public Opinion," *American Political Science Review* 98.4 (2004): 687–701.

5. Green, "Public Opinion versus Public Judgment," 131–154.

6. Johnstone, "Penal Policy Making," 161–180.

7. See for example, Henrik Tham, "Drug Control as a National Project: The Case of Sweden," *Journal of Drug Issues* 25.1 (1995): 113–128.

8. For discussion on varying political cultures and penal regimes in Europe, the United States, New Zealand, Scandinavia, Japan, and South Africa, see Michael Cavadino and James Dignan, *Penal Systems: A Comparative Approach* (London: Sage, 2006). For a debate about the rise of global punitiveness, see John Pratt, David Brown, Mark Brown, Simon Hallsworth, and Wayne Morrison, eds., *The New Punitiveness: Trends, Theories, Perspectives* (Portland, Ore.: Willan, 2005).

Bibliography

Adler, Jeffrey S. "Introduction." In *African American Mayors: Race, Politics and the American City*, eds. David R. Colburn and Jeffrey S. Adler, 1–22. Urbana: University of Illinois Press, 2001.

Allswang, John. *The Initiative and Referendum in California, 1898–1998*. Stanford, Calif.: Stanford University Press, 2001.

Amenta, Edwin. *Bold Relief: Institutional Politics and the Origins of Modern American Social Policy*. Princeton, N.J.: Princeton University Press, 1998.

——. "State-Centered and Political Institutional Theory: Retrospect and Prospect." In *Handbook of Political Sociology: States, Civil Societies and Globalization*, ed. Thomas Janoski, Robert Alford, Alexander Hicks, and Mildred Schwartz, 96–114. Cambridge: Cambridge University Press, 2005.

Amenta, Edwin, Kathleen Dunleavy, and Mary Bernstein. "Stolen Thunder? Huey Long's Share Our Wealth, Political Mediation, and the Second New Deal." *American Sociological Review* 59.5 (October 1994): 678–702.

Amenta, Edwin, and Michael P. Young. "Democratic States and Social Movements: Theoretical Arguments and Hypotheses." *Social Problems* 46.2 (May 1999): 153–168.

American Civil Liberties Union of Southern California. "Three Strikes Reform: Time for the Ballot, 2004." Available at http://aclu-sc.org/News/OpenForum/100443/10445 (August 16, 2007).

American Friends Service Committee Working Party. *Struggle for Justice: A Report on Crime and Punishment in America*. New York: Hill and Wang, 1971.

Anton, Thomas. "Policy-Making and Political Culture in Sweden." *Scandinavian Political Studies* 4 (1969): 88–102.

Aos, Steve, Marna Miller, and Elizabeth Drake. *Evidence-Based Public Policy Options to Reduce Future Prison Construction, Criminal Justice Costs, and Crime Rates.* Olympia: Washington State Institute for Public Policy, 2006.

Austin, James, John Clark, Patricia Hardyman, and D. Alan Henry. "The Impact of 'Three Strikes and You're Out.'" *Punishment and Society* 1.2 (1999): 131–162.

Baldassare, Mark. *PPIC Statewide Survey: Special Survey on Californians and the Initiative Process.* San Francisco: Public Policy Institute of California, October, 2005.

Barabas, Jason. "How Deliberation Affects Public Opinion." *American Political Science Review* 98.4 (2004): 687–701.

Barber, Benjamin. *Strong Democracy: Participatory Politics for a New Age.* Berkeley: University of California Press, 1984.

Bayley, Christopher. "Good Intentions Gone Awry—Proposals for Fundamental Change in Criminal Sentencing." *Washington Law Review* 51 (1976): 529–564.

Beckett, Katherine. *Making Crime Pay: Law and Order in Contemporary American Politics.* New York: Oxford University Press, 1997.

Beckett, Katherine, and Bruce Western, "Governing Social Marginality: Welfare, Incarceration, and the Transformation of State Policy." *Punishment & Society* 3.1 (January 2001): 43–59.

Benjamin, Gerald, and T. Normal Hurd, eds. *Rockefeller in Retrospect: The Governor's New York Legacy.* Albany, N.Y.: Nelson A. Rockefeller Institute of Government, 1984.

Berk, Richard, Harold Brackman, and Selma Lesser. *A Measure of Justice: An Empirical Study if Changes in the California Penal Code, 1955–1971.* New York: Academic Press, 1977.

Berlet, Chip, and Matthew Lyons. *Right Wing Populism in America: Too Close for Comfort.* New York: Guilford Press, 2000.

Beyle, Thad. "The Governors." In *Politics in the American States: A Comparative Analysis,* 8th edition, eds. Virginia Gray and Russell Hanson, 212–213. Washington, D.C.: Congressional Quarterly Press, 2004.

Biles, Roger. "Mayor David Dinkins and the Politics of Race in New York City." In *African American Mayors: Race, Politics and the American City,* eds. David Colburn and Jeffrey Adler, 130–152. Urbana: University of Illinois Press, 2001.

Boerner, David. *Sentencing in Washington: A Legal Analysis of the Sentencing Reform Act of 1981.* Seattle, Wash.: Butterworth, 1985.

——. "Confronting Violence: In the Act and in the Word." *University of Puget Sound Law Review* 15 (1992): 525–577.

Boerner, David, and Roxanne Lieb. "Sentencing Reform in the Other Washington." In *Crime and Justice: A Review of the Research,* ed. Michael Tonry, 71–135. Chicago: University of Chicago Press, 2001.

Bonastia, Chris. *Knocking on the Door: The Federal Government's Attempt to De-Segregate the Suburbs.* Princeton, N.J.: Princeton University Press, 2008.

Bottoms, Anthony. "The Philosophy and Politics of Punishment and Sentencing."
    In *The Politics of Sentencing Reform*, eds. Chris Morgan Clarkson and Rod Morgan,
    17–49. Oxford: Clarendon Press, 1995.
Bourdieu, Pierre. "The Forms of Capital." In *Handbook of Theory and Research for the
    Sociology of Education*, ed. J. G. Richardson, 241–258. New York: Greenwood Press,
    1986.
Braithwaite, John, and Philip Pettit. *Not Just Deserts: A Republican Theory of Criminal
    Justice*. Oxford: Oxford University Press, 1990.
Broberg, Gunnar, and Mattias Tyden. "Eugenics in Sweden: Efficient Care." In *Eugenics
    and the Welfare State*, eds. Gunnar Broberg and Nils Roll-Hansen. East Lansing:
    Michigan State University Press, 1996.
Brown, Darryl. "Democracy and Decriminalization." *Texas Law Review* 86.2 (2007):
    223–275.
Brown, Edmund G. "Report to the Legislature, January 7, 1976." Governor's Office.
    Sacramento, Calif.
Bureau of Justice Statistics. *Sourcebook of Criminal Justice Statistics—1976*. Washington,
    D.C.: U.S. Department of Justice, U.S. Government Printing Office, 1977.
——. *Sourcebook of Criminal Justice Statistics—1986*. Washington DC: U.S. Department
    of Justice, U.S. Government Printing Office, 1987.
——. "Probation and Parole in the United States, 2002." Washington, D.C.: U.S.
    Department of Justice, 2003.
——. "Prisoners in 2005." Available at http://www.ojp.usdoj.gov/bjs/pub/pdf/po5.pdf
    (January 30, 2008).
——. "Prison and Jail Inmates at Midyear 2006." Available http://www.ojp.usdoj.gov/
    bjs/pub/pdf/pjimo6.pdf (January 25, 2008).
——. "Capital Punishment Statistics: Summary Findings." Available http://www.ojp.
    usdoj.gov/bjs/cp.htm (January 21, 2008).
——. "Prison Statistics: Summary Findings." Available http://www.ojp.usdoj.gov/bjs/
    prisons.htm (January 21, 2008).
——. "Jail Statistics." Available at http://www.ojp.usdoj.gov/bjs/jails.htm (June 23,
    2008).
——. "Prisoners in 2007." available at http://www.ojp.usdoj.gov/bjs/pub/pdf/po7.pdf
    (March 12, 2009).
Burrows, Edwin, and Mike Wallace. *Gotham: A History of New City to 1898*. Oxford:
    Oxford University Press, 1999.
Cain, Bruce, and Kenneth Miller. "The Populist Legacy: Initiatives and Undermining of
    Representative Government." In *Dangerous Democracy? The Battle over Ballot
    Initiatives in America*, eds. Larry Sabato, Howard R. Ernst, and Bruce Larson.
    Lanham, Md.: Rowman & Littlefield, 2001.
California Attorney General. "Proposition 66: Official Title and Summary with Analysis
    by the Legislative Analyst." Sacramento, Calif., 2004.

California Council on Criminal Justice. "Memo to Staff, May 19, 1971." California Council on Criminal Justice, Governor Speeches on Crime Control, F3869:106, Sacramento, Calif.

California Department of Corrections. *Historical Trends, 1982–2002*. Youth and Adult Correctional Agency. Data Analysis Unit, Sacramento, 2003.

———. "Time Served on Prison Sentence." Policy and Evaluation Division, Offender Information Services Branch, Estimates and Statistical Analysis Section, Data Analysis Unit. Sacramento, 2004.

———. "Rate of Felon Parolees Returned to California Prisons." Data Analysis Unit. Sacramento, 2004.

California Department of Justice. *Crime in California*. Sacramento, Calif., 2002.

California Field Poll. "Release #554, April 5, 1967." California Field Institute, San Francisco.

———. "Release # 558, May 11, 1967." California Field Institute, San Francisco.

———. "Release #558, February 6, 1968." California Field Institute, San Francisco. Available at the Institute of Governmental Studies Library, University of California, Berkeley.

———. "Release #1128, August 25, 1981." California Field Institute, San Francisco. Available at the Institute of Governmental Studies Library, University of California, Berkeley.

———. "Release #1163, April 22, 1982." California Field Institute, San Francisco. Available at the Institute of Governmental Studies Library, University of California, Berkeley.

———. "Release #1164, April 20, 1982." California Field Institute, San Francisco. Available at the Institute of Governmental Studies Library, University of California, Berkeley.

———. "Release #1547, 1990." California Field Institute, San Francisco. Available at the Institute of Governmental Studies Library, University of California, Berkeley.

———. "Release # 2141, October 13, 2004." California Field Institute, San Francisco. Available at the Institute of Governmental Studies Library, University of California, Berkeley.

California Office of the Governor. Fact Sheet, 2007. Available at Http://gov.ca.gov/index.php?/fact-sheet/6116 (August 17, 2007).

———. "Comprehensive Prison Reform, Fact Sheet: More Rehabilitation, Fewer Victims." Available at http://gov.ca.gov/index.php?/fact/sheet/6089 (March 21, 2008).

———. "Fact Sheet: Governor Signs Prison Agreement." Available at Http://gov.ca.gov/index.php?/fact-sheet/6116 (August 17, 2007).

California Secretary of State. "A History of California Initiatives." Available at http://www.ss.ca.gov/elections/init_history.pdf (July 20, 2006).

Cannon, Lou. *Ronnie and Jesse: A Political Odyssey*. Garden City, N.Y.: Doubleday, 1969.

———. *Governor Reagan: His Rise to Power*. New York: Public Affairs, 2003.

Carey, Hugh. "Annual Message, January 4, 1978." In Public Papers of Hugh Carey, Governor of the State of New York. Albany, N.Y.

Cassou, April Kestell, and Brian Taugher. "Determinate Sentencing in California: The New Numbers Game." *Pacific Law Journal* 9 (1978): 1–106.

Cavadino, Michael, and James Dignan. *Penal Systems: A Comparative Approach.* London: Sage, 2006.

Chartock, Alan. "Narcotics Addiction: The Politics of Frustration," in *Governing New York State: The Rockefeller Years,* eds. Robert Connery and Gerald Benjamin. New York: Academy of Political Science, 1974.

Chorev, Nitsan. *Remaking US Trade Policy: From Protectionism to Globalization.* Ithaca, N.Y.: Cornell University Press, 2007.

Clapp, Elizabeth. *Mothers of All Children: Women Reformers and the Rise of the Juvenile Courts in Progressive Era America.* University Park: Pennsylvania State University Press, 1998.

Clarke, Ronald, ed. *Situational Crime Prevention: Successful Case Studies.* Guilderland, N.Y.: Harrow and Heston, 1997.

Clear, Todd. *Imprisoning Communities: How Mass Incarceration Makes Disadvantaged Neighborhoods Worse.* New York: Oxford University Press, 2007.

Clemens, Elisabeth. *The People's Lobby: Organizational Innovation and the Rise of Interest Group Politics in the United States, 1890–1925.* Chicago: University of Chicago Press, 1997.

Clemens, Elisabeth, and James Cook. "Politics and Institutionalism: Explaining Durability and Change." *Annual Review of Sociology* 25 (1999): 441–466.

Cohen, Jean. "Civil Society and Globalization: Rethinking the Categories." In *State and Civil Society in Northern Europe: The Swedish Model Reconsidered,* ed. Lars Trägårdh, 37–66. New York: Berghahn, 2007.

Coleman, James. "Social Capital in the Creation of Human Capital." *American Journal of Sociology* 94 (1988): S95–S120.

Colla, Piero. "Race, Nation, and Folk: On the Repressed Memory of World War II in Sweden and Its Hidden Categories." In *Crisis and Culture: The Case of Germany and Sweden,* eds. Lars Trägårdh and Nina Witoszek, 131–154. New York: Berghahn Books, 2002.

Cover, Robert. "Violence and the Word." *Yale Law Journal* 95 (July 1986): 1601–1629.

Cuomo, Mario. "Annual Message to the Legislature, January 5, 1983." In Public Papers of Mario Cuomo, Governor of the State of New York, Albany.

———. "Message to the Legislature, November 10, 1985." In Public Papers of Mario Cuomo, Governor of the State of New York, Albany.

Curb, Mike. "Citizen's Committee to Stop Crime." Citizen's Committee to Stop Crime, Sacramento.

Curb, Mike, George Deukmejian, and Paul Gann. "Arguments in Favor of Proposition 8, 1981." California Ballot Measures Database, Hastings Library. Available at http://traynor.uchastings.edu/cgi-bin/starfinder/729.caproptext (July 28, 2006).

Dallek, Matthew. *The Right Moment: Ronald Reagan's First Victory and the Decisive Turning Point in American Politics.* New York: Free Press, 2000.

Diamond, Sara. *Roads to Dominion: Right-Wing Movements and Political Power in the United States.* New York: Guilford Press, 1995.

Didion, Joan. *Where I Was From.* New York: Alfred Knopf, 2003.

Douglas, Mary. *Purity and Danger: An Analysis of the Concept of Pollution and Taboo.* London: Routledge, 1966.

Downes, David. *Contrasts in Tolerance: Post-War Penal Policy in the Netherlands and England and Wales.* Oxford: Clarendon Press, 1988.

Dumm, Thomas. *Democracy and Punishment: Disciplinary Origins of the United States.* Madison: University of Wisconsin Press, 1987.

Dye, Thomas. *Politics in States and American Communities.* Englewood Cliffs, N.J.: Prentice Hall, 1988.

Elazar, Daniel. *American Federalism: A View from the States.* New York: Thomas Y. Crowell, 1966.

Evans, Daniel. "The Courts: Key to Civilizing an Urban Society, November 11, 1966." Speech to Citizens' Conference on Washington's Courts. Office of the Governor, Daniel Evans Gubernatorial Paper, 2S-4-38. Washington State Library and Archive, Olympia.

———. "State of the State Address, January 11, 1967." Office of the Governor, Daniel Evans Gubernatorial Papers, 2S-4-42. Washington State Library and Archive, Olympia.

———. "Speech to the National Council on Crime and Delinquency, September 24, 1968." Office of the Governor, Evans Gubernatorial Papers, 2S-4-38. Washington State Library and Archive, Olympia.

———. Proposal for a Combined Structure for Administering the Juvenile Delinquency Prevention and Omnibus Crime Control and Safe Streets Act, 1968." Office of the Governor, Daniel Evans Gubernatorial Papers, 2S-2-432. Washington State Library and Archive, Olympia.

———. "Richard Nixon Campaign Key Issues 1968." Office of the Governor, Daniel Evans Gubernatorial Paper, 2S-1-21. Washington State Library and Archive, Olympia.

———. "State of the State, January 12, 1971." Office of the Governor, Daniel Evans Gubernatorial Papers 2S-4-42. Washington State Library and Archive, Olympia.

———. "State of the State Address, January 10, 1972." Office of the Governor, Daniel Evans Gubernatorial Papers 2S-4-42. Washington State Library and Archive, Olympia.

———. "The Evans Administration: A Record of Continuing Achievement 1972–1973." Office of the Governor, Daniel Evans Gubernatorial Papers, 2S-I-44. Washington State Library and Archive, Olympia.

———. "State of the State, 1974." Office of the Governor, 2S-4-42. Washington State Library and Archive, Olympia.

Families to Amend California's Three Strikes (FACTS). "150 Stories of Inmates." Available at http://facts1.live.radicaldesigns.org/article.php?list+type&type+20 (August 16, 2007).

Federal Bureau of Investigation. *Uniform Crime Report 1965.* Washington, D.C.: Government Printing Office.

———. "Uniform Crime Report 2006." Available at http://www.fbi.gov/ucr/hc2006/ index.html (February 1, 2008).

Feeley, Malcolm, and Jonathan Simon. "The New Penology: Notes on the Emerging Strategy of Corrections and Its Implications." *Criminology* 30.4 (1992): 449–474.

Foucault, Michel. *Discipline and Punish: The Birth of the Prison.* New York: Pantheon, 1977.

Gardner, Booth. "State of the State Address, 1990." Office of the Governor. Booth Gardner Gubernatorial Papers: Speeches, 8 93-A-24. Washington State Library and Archive, Olympia.

Garland, David. *Punishment and Welfare: A History of Penal Strategies.* Aldershot, U.K.: Gower, 1985.

———. *Punishment and Modern Society: A Study in Social Theory.* Chicago: University of Chicago Press, 1990.

———. "Limits of the Sovereign State." *British Journal of Criminology* 36.4 (1996): 445–471.

———. *The Culture of Control: Crime and Social Order in Contemporary Society.* Chicago: University of Chicago Press, 2001.

Gerber, Elisabeth, Arthur Lupia, Mathew D. McCubbins, and D. Roderick Kiewiet. *Stealing the Initiative: How State Government Responds to Direct Democracy.* Upper Saddle River, N.J.: Prentice Hall, 2001.

Giddens, Anthony. "Problems of Action and Structure." In *The Giddens Reader,* ed. Phillip Cassells, 88–175. Stanford, Calif.: Stanford University Press, 1993.

Gilbert, Richard et al., "Arguments Opposed to Proposition 8, 1981." California Ballot Measures Database, Hastings Library. Available at http://traynor.uchastings.edu/ cgi-bin/starfinder/729.caproptext (July 28, 2006).

Girling, Evi, Ian Loader and Richard Sparks. *Crime and Social Change in Middle England: Questions of Order in an English Town.* London: Routledge, 2000.

Goodwyn, Lawrence. *The Populist Moment: A Short History of Agrarian Revolt in America.* Oxford: Oxford University Press, 1978.

Gottschalk, Marie. *The Prison and the Gallows: The Politics of Mass Incarceration in America.* Cambridge: Cambridge University Press, 2006.

Gray, Virginia, and Russell L. Hanson, eds. *Politics in the American States: A Comparative Analysis.* Washington, D.C.: Congressional Quarterly Press, 2004.

Gray, Virginia, Herbert Jacob, and Robert Albritton. *Politics in the American States.* Glenview, Ill.: Scott, Foresman, 1990.

Gray, Virginia, Herbert Jacob, and Kenneth Vines, eds. *Politics in the American States: A Comparative Analysis.* Boston: Little, Brown, 1999.

Green, David. "Public Opinion versus Public Judgment about Crime: Correction the 'Comedy of Errors.'" *British Journal of Criminology* 46 (January 2006): 131–154.

Greenberg, David, and Drew Humphries. "The Cooptation of Fixed Sentencing Reform." *Crime and Delinquency* 26 (1980): 205–225.

Greenberg, David F., and Valerie West. "State Prison Populations and Their Growth, 1971–1991." *Criminology* 39.3 (August 2001): 615–653.

Greene, Judith A. *Smart on Crime: Positive Trends in State-Level Sentencing and Corrections Policy.* Washington, D.C.: Families Against Mandatory Minimums, 2003.

Griset, Pamala. *Determinate Sentencing: The Promise and the Reality of Retributive Justice.* Albany: State University of New York Press, 1991.

Gutman, Amy, and Dennis Thompson. *Why Deliberative Democracy?* Princeton, N.J.: Princeton University Press, 2004.

Habermas, Jürgen. *The Theory of Communicative Action.* Boston: Beacon Press, 1981.

Hagan, John, John Hewitt, and Duane Alwin. "Ceremonial Justice: Crime and Punishment in a Loosely Coupled System." *Social Forces* 58.2 (December 1979): 506–527.

Haney, Craig. "Psychological Impact of Incarceration: Implications for Postprison Adjustment." In *Prisoners Once Removed: The Impact of Incarceration and Reentry on Children, Families, and Communities,* eds. Jeremy Travis and Michelle Waul, 33–66 Washington, D.C.: Urban Institute Press, 2003.

Heclo, Hugh, and Henrik Madsen. *Policy and Politics in Sweden: Principled Pragmatism.* Philadelphia: Temple University Press, 1987.

Jacob, Herbert, and Kenneth Vines, eds., *Politics in the American States: A Comparative Analysis.* Boston: Little, Brown, 1965.

Jacobs, David, and Ronald Helms. "Collective Outbursts, Politics, and Punitive Outbursts: Toward a Political Sociology of Spending on Social Control." *Social Forces* 77.4 (June 1999): 1497–1523.

Johnstone, Gerry. "Penal Policy Making: Elitist, Populist or Participatory." *Punishment & Society* 2.2 (2000): 161–180.

Katz, Michael. *In the Shadow of the Poorhouse: A Social History of Welfare in America.* New York: Basic Books, 1986.

Key, V. O., and Winston Crouch. *The Initiative and Referendum in California.* Berkeley: University of California Press, 1939.

Kitto, Richard. "Editor's Note, Symposium: Law and the Correctional Process in Washington." *Washington Law Review* 51 (1976): 491–528.

Klatch, Rebecca. *Women of the New Right.* Philadelphia: Temple University Press, 1987.

Knack, Stephen. "Social Capital and the Quality of Government: Evidence from the US States." *American Journal of Political Science* 46.4 (October 2002): 772–785.

LaCourse, Dave. "Hard Time for Armed Crime: Policy Brief, 1997." Washington Policy Center. Available at http://www.washingtonpolicy.org/CriminalJustice/PNHardTimeforArmedCrime97-04.html (August 26, 2007).

Lasch, Christopher. *The True and Only Heaven: Progress and Its Critics*. New York: Norton, 1991.

Liebschutz, Sarah, with Robert Bailey, Jeffrey Stonecash, Jane Shapiro Zacek, and Joseph Zimmerman. *New York Politics and Government: Competition and Compassion*. Lincoln: University of Nebraska Press, 1998.

Loader, Ian. "Policing, Recognition and Belonging." *Annals of the American Academy of Political and Social Science* 605.1 (May 2006): 202–221.

———. "Playing with Fire? Democracy and the Emotions of Crime and Punishment." In *Emotions, Crime and Justice*, eds. S. Karstedt, Ian Loader, and Heather Strang. Oxford: Hart, forthcoming.

Loader, Ian, and Neil Walker. *Civilizing Security*. Cambridge: Cambridge University Press, 2007.

Lockard, Duane. *Toward Equal Opportunity: A Study of State and Local Antidiscrimination Laws*. New York: Macmillan, 1968.

Locke, Gary. "Major Accomplishments: Public Safety." Available at http://www.digitalarchives.wa.gov/governorlocke/accomplish/safety.htm (August 26, 2007).

Lowry, Mike. "State of the State Address, January 9, 1996." Available at http://www.digitalarchives.wa.gov/GovernorLowry/sos1.htm (August 26, 2007).

Madison, James. "Federalist No. 47." In *The Federalist: A Commentary on the Constitution of the United States*, Alexander Hamilton, John Jay, and James Madison, 307–314. New York: Modern Library, 2001.

Manza, Jeff, and Chris Uggen. *Locked Out: Felon Disenfranchisement and American Democracy*. New York: Oxford University Press, 2006.

Marion, Nancy E. *Criminal Justice in America: The Politics behind the System*. Durham, N.C.: Carolina Academic Press, 2002.

Martens, Peter. "Immigrants, Crime and Criminal Justice in Sweden." In *Ethnicity, Crime and Immigration: Comparative and Cross-National Perspectives*, ed. Michael Tonry, 183–256. Chicago: University of Chicago Press, 1997.

Mauer, Marc. "Comparative International Rates of Incarceration: An Examination of Causes and Trends." Sentencing Project, 2003, 2.

Mayhew, David. *Placing Parties in American Politics*. Princeton, N.J.: Princeton University Press, 1986.

McCoy, Candace. *Politics and Plea Bargaining: Victims' Rights in California*. Philadelphia: University of Pennsylvania Press, 1993.

McEleney, Barbara. *Correctional Reform in New York: The Rockefeller Years and Beyond*. Lanham, Md.: University Press of America, 1985.

McGirr, Lisa. *Suburban Warriors: The Origins of the New American Right*. Princeton, N.J.: Princeton University Press, 2001.

McGovern, Stephen J. *The Politics of Downtown Development: Dynamic Political Cultures in San Francisco and Washington D.C.* Lexington: University Press of Kentucky, 1998.

McKinney's Consolidated Laws of New York. 1973 Session Laws of New York.

McKinney's Consolidated Laws of New York. 1978 Session Laws of New York.

McKinney's Consolidated Laws of New York. 2004 Session Laws of New York.

McMath, Robert. *American Populism: A Social History 1877–1898*. New York: Hill and Wang, 1993.

Messinger, Sheldon, and Philip E. Johnson. "California's Determinate Sentencing Statute: History and Issues." In *Determinate Sentencing: Reform or Regression*, 13–58. Washington, D.C.: Government Printing Office, 1977.

Miller, Lisa L. "Looking for Postmodernism in All the Wrong Places: Implementing a New Penology." *British Journal of Criminology* 41.1 (Winter 2001): 168–184.

——. *The Perils of Federalism: Race, Poverty and the Politics of Crime Control*. New York: Oxford University Press, 2008.

Miller, Margaret Ada. *The Left's Turn: Labor Welfare Politics and Social Movements in Washington State, 1937–1973*. Ph.D. diss., University of Washington, 2000.

Mollenkopf, John H. "New York: The Great Anomaly." In *Racial Politics in the American Cities*, eds. Rufus P. Browning, Dale Rogers Marshall, and David H. Taub. New York: Longman Press, 1990.

Morone, James. *Hellfire Nation: The Politics of Sin in America History*. New Haven, Conn.: Yale University Press, 2003.

Morris, Norval. *The Future of Imprisonment*. Chicago: University of Chicago Press, 1974.

New York State Commission on Management and Productivity in the Public Sector. *Violent Attacks and Chronic Offenders: A Proposal for Concentrating the Resources of New York's Criminal Justice System on the "Hard Core" of the Crime Problem*. Albany, 1978.

New York State Department of Correctional Services. "Men and Women Undercustody: 1987–2001." Division of Program Planning Research and Evaluation, Albany, 2002.

——. "Inmates under Custody: By Crime, 1975–1979; 1980–1989; 1987–1992; 1991–2000." Division of Program Planning Research and Evaluation, Albany, 2002.

——. "Pataki Signs Rocky Drug Reform into Law." *DOCS TODAY* 13 (2002): 2.

——. "Press Release, January 23, 2004." Available at http:www/docs.state.ny.us/PressRel/DOCSinitiatives.html (August 31, 2007).

New York State Division of Parole. "Board of Parole 1997–2000." Available at http://criminaljustice.state.ny.us/crimenet/ojsa/cja99/parole.pdf.

——. "The Board of Parole, 1999–2002, Table 4." Available at http://criminaljustice.state.ny.us/crimnet/ojsa/cja_00_01/parole.pdf (March 10, 2008).

——. "Reducing the Number of Parole Violators in Local Correctional Facilities in New York State." Available at http://parole.state.ny.us/PROGRAMpublications.asp (March 10, 2008).

New York State Executive Budget. "Public Safety and Security, 2005–2006." Available at http:www.budget.state.ny.us/archive/fy0506archive/fy0506littlebook/pubSafe.html (September 2, 2007).

New York State Joint Legislative Fiscal Committees on the State 2004–05 Budget. "Testimony of Chauncey G. Parker, New York State Director of Criminal Justice, February 2, 2004." Albany, New York.

New York Statistical Yearbook 1979, Table L-9. Albany, NY: New York State Division of the Budget.

Oregon Department of Corrections. "What Is Community Corrections." Available at http://www.oregon.gov/DOC/TRANS/CC/whatiscc.shtml (June 12, 2008).

Orloff, Ann Shola. "The Political Origins of America's Belated Welfare State." In *The Politics of Social Policy in the United States*, eds. Margaret Weir, Ann Shola Orloff, and Theda Skocpol, 37–80. Princeton, N.J.: Princeton University Press, 1988.

Paul Gann Archive. Letters. Proposition 8: Analyses and Correspondence, Box 1392–1395. California State Library, California History Section, Sacramento.

Peirce, Neal R., and Jerry Hagstrom. *The Book of America: Inside the 50 States Today.* New York: Norton, 1983.

Petersilia, Joan. *When Prisoners Come Home: Parole and Prisoner Reentry.* New York: Oxford University Press, 2003.

Pierson, Paul. *Dismantling the Welfare State? Reagan, Thatcher, and the Politics of Retrenchment.* New York: Cambridge University Press, 1994.

——. "Big, Slow-Moving, and Invisible: Macrosocial Processes in the Study of Comparative Politics." In *Comparative Historical Analysis in the Social Sciences*, eds. James Mahoney and Dietrich Rueschemeyer, 177–207. Cambridge: Cambridge University Press, 2003.

Portes, Alejandro. "Social Capital: Its Origins and Applications in Modern Sociology." *Annual Review of Sociology* 24 (1998): 1–24.

Pratt, John. "Emotive and Ostentatious Punishment: Its Decline and Resurgence on Modern Society." *Punishment & Society* 2.4 (October 2000): 417–439.

Pratt, John, David Brown, Mark Brown, Simon Hallsworth, and Wayne Morrison, eds. *The New Punitiveness: Trends, Theories, Perspectives.* Portland, Ore.: Willan, 2005.

Public Policy Institute of California. "PPIC Statewide Survey: Californians and Their Government." Public Policy Institute of California and James Irvine Foundation, San Francisco, 2007.

Putnam, Robert. *Making Democracy Work: Civic Traditions in Modern Italy.* Princeton, N.J.: Princeton University Press, 1993.

——. *Bowling Alone: The Collapse and Revival of American Community.* New York: Simon & Schuster, 2000.

Ramakrishnan, S. Karthick, and Mark Baldassare. *The Ties That Bind: Changing Demographics and Civic Engagement in California.* San Francisco: Public Policy Institute of California, 2004.

Reagan, Ronald. "The Morality Gap at Berkeley, Speech at Cow Palace, May 12, 1966." In *The Creative Society: Some Comments on Problems Facing America.* New York: Devin-Adair, 1967.

Reagan, Ronald. "Address before the Merchants and Manufacturers Association, Los Angeles," and "Speech at the Republican State Convention, Anaheim." In *The Creative Society: Some Comments on Problems Facing America*. New York: Devin-Adair, 1967.

———. "Joint Conference of California School Boards Association and California Association of School Administrators, December 8, 1968." California Council on Criminal Justice, Governor Speeches, 1968, F3869:106, Sacramento.

Reynolds, Mike. "Three Strikes and You're Out: Stop Repeat Offenders: An Official Online Resource." Available at http://www.threestrikes.org/index.html (August 16, 2007).

Rockefeller, Nelson A. Nelson A. Rockefeller Gubernatorial Papers, Rockefeller Family Archive, Rockefeller Archive Center, Sleepy Hollow, New York.

———. "Special Message to the Legislature, March 23, 1962." NAR Gubernatorial, Press Office, Folder 1907, Box 91, Series 25. Rockefeller Family Archive, Rockefeller Archive Center, Sleepy Hollow, New York.

———. "Annual Message to the Legislature, January 5, 1966." In Public Papers of Nelson A. Rockefeller, Governor of the State of New York. Albany, New York.

———. "Annual Message to the Legislature, January 6, 1971." In Public Papers of Nelson A. Rockefeller, Governor of the State of New York. Albany, New York.

———. "Annual Message to the Legislature, January 3, 1973." In Public Papers of Nelson A. Rockefeller, Governor of the State of New York. Albany, New York.

———. "News Conference with Governor Nelson A. Rockefeller, January 22, 1973." NAR Gubernatorial, Press Office, Folder 1837, Box 89, Series 8, Record Group 15. Rockefeller Family Archive, Rockefeller Archive Center, Sleepy Hollow, New York.

Rosenberg, Göran. "The Crisis of Consensus in Post-War Sweden." In *Crisis and Culture: The Case of Germany and Sweden*, eds. Lars Trägårdh and Nina Witoszek, 170–201. New York: Berghahn, 2002.

Rothman, David. *Conscience and Convenience: The Asylum and its Alternatives in Progressive America*. Glenview, Ill.: Scott, Foresman, 1980.

Sabato, Larry, Howard Ernst, and Bruce A. Larson, eds. *Dangerous Democracy? The Battle over Ballot Initiatives in America*. Lanham, Md.: Rowman & Littlefield, 2001.

Sasson, Theodore. *Crime Talk: How Citizens Construct a Social Problem*. New York: Aldine de Gruyter, 1995.

Savelsberg, Joachim J. "Knowledge, Domination, and Criminal Punishment." *American Journal of Sociology* 99.4 (January 1994): 911–943.

Scarry, Elaine. *The Body in Pain: The Making and Unmaking of the World*. New York: Oxford University Press, 1987.

Scheingold, Stuart. *The Politics of Street Crime: Criminal Process and Cultural Obsession*. Philadelphia: Temple University Press, 1991.

———. "New Political Criminology: Power, Authority, and the Post-liberal State." *Law & Social Inquiry* 23.4 (Fall 1998): 857–895.

Scheingold, Stuart, Toska Olson, and Jana Pershing. "Sexual Violence, Victim Advocacy, and Republican Criminology: Washington State's Community Protection Act." *Law & Society Review* 28.4 (1992): 729–763.

Schneier, Edward, and John Murtaugh. *New York Politics: A Tale of Two States.* Armonk, N.Y.: M. E. Sharpe, 2001.

Schofer, Evan, and Marion Fourcade-Gourinchas. "The Structural Contexts of Civic Engagement: Voluntary Association Membership in Comparative Perspective." *American Sociological Review* 66.6 (December 2001): 806–828.

Schwarzenegger, Arnold. "Swearing-In Remarks, November 13, 2003." Sacramento, CA. Available at http://gov.ca.gov/index.php?/print/version/speech/3086 (August 21, 2007).

Scott, Garrett. *Cul de Sac: A Suburban War Story.* USA: First Run/Icarus Films, 2002.

Sentencing Project. "Comparative International Incarceration Rates: An Examination of Causes and Trends." Report to U.S. Commission on Civil Rights, June 20, 2003.

———. "Incarceration." Available at http://www.sentencingproject.org/IssueAreaHome.aspx?IssueID=2 (June 23, 2008).

Simon, Jonathan. *Poor Discipline: Parole and the Social Control of the Underclass.* Chicago: University of Chicago Press, 1993.

———. *Governing through Crime: How the War on Crime Transformed American Democracy and Created a Culture of Fear.* Oxford: Oxford University Press, 2007.

———. "The Professor and the Governor." Blog posted May 11, 2007. Available at http://governingthroughcrime.blogspot.com/2007_05_01_archive.html (August 21, 2007).

Skinner, Kiron, Annelise Anderson, and Martin Anderson, eds. *Reagan, in His Own Hand.* New York: Touchstone Books, 2002.

Skocpol, Theda. *Protecting Soldiers and Mothers: The Political Origins of Social Policy in the United States.* Cambridge: Cambridge University Press, 1992.

———. *Diminished Democracy: From Membership to Management in American Civic Life.* Norman: University of Oklahoma Press, 2003.

Skowronek, Stephen. *Building a New American State: The Expansion of National Administrative Capacities, 1877–1920.* Cambridge: Cambridge University Press, 1982.

Spitzer, Eliot. "Inaugural Address, January 1, 2007." Available at http://www.ny.gov/governor/keydocs/0101071_speech_print.html (August 31, 2007).

———. "Executive Order No. 10: Establishing the New York State Commission on Sentencing Reform, March 5, 2007." Available ay http://www.ny.gov/governor/executive_orders/exeorders/10_print.html (August 31, 2007).

Stack, Jonathan, and Liz Garbus. *The Farm: Life Inside Angola Prison.* New York: A&E Home Video, 1998.

Starr, Kevin. *Inventing the Dream: California through the Progressive Era.* New York: Oxford University Press, 1985.

Sutton, John. "Imprisonment and Social Classification in Five Common Law Countries." *American Journal of Sociology* 106.2 (September 2000): 350–386.

Sykes, Gresham. *Society of Captives: A Study of Maximum Security Prison.* Princeton, N.J.: Princeton University Press, 1958.

Taylor, Quintard. *The Forging of a Black Community: Seattle's Central District from 1870 through the Civil Rights Era.* Seattle: University of Washington Press, 1994.

Tham, Henrik. "Drug Control as a National Project: The Case of Sweden." *Journal of Drug Issues* 25.1 (1995): 113–128.

Tilly, Charles. "Parliamentarization of Popular Contention in Great Britain, 1758–1834." *Theory & Society* 26.2/3 (April 1997): 245–273.

Tonry, Michael. *Malign Neglect: Race, Crime, and Punishment in America.* New York: Oxford University Press, 1995.

Trägårdh, Lars. "Democratic Governance and the Creation of Social Capital in Sweden: The Discreet Charm of Governmental Commissions." In *State and Civil Society in Northern Europe: The Swedish Model Reconsidered,* ed. Lars Trägårdh, 255–270. Oxford: Berghahn, 2007.

Tyler, Tom, and Robert J. Boeckmann. "Three Strikes and You Are Out, but Why? The Psychology of Public Support for Punishing Rule Breakers." *Law & Society Review* 31.2 (1997): 237–266.

Underwood, James, and William Daniels. *Governor Rockefeller in New York: The Apex of Pragmatic Liberalism in the United States.* Westport, Conn.: Greenwood Press, 1982.

U.S. Census Bureau. "The 1966 Statistical Abstract." Available at http://www2.census.gov/prod2/statcomp/documents/1966-01.pdf (February 1, 2008).

———. "The 1978 Statistical Abstract." Available at http://www2.census.gov/prod2/statcomp/documents/1978-01.pdf (February 1, 2008).

———. "Persons Reported Registered and Voted by State: 2000, No. 420." Statistical Abstract of the United States. Available at http://www.census.gov/statab/www.

———. "Statistical Abstract of the United States: State and Local Government—Expenditures and Debt by State 2000, No. 447." Available at http://www.census.gov/statab/www.

———. "Statistical Abstract of the United States: State Unemployment Insurance by State and Other Area: 2002, No. 555." Available at http://www.census.gov/statab/www.

———. "Statistical Abstract of the United States: State Governments—Expenditures and Debt by State 2004, Table 440." Available at http://www.census.gov/compendia/statab/tables/08s0440.pdf (March 10, 2008).

———. "Statistical Abstract of the United States: State and Local Government Employment and Average Monthly Earnings by State 1995 and 2004, Table 452." Available at http://www.census.gov/compendia/statab/tables/08s0452.pdf (March 10, 2008).

———. "Participation in Elections for President and US Representatives: 1932–2006, Table 406." Available at http://www.census.gov/compendia/statab/tables/08s0406.pdf (January 30, 2008).

———. "Persons Reported Registered and Voted by State: 2006, Table 405." Available at http://www.census.gov/compendia/statab/tables/08s0405.pdf (January 30, 2008).

——. "The 2007 Statistical Abstract." Available at http://www.census.gov/compendia/statab/index.html (February 1, 2008).

——. "California: Quick Facts." Available at http://quickfacts.census.gov/qfd/states/06000.html (February 13, 2008).

Wacquant, Loïc. "Deadly Symbiosis: When Ghetto and Prison Meet and Mesh." *Punishment & Society* 3.1 (2001): 95–134.

Walker, Samuel. *Taming the System: The Control of Discretion in Criminal Justice, 1950–1990.* New York: Oxford University Press, 1993.

Washington Association of Prosecuting Attorneys. "Justice in Sentencing, 1981." House of Representatives, Committee on Institutions, Washington State Archive and Library, Olympia.

Washington State Citizens Council on Crime and Delinquency. "Council Minutes, February 22, 1966." Office of the Governor, Daniel Evans Gubernatorial Papers, Washington State Library and Archive, Olympia.

Washington State Commission on the Causes and Prevention of Civil Unrest. "Report on Race and Violence in Washington, 1969." Office of the Governor, Daniel Evans Gubernatorial Papers, Washington State Library and Archive, Olympia.

Washington State Department of Corrections. "Community Corrections Population Characteristics." Available at http://www.doc.wa.gov/general/communitypopcharacteristics.htm (December 10, 2003).

——. "Community Corrections." Available at http://www.doc.wa.gov/aboutdoc/communitycorrections.asp (February 22, 2008).

——. "The DOC Re-entry Initiative: Smart on Crime." Available at http://www.doc.wa.gov/docs/reentrywhitepaper.pdf (March 10, 2008).

——. "Offender Crews." Available at http://www.doc.wa.gov/aboutdoc/offendercrews.asp (February 25, 2008).

Washington State Department of Social and Health Services. "Statistics on the Number of Persons Civilly Committed to the Special Commitment Center Program." Available ay http://www.1dshs.wa.gov/hrsa/scc/Stats.htm (September 23, 2006).

Washington State Governor's Task Force on Community Protection. "Report, November 28, 1989." Office of the Governor: Booth Gardner Gubernatorial Papers, Washington State Library and Archive, Olympia.

Washington State Institute for Public Policy. "Sex Offender Sentencing in Washington State: How Sex Offenders Differ from Other Felony Offenders." Olympia, September 2, 2005.

——. "Sex Offender Sentencing in Washington State: Initial Sentencing Decision." Olympia, September 16, 2005.

Washington State Law and Justice Planning Division. "Comprehensive Plan for Law Enforcement, 1970." Office of the Governor: Planning and Community Affairs, Washington State Library and Archive, Olympia.

Washington State Law and Justice Planning Division. "William Henry's Testimony to the House Institutions Committee, July 28, 1978." Office of the Governor, Dixie

Lee Ray Gubernatorial Papers: Governor's Council on Crime and Justice, 2T4012, Washington State Library and Archive, Olympia.

Washington State Office of Crime Victim Advocacy. Available at http://www.cted.gov/ portal/alias_lang_en/tabID_244 (September 23, 2006).

Washington State Revised Code, "Sentencing Reform Act of 1981, 9.94A.010." Available http://apps.leg.wa.gov/RCW/default.aspx? (February 22, 2008).

Washington State Senate Law and Justice Committee. "Public Hearings on Community Protection, January 9–12, 1990." Audiotapes. Washington State Library and Archive, Olympia.

Washington State Senate Committee on Ways and Means. "Senate Bill Report: SI 159, 1995." Olympia.

Washington State Sentencing Guidelines Commission. "Sentencing Guidelines Public Hearings and Written Testimony, 1981–1983." Office of the Governor: John Spellman's Gubernatorial Papers, 2U-08–045, Washington State Library and Archive, Olympia.

——. "The Sentencing Reform Act at Century's End: An Assessment of Adult Felony Sentencing Practices in the State of Washington." Report to the Governor and the Legislature, January 2000, Olympia.

Washington State Secretary of State. "Elections: Index to Initiatives and Referendum History and Statistics, 1914–2005." Available at http://www.secstate.wa.gov/ elections/initiatives/statistics.aspx (July 20, 2006).

Weber, Max. *Politics as Vocation.* Philadelphia: Fortress Press, 1965 [1919].

——. *Economy & Society,* eds. Guenther Roth and Claus Wittich, 4–5. Berkeley: University of California Press, 1978.

Western, Bruce. *Punishment and Inequality in America.* New York: Russell Sage, 2006.

Western, Bruce, and Katherine Beckett. "How Unregulated Is the US Labor Market? The Penal System as a Labor Market Institution." *American Journal of Sociology* 104 (1999): 1135–1172.

Whitman, James Q. *Harsh Justice: Criminal Punishment and the Widening Divide between America and Europe.* Oxford: Oxford University Press, 2003.

Willis, James J. "Transportation versus Imprisonment in Eighteenth- and Nineteenth-Century Britain: Penal Power, Liberty, and the State." *Law & Society Review* 39.1 (2005): 171–210.

Wolfinger, Raymond, and Fred Greenstein. "Repeal of Fair Housing in California: An Analysis of Referendum Voting." *American Political Science Review* 62.3 (September 1968): 753–769.

Wooddy, Carroll H. "Populism in Washington: A Study of the Legislature of 1897." *Washington Historical Quarterly* (1930): 108.

Zimring, Franklin, and Gordon Hawkins. *The Scale of Imprisonment.* Chicago: University of Chicago Press, 1991.

——. *Prison: Population and Criminal Justice Policy in California.* Berkeley, Calif.: Institute of Governmental Studies Press, 1992.

Index